D0310494

ROBERT
RUNCIE

ROBERT
RUNCIE

ADRIAN HASTINGS

MOWBRAY

Mowbray
A Cassell imprint
Villiers House, 41/47 Strand, London WC2N 5JE, England

© Adrian Hastings 1991

All rights reserved. No part of this manuscript may be reproduced or
transmitted in any form or by any means, electronic or mechanical
including photocopying, recording or any information storage
or retrieval system, without prior permission in writing
from the publishers.

First published 1991
Reprinted 1991

British Library Cataloguing in Publication Data
Hastings, Adrian
    Robert Runcie
    1. Church of England. Runcie, Robert. Biographies
    I. Title
    283.092

ISBN 0–264–67209–7

Typeset by Saxon Ltd, Derby
Printed and bound in Great Britain by Mackays of Chatham Plc.

❧CONTENTS❧

ACKNOWLEDGEMENTS

Extracts from *Windows onto God* and *One Light for the World* by Robert Runcie reprinted by permission of Society for Promotion of Christian Knowledge.

Extracts from *The Unity We Seek*, copyright ©Robert Runcie 1989, are used by permission of the publishers: Darton, Longman and Todd, and Morehouse Publishing.

In memory of Theodore,
Greek Archbishop of Canterbury (668–690)
and his friend and collaborator,
Adrian the African

If anybody thinks that it is easy and it doesn't cost very much to your personal soul to pursue the middle way, if anybody thinks that it's simply trying to please everybody like a chameleon, let them come and try and ponder the scripture and say their prayers and try to hold the Church together. They will find it's much easier to align yourself with one particular insight into religion, one particular dogmatic group and devil take the hindmost.

(Archbishop Runcie to Walter Schwarz,
The Guardian, 23 March 1990)

❧ PREFACE ❧

Many names were suggested when Mowbray decided it was time to prepare an account of Dr Runcie's work but the outcome was that the Archbishop himself suggested me, whom he had hardly met. I was honoured at this choice but at first taken aback: several of the more important people in any history of the Church of England in this decade, let alone the Anglican Communion, I have never met. I did not attend the Lambeth Conference of 1988. But distance has its own rewards. Mine is clearly an outsider's view.

This is not a Church history of these ten years. It is not even an account of all the important things Dr Runcie has said and done. Instead, I have picked out the issues which have seemed to me nearest to the heart of his own strategies, the issues most characteristic of the Runcie years. Across these issues I have attempted to focus on what the central role of the Archbishop of Canterbury is, what it should be, what he has tried to make of it. I have been encouraged in this by the feeling that he has himself been continually preoccupied with the nature and limits of religious authority and its appropriate functioning ever since his enthronement in 1980. It seems to me that this focus is of theological value as well as being historically correct.

I only agreed to write this book because I sensed a quite considerable degree of common ground between us. Such a sense of affinity is helpful if one is to get inside a subject, but it can also be misleading. I have, of course, endeavoured to make of it as fair a delineation of his beliefs and policies as I can, but it remains my delineation and cannot but be faithful to my own controlling vision as to what matters most.

I have also tried to structure the book somewhat as a dialogue between the Archbishop and myself in which his own voice can be heard at some length. So I have given him the last word but ensured that he would, characteristically, turn it rather in my direction, that of the scribbler of the written word. Perhaps to imagine an absurd romantic parallel it could be compared with some long rambling conversation held in a Canterbury cloister on a feast day in the year 690 from Vespers to Compline between the aged Theodore, our only Greek Archbishop, at the close of his archiepiscopate, and his dear friend, the more Roman-minded African monk Adrian, abbot of the Canterbury monastery of St Peter and Paul, surveying the ups and downs of Christianity in this still very pagan land of England — the authority of Canterbury, the establishment of the parochial system, the calibre of the new bishops, the difficulties with Wilfrid of York, the touchiness of Rome, but above all the growth of the spiritual life, of scholarship and sound theology in monasteries and schools. Theodore is one of Archbishop Runcie's favourite predecessors, and this September he has commemorated the thirteenth centenary of his death at Canterbury, while Adrian has long been a favourite of mine: an African who became for forty years one of the most influential teachers the English Church has ever known.

The conversations between the Archbishop and myself over the past year have not been long and rambling: in the nature of his work that would be impossible. But for the time he has found to set aside I am very grateful. I am also grateful to Canon Graham James, the Archbishop's Chaplain, for providing me with copies of many hundreds of his sermons, lectures and addresses. They have been a major source available to me. Central to these are the annual sermons for the principal feast days at Canterbury and other sermons for a variety of special occasions. No less important are the presidential addresses he has given to General Synod, to Canterbury Diocesan Synod and the Lambeth Conference. There are, next, a number of major lectures given mostly in the latter years of his primacy, such as the Younghusband Memorial Lecture of 1986 on 'Christianity and World Religions', a lecture inaugurating the Centre for the Study of Theology at the University of Essex in 1987 entitled 'Theology, the University and the Modern World', two lectures on authority given in New York in January 1988, lectures in 1989 at Heythrop College on Anglican–Roman Catholic relations, at Lambeth on Thomas Cranmer and two others in Dallas on religious experience. A number of speeches in the House of Lords and annual after-dinner speeches at the Lord Mayor's Banquet, as well as sermons given in the course of the Archbishop's overseas tours and at festivals, centenaries and special occasions of all kinds, are also, many of them, of importance.

Lambeth Palace has helped me in many other ways too, especially by checking my text for factual accuracy, and I am most grateful. But the assessment is mine alone. This is not an official account, and doubtless an official, far longer, life will some day be written. Dr Runcie has in no way attempted to shape the book or influence my interpretation, of which he has been aware. It is simply one account of a distinguished Archbishop of Canterbury of liberally Anglo-Catholic temperament and a historian's mind by a liberal Roman Catholic theologian, historian and near contemporary. We studied history at

Oxford at the same time. In October 1946 he returned from the army to Brasenose and the School of Classics. The same month I came up from school to Worcester and the School of Modern History. But we first met nearly thirty years later. This book has been an honour to write. I can only hope it will serve, not only to make the work of an exceptionally self-regardless and godly man better understood, but also to the on-going health of that greater *Ecclesia Anglicana* and *Ecclesia Catholica* too, to each of which, I trust, we both belong.

Chapter 1 owes a great deal to Margaret Duggan's excellent biography of Dr Runcie and the whole book owes a considerable debt to Owen Chadwick's recent life of Michael Ramsey, not least for the story about Ramsey and Roland Walls on page 46.

I am most grateful to many people whom I have consulted and who have been without exception unstinting in their help, especially the Archbishop of York, Lord Prior, Sir Richard O'Brien, Margaret Duggan, Bishop Mark Santer, Bishop John V. Taylor, Bishop Oliver Tomkins, Canon Sam Van Culin, Canon Martin Reardon, Canon Eric James, the Rev. Richard Chartres and Canon Christopher Hill. I must also express my thanks for support and hospitality to Dean James Annand and the Berkeley Theological College at Yale where the book has been completed.

My wife has commented upon the whole book, typed parts of it and sustained a more than usually irritable husband while I have been engaged upon it. A quite special word of thanks is owed to Jean Rowland who has typed and retyped it at great speed and to her husband Jim who has acted as proof-reader and conveyor of texts back and forth between us. May all typists have such supportive husbands.

September 1990   ADRIAN HASTINGS
                                                    Leeds

❦ PROLOGUE ❦

The vision of the Kingdom and the place of the Church

(Extracted from an address by the Archbishop to diocesan clergy,
Manchester Cathedral, February 1989) ·

I have reached the age when I tend not to turn to the latest theological book, but to some of the classics of the past to remind me of fundamental truths of the Christian faith. The classic analysis of the relationship of the Church to the Kingdom is still, I believe, Richard Niebuhr's study *Christ and Culture*. Written forty years ago in the wake of the last war, it still reads as though the contemporary situation is being described. His analysis of the possible relationships between Christianity and wider society is one of those studies where you keep feeling slightly uneasy. Again and again he seems to describe the position which you have adopted or which you recognize in the Church around you. For example, he talks about *Christ against culture*, a position adopted when the Church maintains almost entirely a prophetic or sectarian role. By contrast, there is the *Christ of culture* where it becomes difficult to disentangle the Church from wider society and to get any feeling of challenge or prophetic ministry. In chapter after chapter he explores other ways in which the Christian faith and the modern world might relate.

The long and the short of it is that the Church can either cut itself off completely and become isolated from the secular world, or it might immerse itself totally, identifying with every trend that comes its way. Niebuhr's point is that none of the descriptions which he offers provides a final answer. The witness of the Church should include something of each, and indeed these different approaches should criticize one another and provide a necessary corrective in the proclamation of the gospel. It is the sort of book that acts like a cold shower. It dispels complacency.

What are the signs of *Christ against culture*, and *the Christ of culture*, in the life of our Church today? There are, I believe, a number of developments which, when taken to their ultimate conclusion, create a mood of Christ *against* culture. Take, for example, the increasing sense of the importance of liturgy in the life of the Church.

1

There are several ways in which this manifests itself in our parishes. Most vividly, it is seen in the revived Holy Week ceremonies — a new part of the round of worship in many a parish in the last decade or so. It is there again in the so-called catechetical movement which has its roots in the Early Church and its revival in modern Roman Catholicism. In this movement baptism and initiation, and a continuing reflection upon their significance, become central to the Christian agenda. Our own Liturgical Commission is working away to produce more texts for us which will offer the opportunity of vivid liturgical celebrations throughout the year.

I am not being critical of this, for I believe we must take care over our liturgy if it is to be a worthy offering to God. It is through liturgy that so much Christian formation takes place. Many of the new rites have increased our consciousness of the *identity* of the Church, for they reaffirm our commitment and emphasize the corporate character of Christian believing. *But* pursued with too much zeal, the good things in this movement may so sharpen the edges of the Church that those outside find it difficult to break through the barriers which we have erected. This sort of process has the danger of *identifying* the Church with the Kingdom. It cannot be said often enough that the Church of God and the Kingdom of God are *not* one and the same.

In the Acts of the Apostles St Peter proclaims that Jesus Christ is Lord of *all*. The Church is that part of the world which has accepted for itself that message and responded to it in faith and trust.

The dangers in such identification are found in those tell-tale signs exhibited by committed and zealous ecclesiastical communities. Take, for example, the 'Christian' approach to Christmas. I am, frankly, rather tired of the tendency of Christians to berate the world for its commercialism and lack of appreciation of what the Feast of Christmas is all about. You know the sort of thing I mean. It's those sermons and parish magazine articles, read curiously by only the most devout, in which Christmas trees are dismissed as pagan cult objects; it's the obsessiveness which bans the singing of any carols before Christmas Eve; it's the encouragement to Christians to challenge the surrounding culture with the 'real message' of Christmas.

All this is part and parcel of a tendency within the Christian community to despise the folk festival. Two other examples are the sneering references often made to Harvest Festival and Mothering Sunday. Neither are exactly central to the Christian calendar, but there is an increasing movement in some parts of the Church to give no more than a grudging place to such celebrations in the round of Christian worship. None of this is particularly new. There is a telling little story in George Orwell's *A Clergyman's Daughter* where every year a local tradesman is allowed to set up in the parish church a veritable Stonehenge of vegetable marrows. Such is the anger of the new vicar at seeing his church decorated to imitate a coster's stall that he banishes the display and the man is lost to the Church forever!

This is an attitude which has not died. Yet I am encouraged by those clergy and congregations who make imaginative use of these folk festivals. On many a council estate it is the Mothering Sunday family service which is one of the best attended of the year. It is *not* Mothering Sunday and its ecclesiastical appeal which has created this. It is the commercial Mother's Day. Yes, it has sentimentalized notions of family life and motherhood, but the sheer fact that people want to put these into a religious context means that the folk festival can be fed with the resources of the Christian gospel. Christ is in culture, as well as against it. And of course you could illustrate that from customs surrounding marriage, or elsewhere from the radical way in which Indian Jesuits have developed a strategy for Christianizing Hinduism.

My point is not that we should lose the significance and distinctiveness of the Christian calendar, but rejoice at the 'rumours of God' which are stirred in the spirit of all people at these various times during the year. We do well to remind ourselves that Christmas was originally a pagan winter festival taken over by the Church fairly late. We do well also to remind ourselves that through the feasting of that time of year numerous other ventures have arisen which presumably we would see as running with the tide of Christian teaching. I think of the extraordinary scene of the first Christmas Day during the First World War when Germans and British played football together between the trenches. I think more recently of the establishment of Crisis at Christmas — supported by politicians as much as churchmen. And there is much to rejoice at when we see society giving thanks for creation in the gifts of the harvest and expressing gratitude for motherhood and nurture within families. Our task is to 'church' these sentiments, not to belittle them.

But folk customs are one thing; philosophies and dogmas are another. Some attitudes have become so commonplace in our culture that we fail to see how much they conflict with Christ and the values of the Kingdom. Let us take just two examples: the notion of individual autonomy and the ascendancy of economic factors in moral decision making.

What is wrong with individual autonomy? Don't we all want to be free, to be responsible for our actions, to determine things for ourselves? A Christian can say at best to this, 'up to a point'. For, though

3

we have free will, we are *not* free agents. We are accountable — to God and to each other. Christianity is a corporate religion, rooted in life within a community, and our Christian character is revealed in our love of justice and love of others. The autonomous individual is on his or her own. We are not. We live by the grace of God, and in God we live, move and have our being. So a Christian is always likely to challenge a prevailing spirit of individual autonomy. It is a spurious freedom which neglects the demands of God. Remember those words of Alexander Solzhenitsyn when he diagnosed so accurately the sickness of Western society, 'Why have all these troubles come upon us? Because we have forgotten God.'

Perhaps we see more easily what is wrong with economic factors in moral decision making. In contemporary society, if a value or conviction is deemed 'uneconomic' it is too often regarded as worthless. Until recently this characterized our attitude to the environment. It was treated as a free resource. Since it had no economic price-tag, little else mattered. Aesthetic, moral, social, ecological and religious reasons for respecting the environment counted for little. And the growing change in attitude now may have more to do with the discovery of economic implications than perhaps we recognize.

Schumacher makes this point passionately in one of his books:

In the current vocabulary of condemnation there are few words as final or conclusive as 'uneconomic'... call a thing immoral or ugly, soul destroying or a degradation of man, a peril to the peace of the world or to the well-being of future generations; as long as you have not shown it to be 'uneconomic' you have not really questioned its right to exist, grow and prosper.

Is Christ against this element of culture? Certainly concepts like stewardship challenge it fundamentally because they contain a sense of accountability to the Creator. And it is accountability to God that contemporary Western culture finds hard to swallow. Yet our vision of the Kingdom must help us sense that God has given us a rich creation, that we live in a universe soaked in non-economic values, one in which beauty, truth and communal responsibility go alongside our stewardship of the earth's resources.

Last night I spoke of another area in which Christ may be more against culture than within it. A week ago a Government Minister called for the Church to develop a theology of success. It is a tempting invitation. But where in the New Testament is success a criterion for godliness and grace? As I said last night, 'What do you do with the crown of thorns and Christ's shed blood when you create a theology of success?'

Perhaps here we see why there is a degree of tension between the Church and the Government at the present time. That tension is much, much overstated. But the Church, if it is to be faithful, cannot espouse the cult of individual autonomy, or cloak economic factors and worldly success with a divine approval. The values of the Kingdom are much greater. God has to be reckoned with as a loving judge and merciful saviour.

Yet the Church of England has long worked less with the model of Christ against culture than with the model of the Christ of culture. What else might be expected of an Established Church? Dissenters dissented precisely because it sometimes went too far in identifying the Church of God with the society in which it was set. Nowadays, though, the establishment of the Church of England is frequently, sometimes wilfully, misunderstood. It has become a derogatory term, tossed out when the Church of England is accused of standing on privilege. That is one way of avoiding the examination of the complex interaction between the Church of England and the English people. The establishment of our Church is contained not merely in the relationship of the Church as an institution with other institutions within the State, but in the unexamined relationship between the citizens of our land, whatever their beliefs, and a Church which defines itself by offering them service. In this area I believe we must maintain the model of the Christ of culture if we are to be an accessible Church to the English people.

Let me illustrate what I mean by examples which have been recently in the news. On the Sunday following the crash of the British Midland plane on the M1, the second item on an early radio news bulletin was that the Vicar of Kegworth would be saying prayers for the victims, their families and friends at the Morning Service in the parish church that day. Just a week before, the nation had paid attention to the Service in Lockerbie parish church at which the Moderator of the established Church in Scotland preached at an occasion which was described by social workers and journalists as the time when the people of that area could close one chapter in their mourning, and begin to look to the future again. And the Memorial Service in Winchester Cathedral for the victims of the Clapham rail crash did exactly the same thing.

Even in a society which church people, as much as others, commonly call 'pluralist', sources of overarching religious authority are needed. Yes, our society struggles about acknowledging them, but it cannot be doubted that they are sought. Authority is a sign to the Church to handle the area of meaning and belief and symbolism in human life.

That our culture remains shot through with Christianity and pluralism does not undermine this in the way some social commentators imagine. I was struck, for example, by the way in which other faith communities looked to the Archbishop of Canterbury in the House of Lords as a protector of their own faith interests during the passage of the Education Act. That is but one example of the way in which the establishment of the Church of England assists the handling of religious pluralism, rather than works against it. Indeed, I have had a brief meeting with members of the Islamic community here in the last two days. They understand our condemnation of incitement to murder, but feel we have been too silent over the hurt to their faith which the publication of *The Satanic Verses* occasioned.

Our society still looks to the Church as a body able to handle the great questions of life and death when their enormity becomes too great for easy answers. Often the bereaved family expresses thanks to the vicar after a funeral service which is out of all proportion to the extent of his ministry. But their gratitude lies in the security they feel in finding someone who can handle these perplexities of life and death. Likewise, I believe that the Church needs to discern signs of the Kingdom in the world and should attempt to identify where God is already working well outside the agencies of the Church. The hope is that we may use the resources of the gospel to support and strengthen encouraging movements of the human spirit wherever they are found.

What must concern us is how the Church of England should organize itself so that the resources of the Christian faith are made accessible to the English people. For only then can those signs of God's Kingdom which we discern in the world around us be nourished and nurtured by the gospel of Christ.

Our Church has traditionally undertaken this task through its system of authorized ministerial leadership — namely, that exercised by bishops and vicars. I choose the latter word deliberately because it so closely identifies the minister with the parish. The vicar is a person whose profile is much higher in the mind of the public than that of the priest, deacon or lay worker. English people generally have only the most blurred notion of ecclesiastical structure but they do recognize the *trusted person*. For that is what the vicar is. He is someone authorized, someone whom people may confidently approach.

People find their generalized expectations of 'God' and 'the Church' met in a trustworthy person, whether bishop or vicar. But those who are perceived to live such a trustworthy or reliable existence must themselves feel, and in fact be, trusted. That is the essence of functional episcopacy: an individual is trusted and the limits of that trust are very wide.

We must be careful not to belittle that trust.

The gospel is not something we *possess* to bring to people. The gospel has no independent life of its own. It is a saving work, discovered through proclamation. In the Church of England's mission in the past a central feature of its proclamation of the gospel has been the pastoral work of its parish clergy, and the witness in home, community and work place of its laity. In general, Anglican clergy have not been great preachers, and the laity not vocal evangelists, but the gospel has been generated in the discipleship evident in pastoral work and daily encounter.

If we are to serve the Kingdom of God I am sure we must not abandon the vision of our Church as a public body, at the service of the whole nation, serving those in the outer court as well as those in the sanctuary; a Church pervasive, guarding the roots and the memories, pointing to eternity amid a time of restlessness, distraction and ephemeral social change.

1

From Crosby to Canterbury

Robert Alexander Kennedy Runcie was born in Crosby on the outskirts of Liverpool on 2 October 1921. His father, Robert Dalziel Runcie, was a Scot, fond of bowls and golf, chief electrical engineer at the Tate and Lyle sugar refinery in Liverpool. His mother Nancy, a hairdresser, was of Irish blood. They lived in a semi, large and comfortable enough for the four children, but not very grand. The family had no special pretensions. None of its members had been to a university. There was no money for holidays away from home. There was also no church connection beyond formality. They had been married in church. The children were baptized, but they were not regular church-goers though Runcie's grandfather remained a sturdy communicating Presbyterian. In all this, Runcie's background was thoroughly typical of lower middle-class urban England of the inter-war years, with its strongly secularizing character, but not at all typical of Archbishops of Canterbury. His class background was lower than that of any of his predecessors for a century or more. It was also far less ecclesiastical than that of most of them. William Temple was, of course, at the other extreme in having an Archbishop of Canterbury as his father, but most archbishops and many bishops had plenty of clergy in their ancestry, so that a man like Bishop John Robinson had so many he might hardly have been able to imagine *not* becoming a priest himself! Runcie was quite different, lacking any inherited link with either the Church or the academic world. Quiet as he has mostly been about his family and early background, it is a point of considerable importance for understanding Runcie and his relationship to the Church and society.

Robert's sisters and brother were half a generation away from him, Kathleen being twelve, Marjorie ten and Kenneth eight when Robert ('Robin', 'Bobby' or 'Bob') was born. They were all very fond of their baby brother. His parents were affectionate but also a little distant. With siblings so many years older than himself, Runcie started life very much a loner. He developed a deep friendship with an imaginary companion, 'Bonner', with whom he played games and for whom a place had always to be laid at table. However, when the time for school came — the Primary in Coronation Road — Bonner's days were up. He

8

was discreetly dispatched to another school. Insistence upon both his presence at table and his disappearance when he was becoming troublesome illustrated a certain firmness already present. Conversation with Bonner was replaced by more self-conscious discussion with himself; a habit of arguing things out, not with others, but alone, yet rather deliberately. Perhaps a consciousness of incipient intellectualism, of being brighter and more academic than the rest of the family, had something to do with it too.

Like his brother Kenneth, Runcie went to the local grammar school, Merchant Taylors', founded by a seventeenth-century worthy, John Harrison, and he went there on a Harrison Scholarship. His sisters had been at its companion girls' school. They were good schools and the then headmaster, the Rev. Charles Russell, a former Fellow of Pembroke College, Cambridge, was determined to improve the style and academic achievement. Gowns, prizes, boards of honour, societies and houses were the order of the day, and Runcie was the sort of boy to respond and be appreciated. Highly competitive in spirit and with a great will to succeed, the absolute all-rounder, cricket, rugby, athletics and classics, he shone in everything. Sport might appear to dominate, but it was the classics and things of the mind which mattered most. Runcie's classics master was outstanding and undoubtedly, for a while, influenced him considerably. He was also a Communist, and Runcie thought himself a Communist too — a natural phase in the life of a thoughtful young man in the 1930s.

Russell was a modern churchman of some distinction, a member of the Church of England's Doctrine Commission chaired by William Temple. He wanted his boys to think and to be Christians too. With Runcie at least he succeeded. One term he spent entirely on the Book of Job. The issues came alive and, fifty years later, it is still the book of the Old Testament that Runcie knows best. He also gave him B. H. Streeter's *The Four Gospels* to read, a work of quite serious biblical criticism. Runcie read it like a detective story and it converted him at one go to a critical faith. He would in his mind ever after, odd as it may seem, be intellectually a Streeter Christian.

The wider Liberal Protestant form of religion practised by Russell and Streeter did not appeal to him. He needed something a good deal richer in symbolism. He had a great-aunt who was a Roman Catholic and his very earliest recollection of religion was being taken into the local Catholic church and sitting there while she prayed: 'I don't know much about the chemistry of the subconscious, but I do know that the experience had a deeper effect on me than the subsequent effort to drum a wordy religion into me at Sunday School.' Later his sister

helped. Kathleen had already been confirmed in the Church of England and become an active member of the Anglo-Catholic congrega-
tion of St Faith's on the corner of the Liverpool Road. Here Runcie
joined her, making his first communion next to her. Russell, as a
member of the Modern Churchmen's Union, did not approve, but he
let the boy have his way; a certain sensible quiet firmness in Runcie
will have prevailed then, as it often prevailed later. Not long afterwards, he realized that he wished to be ordained. He defended T. S.
Eliot in the school literary society, was in with the SCM, and by the
time he left school rather thought of himself as a Christian socialist.
The shape of his mind, give or take a point here and there, was clearly
already formed.

It was clear that a boy of his intellectual ability should go to
university. Liverpool and Manchester were doing well with respectable departments of classics, but it was Oxford or Cambridge which
seemed obviously right for someone of Runcie's calibre — at least in
the eyes of Russell and in the eyes too of Kathleen. In 1937 she married
an Anglican priest, Angus Inglis, a curate in Nottingham, who had
himself studied at Oxford. So Runcie sat the entry examinations in
1940 for Cambridge and Oxford colleges. It was eventually to
Brasenose at Oxford that he went, early in 1941, with the help, once
more, of a Harrison as well as a university scholarship. The scholarship was important — there was little spare family money, even for
the university education of its brightest member. The other children
had long ago left home, while Runcie's father was ill and had to take
early retirement. By early 1939 he was completely blind and in 1940
the family home was sold, and Runcie spent his last two terms at
school as a boarder. Coping with his father's blindness and the loss of
a home provided his first major experience of the pain of living.

The move to Oxford after Easter 1941, when he was nineteen and a
half, was one of the most decisive moments in Runcie's life. The spell
was a strong one. For the next thirty years, he would be for the greater
part of the time in or around Oxford or Cambridge. His was a natural
Oxbridge spirit, adapting almost instantly to its characteristic moods
— infinitely confident, enthusiastic, critical, amused. His ability to
adapt has always been outstanding. It is indeed perhaps his most
striking quality. He takes on the very colour of the vegetation almost
without trying, chameleon-like. Whereas others have characteristics,
idiosyncrasies, which stick out in every situation and through which
one comes to seek the person's character, Runcie is rather the other
way round. He enters perfectly into every environment. Indeed his
most memorable personal gift is a sort of caricature of this very

characteristic of chameleonship: his outstanding power of mimicry. The ability to take off anyone — to produce the tone of voice, the mannerisms, the movements of hand and arm of almost any colleague, so convincingly as to be deliciously absurd — is a great, almost irresistible party gift and one reason why Runcie could move so easily into new social groupings. He had no Oxbridge background, but became, almost at once, a quintessentially Oxbridge young man, not in any exaggerated or stylized way, but simply because he fitted the part, enjoyed it, and could do it so well.

The Anglo-Catholicism he had already embraced at St Faith's, Crosby, flourished in Oxford. He served at Pusey House, in Christ Church Cathedral and in St Mary's, the University Church. He made theological friends. His intention to become a priest when the war was over was strengthened but kept very much to himself.

He was reading 'Greats' — the most distinguished of Oxford courses: Greek and Latin language and literature, philosophy, ancient history. He enjoyed the contact with K. J. Spalding, a rather unusual tutor for a Greats man, a specialist in Eastern religion as well as in philosophy, and he learnt a lot from his tutor of ancient history, Hugh Last. But neither then nor later was Runcie a person to be very obviously influenced by anyone past or present. Beneath the adaptable surface lay already a mind not lightly fathomed, nor perhaps easily interpreted even by its possessor. We often only discover our thoughts by writing them at length, and Runcie has never been a writer.

England was at war, and even Oxford, unchanging as it always liked to appear, was in considerable disarray. Many of the colleges had been taken over for war work. The students were few in number, their courses were abbreviated; they came and went at any time. Though Runcie was an undergraduate of Brasenose (BNC), in fact he lived in Christ Church, as Brasenose was under military occupation. And he stayed only four terms. No time for more. Once he was past his twentieth birthday, conscription could not be far off, and he visited the Oxford recruiting office.

An Oxford undergraduate, obviously very bright, an excellent all-rounder in sports, he was just the kind of officer material the army needed. But which regiment? Runcie had no pretensions, but a sense of still being enough of a Scotsman to suggest a Scottish one. 'What about a commission in the Scots Guards?' he was asked. In peacetime someone of his social background would hardly have been welcome. But 1941 was not peacetime, and the Scots Guards had recently suffered heavy casualties in North Africa. The gaps needed to be filled. Robert Alexander Kennedy Runcie sounded quite sufficiently Scottish and the Commanding Officer, Col. Bill Balfour, took to him at once and firmly reassured him that, in time of war, the absence of a private income in a Guards officer could easily be overlooked.

In consequence, in early June 1942, Robert Runcie left Oxford and entered the army by way of Pirbright Camp in Surrey. A few awful weeks followed before Runcie could adapt sufficiently and be accepted. Socially, his was simply the wrong background. While his future fellow officers had been learning to lead army, kingdom and empire via the playing fields of Eton, he had been hanging around the Regal at Crosby to watch Laurel and Hardy or the Marx Brothers or going on the odd day trip to Blackpool or Manchester. Beneath Colonel Balfour, the regiment was divided into four: Right Flank (to which Runcie would belong) commanded by Lord Cathcart; Left Flank, the Hon. Michael Fitzalan Howard; 'S' Squadron, Willie Whitelaw; and Headquarters Squadron, Sir Charles Maclean, Chief of Clan Maclean, and later on, Chief Scout and Chief almost everything else too.

It was a colossal social leap. At the close of 1940, Runcie was still a lower-class Lancashire lad, shining at the top of a provincial grammar school, and very conscious of the slums of Liverpool where his sister was a social worker. By the close of 1942, he was a polished Guards officer, with an Oxford background, quite at home with the nation's aristocratic and military *crème de la crème*. It could only be possible in war time. But, equally, it could only be possible with someone as adaptable, as clever and as nice as Robert Runcie. Even snooty young Etonians could not long resist his power of mimicry, the quality of his cricket or his sheer competence and underlying toughness. Of course, he did not parade his Crosby past, or even his Anglo-Catholic convictions, though that was not a matter of denying them — just as later on as a priest he was not the sort of one who would parade his military experience; he just naturally and quickly put on the new mask almost unconsciously, while getting on with the job in hand. Most people relate jobs to themselves, at least as much as they relate themselves to the job. Runcie has all his life been, from this point of view, an extreme case of non-egotism: the work required, the social milieu it goes with, the expectations of others here and now, have an immense priority. Thus, the commander of a troop of three Churchill tanks quickly emerged. Two years later Europe was invaded and the Scots Guards crossed to Normandy. A few weeks earlier, 30 May 1944, the whole brigade attended a 'Service before Battle' in Canterbury Cathedral. The 'Red Dean', the Stalinist Dr Hewlett Johnson, a fine liturgist, led the service. The Archbishop, William Temple, preached and the band of the Scots Guards played. Young Lieutenant Runcie was in his future Cathedral for the first time.

In the last days of July in the battle of Caumont, he was under fire for the first time. The heavy tanks slowly advanced through the hedges, ditches, orchards and copses of the Normandy countryside. It was a breakthrough of a sort, but one involving heavy casualties. At one point, twelve of their tanks were destroyed in just five minutes and the second-in-command of the battalion killed. The strain, the discomfort, the noise, the sheer intensity of the struggle to advance, to survive, to keep one's tank functioning and one's companions (if possible) alive — all this was a new experience, one immeasurably heightened beyond the months of training in Yorkshire or Salisbury Plain the year before.

Major Whitelaw took over as battalion second-in-command and the front moved on across France and Belgium and Holland and into Germany. More battles, more casualties, endless mud, occasional dances with local girls, occasionally Mass in a local church. New Year 1945 saw them advancing into Germany. In March, one of Runcie's other tanks was hit under heavy fire. The crew, all but one, were able to scramble out and rush for cover, but the one was caught, dazed in a jammed turret and unable to get out. Runcie jumped from his own tank, ran across, turned the turret and dragged the driver out. Next day, in the early evening of 2 March, they attacked the town of Winnekendonk. The first line of tanks was knocked out under heavy fire and Runcie was in the second line, advancing to replace them. To see where the shells were coming from, he took his tank into a highly exposed position with the German guns 500 yards away, and quickly opened fire. They had the shortest amount of time before they were bound to be destroyed, but it was enough. The German guns were silenced and the march went on. In Winnekendonk hours later, Runcie walked over to a German Tiger Tank, most likely knocked out by his own guns. There were four dead young men inside it.

In May the war was over. Runcie was one of the first troops to enter the Belsen Concentration Camp. It made an indelible impression on his consciousness. He also distinguished himself as a tank commander by taking the surrender of a German U-boat. The next day, Colonel Dunbar, the battalion commander, came into the mess with the news that he had been awarded the Military Cross for his courage at Winnekendonk with the following citation:

During the attack on Winnekendonk on 2 March 1945, Lieutenant Runcie's troop was in support of the leading wave of tanks when

13

they came under heavy and close fire of concealed 88 mm and self-propelled guns from the front and both flanks, all three tanks being hit.

Lieutenant Runcie unhesitatingly took his tank out into the open which was the only place from which he could see the enemy weapons, and engaged them so effectively that he knocked out two 75 mm SPs, one 88 mm, also causing the enemy to abandon a nest of 50 mm guns. During this time not only was he shot at with armour-piercing shells from a range of not more than 500 yards, but was also being subjected to very heavy shell and mortar fire. A short time later, while still being fired upon, he personally and successfully directed the fire of our artillery on to an area from which fire was holding up our advance. There is no doubt that Lieutenant Runcie's courageous leadership and the magnificent marksmanship of his troop dealt so successfully with this strong enemy anti-tank screen that our tanks and infantry were able to get on into the town.

In June, the Churchill tanks were paraded for the last time with all their dents and then abandoned. Runcie moved to Cologne, attended the opera with a German girl-friend, and in his final months in the army was sent to Trieste to help define and keep the peace on the Italian–Yugoslav border, the line also of what was already becoming the 'Iron Curtain', and participate in a bit of international diplomacy. In August 1946, he was demobbed. Four years of soldiering had made an enormous difference. The experience was vast, very tough, requiring every skill of mind and body. And he had come through it to perfection. The job had been done. Ever so many friends had been acquired. But there remained a secretness about him, hard to explain. The inner core of his being had been fortified but had, hidden, remained essentially unchanged. None of his friends in the army ever guessed his intention to be a priest. His religious life had been kept quietly fed on his bible and the regular reading of J. H. Oldham's *Christian Newsletter*. He could now move on, with the confidence of a Guards officer, back to Oxford but forward to the Church.

October 1946, Michaelmas term, Runcie was settling into his rooms in BNC and a rather odd Oxford, where 90 per cent of the male undergraduates were warriors back from the forces, only 10 per cent direct from school, but where the University would not admit that anything had changed or that rules should be revised. Gowns had to be worn for lectures and tutorials, in hall for dinner and in the evenings, college doors were locked at 9.00 p.m., the proctors and their human 'bulldogs' patrolled the streets to ensure academic decorum. 'In the present state of the world', Runcie wrote to his brother-in-law, Angus, 'it is comforting beyond all measure to return here where nothing has changed or ever looks likely to change; where the battle of Marathon is still fought over daily. . . . I have very pleasant rooms with a very academic view from the window, of the Camera and St Mary.' But the eyes of the dead lads in the tank at Winnekendonk, the friends killed in battles more recent than Marathon, would take their time to be laid to rest, and for the mind truly to move on. The academic calm of Oxford was too strange a contrast for all to stomach, and some ex-servicemen preferred to leave. For those who stayed, however, it could prove the best of therapies.

The undergraduates of those years were not very politically inclined. Runcie had now moved, mildly, into the Conservative Association, and was even briefly its college secretary, but a certain lack of commitment could not be concealed from the eyes of the truly dedicated, such as Margaret Roberts (later Thatcher), his contemporary at Somerville, and he was dropped. Politics, he admits, was never ever a first interest. The heights of Anglo-Catholicism too were no longer very appealing and Pusey House was quietly abandoned, but the middle-of-the-road services of St Mary's, and the mystical tutorials of Spalding, continued to be savoured. What, however, chiefly concentrated the mind was the struggle to get to grips with what seemed most challenging in the Greats course, post-Cartesian philosophy and especially the exigencies of current Oxford philosophy, Logical Positivism. This required all his time.

Runcie's commitment was to the Church, a very unwavering one, but his decisive training was exceedingly unchurchy: the army and Oxford philosophy, both at their most rigorous. If he came through the former with an MC, he mastered the latter at Christmas 1948 with a First in Greats.

An Oxford graduate, destined for the Church of England's priesthood, is likely enough to go to Westcott House, Cambridge, for his ordination training, just as a Cambridge graduate is likely to go to Cuddesdon, near Oxford: then you have had at least a touch of both places, the two traditional pillars of England's social, academic and also ecclesiastical establishment. Few and far between, at least until very recently, are the bishops who have been to neither. So it was certainly less than surprising that Runcie should immediately on graduation at Oxford have gone to Westcott and to Cambridge. We are entering, indeed, the most predictable part of his career.

Westcott was well, indeed excitingly, staffed: its principal, Kenneth

Carey, its vice-principal, Alan Webster, its chaplain, Harry Williams. Many of Runcie's fellow students were very able and included a number of future bishops. Outside Westcott's doors, there was the university in which the post-war religious revival was booming, the churches and college chapels full, the theological faculty distinguished. College life could continue for a couple more years, more prayer, less socializing, theology rather than philosophy, but an ongoing sense of belonging to an inner élite of intellectual and spiritual excellence.

It is, however, important to note that Runcie did not wish to take a degree in theology and never did so. In some way, which he might even now find hard to explain, he did not quite get on with theology. There was a sense of underlying unease here, even of rejection of something now proving a little alien to the formation of his mind. The great theological systems of German origin simply wearied him. He had been inoculated against them too successfully by Ayer's *Language, Truth and Logic,* and in any case his mind simply did not work that way. It was intuitive, not systematic. He also felt no inclination to develop into a biblical or patristic scholar, despite his excellent classical grounding. Years later, in 1960, he would write to his brother-in-law, 'My ambitions are not — because I haven't the gift — book writing and professorial chairs'. That was an accurate piece of self-knowledge. He could, of course, have spent his life as a perfectly passable academic and he has certainly a sensitive sense of history, though of a more anecdotal than analytical sort, but at least theology was out, and it is noticeable that it is T. S. Eliot, not Barth or Tillich, whose name and quotations recur in his speaking. Literature, history, philosophy, all these three, and each in a fairly secular form, have shaped his mind, his intellectual approach to the understanding of things. Always careful of his sources and his arguments, anxious not to claim too much, aware of the agnostic dons further along the table, glad to throw light upon particularities rather than attempt any over-large approach, Runcie remained intellectually the classics man he had become at Brasenose. Westcott clericalized him socially and prepared him for pastoral ministry; for a time it set him on perhaps almost too churchy a road, but it affected the structural boundaries of his thinking remarkably little.

Christmas Eve, 1950. Runcie was ordained deacon in Newcastle Cathedral and began two years of curacy at Gosforth on Tyneside, about as far from Oxbridge as he could go. It is customary for Anglican high-fliers to do their stint first in a northern industrial parish. Hugh Montefiore, a friend of his from Westcott, was a curate nearby. Here

Runcie baptized his first babies, led confirmation classes, preached regularly and, on Christmas Day 1951, celebrated Holy Communion for the first time. For him, as for many a priest, that was an extraordinarily tense experience: to hold the bread and the wine in his hands, to say the words of institution, and to believe them now the Body and the Blood of Christ. Everything came together at that point. In this he stood and has always continued to stand fully in the Catholic sacramental tradition. There are shadows in plenty one cannot well interpret, but at the heart of things remains the luminous, on-going power of the Eucharist.

His ministry at Gosforth was not to last. In less than two years, he had a telephone call from Kenneth Carey asking him to return to Cambridge, to the staff of Westcott House. Alan Webster was leaving. Hugh Montefiore was already back on the staff. Would he join them? Neither his vicar nor his Bishop was very pleased at so hasty a departure, following in Montefiore's wake, but they could see the point, though three years as a curate is normally the minimum. Theological colleges can claim a certain priority and probably Runcie already looked only too clearly a man marked for early promotion. He was, moreover, well over thirty, and far more mature than the normal curate. So he left Gosforth — perhaps too soon for his own long-term benefit, because he would never have another opportunity for straight, grass-roots, pastoral work.

For the next eight years, Runcie worked in Cambridge, first as Chaplain, then Vice-Principal, of Westcott House and later, from 1956, as Dean of Trinity Hall. He felt wonderfully at home in Cambridge — as many Oxford men do. Westcott and then Trinity Hall gave him constant opportunities of the sort he used so well, for pastoral guidance coupled with friendship, a humane mix of spiritual life, teaching of a not too adventurous kind, and the almost hidden ability to ensure that a human community is functioning happily and efficiently. One example may be given. There was, among the summer students, a young clearly awkward, but highly intelligent, history graduate, Gary Bennett. Bennett found Kenneth Carey unsympathetic and no help at all in resolving his problems, but Runcie was quite different. 'He was the one member of the staff who actually seemed to think that it was a good thing that I was an academic, and we had a number of humorous conversations. . . . He thought that all priests should have a secular side to them, and a false or intense piety was an enemy to real religion. He took a kind of benevolent oversight of me which was more that of equal to equal than I deserved. He was always cheering me up by asking my advice on this or that theological problem. I became quite devoted to him, and my diary is full of reference to his kindness. He had intelligence, wit and style.' This description of the young Runcie at work is all the more valuable in coming from the future author of the ill-fated Crockford Preface. But there are scores of people from this and later periods of his life who would describe Runcie in almost exactly similar words.

Carey, Montefiore and a group of Westcott-linked friends decided to write a book of essays about the Anglican understanding of episcopacy — a contribution to resolving the Church of England's attitude to the Church of South India and its ministry, an issue which was causing great unease at the time among Anglo-Catholics. Most held that the CSI's view of the episcopate was seriously inadequate, and must prevent communion between the two Churches, especially while many of its clergy were not ordained episcopally at all. Low Church Anglicans, on the other hand, held that episcopal ordination, while a good thing for Anglicans, is not really a necessity for a Christian Church and one may be in communion with those who do not have it, or, still more, with those who do have the episcopate but also (temporarily) have some ministers not episcopally ordained. The point of the book, *The Historic Episcopate*, was to argue a middle way. While stressing, in Anglo-Catholic terms, the great value of having bishops, it argued more ecumenically against the necessity for episcopal ordination in all circumstances. As a staff member of Westcott House, a historian at heart, and a close friend of Montefiore especially, Runcie was expected to take part. He declined to do so. Deep down, all his life he has been a non-writer. Why, perhaps he could hardly say. He loves beautiful writing and has a great gift for the construction of elegant sentences even in impromptu speech, but 'I'm such a slow writer', he admits, always seeking further to perfect his phrases. Temperamentally he seems antipathetic to committing himself to any piece of extended theory. It was probably this, rather than any chunk of hardline Anglo-Catholicism in his soul, which formed the ground for his abstention. It was, nevertheless, a signal of some significance for the future: he played his cards quite close to his chest, but, in part at least, because he was less confident than most of his colleagues as to exactly which theological cards he actually held.

The move from Westcott to Trinity Hall is to be noted. Owen Chadwick was Dean of Trinity Hall and had just been elected Master of Selwyn College. He would become, in due course, Regius Professor of Modern History in the University, Vice-Chancellor and very much else: the ablest of modern Church historians and a very great power indeed in a quiet way, both in the ecclesiastical and the academic world. He was and is a man exceptionally good at weighing up other men. Naturally enough he wanted a good successor and felt he had found one in Runcie. Runcie hardly knew him, but when Chadwick called on him at Westcott and suggested the idea of his becoming Dean of Trinity Hall, Runcie liked the idea, was interviewed and appointed. John Habgood succeeded him as Vice-Principal of Westcott.

Trinity Hall is strong on law and when Runcie needed a secretary, he found one in the daughter of a distinguished legal don and editor of several books on criminal law, Rosalind (Lindy) Turner. Within a year they were married. Lindy had some interest in religion, but almost none in the professional in-talk of the clergy. The rest of her family was decidedly agnostic. She enjoyed music and gardens and a sort of moderately liberated modern domesticity. She was always deeply loyal to Robert, his work and all that followed from his work, but she regularly made it clear that she wanted a life of her own too. She would not be the silently dutiful wife. On the contrary, she would make a point of nonconformity loudly enough but then, again and again, do as she knew Robert's wife needed to do. Above all, she stopped him sinking into the bog of an unquestioning churchiness, a fate he was not incapable of succumbing to. 'Her mixture of extreme honesty and extreme domestic efficiency', he would write later, 'can often be explosive and difficult to live with but it enables her to communicate with and win the respect of people with whom the church is seldom in touch.' She and their two children would be a decidedly lay presence within a life one of whose principal temptations could have been to grow remote from any genuinely lay concern.

But of course, as we have seen, she had a very considerable ally within Runcie himself — the rather lay and secular cast of his intellectual formation, as well as his family background. It was in the years around his marriage, as a don of Trinity Hall, that this found its fullest natural scope. He taught not theology but classics. He interpreted Herodotus and Thucydides. Here he could use his sharp mind, historical skills and ability to communicate imaginatively without worrying whether his conclusions involved believing or not believing this or that. While his scholarship undoubtedly fed his religion, there was also a certain distance between them, but he was very clearly a priest as well as a don, and a priest already demonstrating particular skills in relating to the non-believer.

Three years later, in 1960, Runcie moved back into a theological college and back also to Oxford. He became Principal of Cuddesdon, just outside Oxford, most prestigious of moderately Anglo-Catholic colleges. Westcott and Cuddesdon between them have provided by far the largest number of bishops — and scholars — over the last hundred years, though, in the last quarter century or so, their relative distinction *vis à vis* other Anglican colleges has probably declined a little, just as the relative social weight of Oxford and Cambridge has declined a little *vis à vis* other English universities. It was nice being Dean of Trinity Hall, but it was still a relatively junior job and Runcie was now not far off forty. It was inevitable that people concerned with promoting able men in the Church should have had their eyes on Runcie by this time and be looking for a fairly senior post in which his manifest abilities would find fuller scope. It was, it seems, once more Owen Chadwick who took the lead and approached Runcie early in 1960 about the possibility. The suitability was obvious. Runcie was not going to be a leading academic, it was already clear, so while staying indefinitely at the university would be pleasant enough, it could hardly lead there to anything very senior. His best skills needed a different field.

At Cuddesdon Runcie was not only Principal of the theological college, he was also vicar of the parish and the Runcies lived in the vicarage. This side of these ten years is largely overlooked by others, but never by him. It is not in his nature to under-respond to any task and he took his job as parish priest of Cuddesdon very seriously. It is to Cuddesdon, rather than to Gosforth, that he later looked back to earth his teaching about the pastoral ministry. It convinced him of the truth of William Blake's line, of which he has long been specially fond, 'He who would do good must do it by minute particulars'. For him the parson should be 'a living symbol — faint and imperfect but the only living symbol we have — of the attitude of God himself'. He experienced the need for that, taking seriously the most 'minute particulars', as vicar of Cuddesdon.

Runcie was at Cuddesdon for almost ten years — by far the longest stretch he had been anywhere since he left Crosby in 1941 — and as Principal of Cuddesdon we can see rather well both his strengths and his weaknesses. It was an old-fashioned countryside seminary in the Tractarian mould. The day began with Mattins at 7.00 a.m. followed by meditation and the Eucharist. Evensong was at 4.30 p.m., Compline at 9.30 p.m. The 'Great Silence' extended from Compline to breakfast. Mattins, meditation and Compline seven days a week were compulsory. All meals had to be taken in the college except for Saturday lunch. This was the regime of a Roman Catholic seminary, but many of these men were married, and in a RC seminary they were not. Though wives were allowed to exist, they could not appear in college and they had to sleep at least two miles away. It was decidedly hard for a married student to have to live at that distance, be in the college chapel every day at 7.00 in the morning and 9.30 in the evening, and never eat with his wife except at Saturday lunch. Runcie's predecessor was unmarried. Runcie was not and he had, too, a baby son; but at first he followed quite the same routine as his students and his predecessor, leaving home — the Cuddesdon vicarage — before 7.00, returning after Compline and having all his meals in college. His marriage survived it, but those of some of his staff suffered greater strain.

Little by little things changed, Saturday Mattins ceased to be compulsory and up to a point Lindy managed to make women appear natural in Cuddesdon and even welcome; weekend eating rules were relaxed a good deal; but there was very little attempt to alter the structures at all systematically. Women remained extraordinarily excluded even from the prayer life of the college, apart from the Sunday Eucharist. Runcie was a temperamental conservative within the Anglo-Catholic tradition, intellectually almost unflappable but with no belief at all in radical change of rules and liturgies. Despite the wider radical ethos of the 1960s, the shape of Cuddesdon remained largely unaltered.

What did concern Runcie was a first-class intellectual training, good spiritual direction and happy human relationships. And he was very good at achieving all three. David Jenkins, Oxford's most lively theologian at that time, came over for a weekly lecture, as did the patristic scholar and Dean of Christ Church, Henry Chadwick, the Jesuit biblical scholar, Robert Murray, and the historian of spirituality, Donald Allchin. The internal staff of Cuddesdon also included some interesting appointments such as Mark Santer and Peter Cornwell. Runcie did not see himself as a theologian but he was extremely anxious to train his students to think theologically as vigorously as could be. While *Honest to God* rocked the Church of England and the Second Vatican Council the Church of Rome, Runcie wrote nothing and said remarkably little. Yet undoubtedly he was wrestling mentally with the problems of the day, even if the wrestling seldom produced intellectual conclusions which satisfied him. He felt happy neither with new and radical theologies, nor with fundamentalist simplicities. There was no streak of evangelicalism in him, but no streak either — despite his spiritual Anglo-Catholicism — of any special inclination for Rome. Again, he was by no means the child of Temple and still less enthused by the stirrings of liberation theology; it would be very hard indeed to find in him a special inclination towards any particular social or political theology. 'We cannot choose

21

the ground on which to fight the Lord's battle, but it is possible to fight on the wrong ground', he wrote in 1965. He was better able to detect the wrong ground than the right but perhaps the Second World War tank commander and interpreter of Thucydides may have felt at times that any unchosen ground on which he might be compelled to fight was likely to be the wrong one.

In so far as one could alter the ground, he seemed to feel that it was 'prayer and wise, experienced direction' which would make the difference, changing the wrong ground into the right. The ground, of course, cannot change: it is as it is, the world in all its secularity. What is different is how it is perceived and that change of perception, of symbolic understanding may be achieved — Runcie has consistently believed — less by any change in structure than by a combination of spiritual with intellectual maturity. He encouraged links with the Sisters of the Love of God at Fairacres in Oxford and parties of students regularly visited the convent. He himself developed as a spiritual director of sensitivity and wisdom. It may well be as such that those who know him best rate him most highly, but this is of its nature a hidden role, not open to detailed report or analysis.

Runcie spent a very large part of his adult life in theological education — four years at Westcott and ten at Cuddesdon. Moreover, while Bishop of St Albans he chaired a Commission on theological education. Nothing, then, has occupied him more. Years later he reflected on it all in an address to members of Westcott House and Ridley Hall. He quoted a saying of F. R. Barry, 'Once get the Ministry right and nearly everything else will get itself right', and commented, 'Too strong, perhaps, but a maxim worth pondering'. He stressed the need for 'theological coherence' and admitted that it had often been lacking: what was needed was 'not *less* academic theology . . . but academic theology focused on those areas of theology which need to be studied for the sake of the spiritual and intellectual integrity of the community of faith'. The good minister is good, less because of what he does, but because of what he is, one who can convey 'a sense of being involved in a serious and costly endeavour' but who still does this largely through 'harnessing, directing and consecrating our natural gifts'. That includes playing cricket, and Runcie quoted Martin Thornton's remark that 'the English priest plays cricket on the green not in spite of his priesthood but because of it'. In 1986 he recognized that some aspects of theological education had rightly changed since his day but these later reflections probably remain faithful enough to the spirit of his years at Cuddesdon.

Cuddesdon prospered under Runcie's leadership, despite the general disjointedness of 1960s religion. It is hardly surprising that in 1968 he became Chairman of the Conference of Theological College Principals. He had a very firm sense of the relationship of theology and spiritual life to pastoral ministry. He had shown himself a leader — not in terms of any special idea, cause or party: in such terms he was perhaps harder than ever to identify, but in terms of generating an effective, confident and happy community. By the end of the decade, when he was nearly fifty years old, his name was put forward for a bishopric. On 10 October 1969 a letter from Harold Wilson offered him the See of St Albans — a nice bishopric of middling importance, close to London and, as the Archbishop's Appointments Secretary helpfully stressed, just midway between Oxford and Cambridge! He would still not need to forgo the image of the Oxbridge man. 'I always thought you were a natural diocesan', wrote his old friend, Hugh Montefiore, 'as you have a great gift for the Ministry of Encouragement.'

Runcie was consecrated a Bishop in Westminster Abbey by Archbishop Michael Ramsey in February 1970. His old Cambridge friend Harry Williams, now at Mirfield, preached a sermon of quite inordinate length. It was meant to last twelve minutes and continued for a full forty, throwing the day's programme into disarray. It can still be read, slightly cut down, in the pages of *Theology* for the following August. He began by remarking that 'it is difficult to know what to say at the consecration of a bishop' and went on, some thirty minutes later, to offer 'a few brief suggestions'. It was in fact an exciting, if somewhat rhetorical, analysis of the nature of a bishop's authority in the light of the Resurrection. He rejected the idea that the modern world is scornful of authority. It is scornful only of bogus authority, but the authority of a genuine competence is not despised. Again, 'although people may laugh at holy and humble men of heart and make fun of them, it is often the sort of fun and laughter which conceals astonishment and alarm leading to respect and admiration'. Authority will flow from 'the manner of man' one is. Later on, as Bishop and still more as Archbishop, Runcie often ruminated on the problem of authority and Harry Williams's words at his consecration may, at times, have come back to him with their final line, 'His sheep will follow him, for they will know his voice'.

On the evening before his consecration, the Confirmation of the Election was held in St Margaret's Westminster, an odd legal ceremony in which Runcie's Advocate was his barrister sister-in-law, Jill: 'I think it is the first time in history it has been done by a woman', he wrote. So, if his years at Cuddesdon were certainly not revolutionary in terms of the changes they made in the relationship of women to the college, they ended all the same with a small, significant, but wholly untheological and slightly humorous recognition that the role of women in the Church was changing and needed to change.

The ten years of St Albans appear to the observer almost as energetically uneventful as the ten years at Cuddesdon. Runcie is not perhaps temperamentally a workaholic but he is temperamentally a perfectionist and as each of his jobs has been larger and more demanding so has he met the demands by becoming in practice a workaholic. If he does something it must meet his own exceptionally high standards. A small but interesting example is the book on St Albans which he edited in 1977 on the occasion of the centenary of the diocese, *Cathedral and City: St Albans, Ancient and Modern*. The contributions to it are all by outstanding scholars, each in his own field: Asa Briggs on the Victorian city, Owen Chadwick on the Victorian diocese, Christopher Brooke on the medieval abbey, Martin Biddle on the early Anglo-Saxon church, Sheppard Frere on the Roman origins and St Alban himself. Diocesan centenary volumes and such like are often produced, rarely do they last. *Cathedral and City* is different. It remains both authoritative and very readable. It is the only book prior to his appointment to Canterbury to be found under Runcie's name and even his own chapter in it, 'The Future of the Diocese', does not really tell one much about him — except his professionalism and perfectionism in regard to the job in hand.

A centenary history was, of course, only a tiny side of his concern with the diocese. Much of that concern had to do with education — lay Christian education and ministerial training. Here he felt himself an expert. He chaired an Archbishop's Commission for the Reorganization of the Theological Colleges. He established a diocesan Ministerial Training Course of a rather radical sort. He appointed Eric James as his 'Canon Missioner' to keep the diocese thinking. The appointment is significant. James was quite a different sort of animal to Runcie — a natural radical, and ally of John Robinson. He had been a principal agitator for the reform and renewal of the Church in the early 1960s. They had been friends in Cambridge and Runcie had always kept in touch. Without being a radical himself, Runcie could appreciate radicalism in others and see the value of harnessing it creatively. Of James, Runcie remarked, 'it was worth having someone with a stronger sense than I possessed that progress is made by honest conflict'. The comment is revealing. Runcie is temperamentally the last person in the world to work through conflict, but as his wider sense of strategic leadership developed, he had come to recognize that his own gifts of the both–and type needed to be balanced by other more

24

conflictual contributions. At St Albans, even though it was not the greatest of dioceses, Runcie was starting to emerge as the ecclesiastical statesman he would become, especially through the selection and use of outstandingly able people with gifts very different from his own.

In 1973, Archbishop Ramsey invited him to join the Committee for Anglican–Orthodox Joint Doctrinal Discussions. It was to be a fateful development. Runcie was a Greek scholar with a great personal interest in Eastern Orthodoxy. The following year he succeeded Bishop Carpenter as Anglican co-chairman and from then on this would be a central and often determining concern in his life. He probably feels more spiritually at home in Greek Orthodoxy — so long as it is not being too rigidly traditionalist — than in any Christian tradition other than his own. Occasionally, perhaps, even the last qualification might be omitted. Anglican–Orthodox relations have been important throughout the twentieth century from both sides: each can, in its way, find support from the other for a traditionally 'Catholic' and episcopal position which, however, rejects the claims of the papacy. Nevertheless, these relations while mostly friendly have seldom greatly advanced. Both the more Protestant and the more liberal elements within the Church of England have been sufficient to deter the Orthodox from moving very decisively towards unity. There is also the great practical difficulty of achieving agreement within the network of Orthodox Churches, each autocephalous.

By the 1970s, however, a great new shadow threatened to exclude whatever light and accord years of friendly conversations had generated: the ordination of women. Most Protestant Churches had been ordaining women for up to 60 years. The Anglican Communion had never done so, but now, affected by both Protestant example and the vast secular change in the general social position of women in the Western world which had accelerated since the early 1960s, an increasing number of parts of the Anglican Communion — Hong Kong, the United States, Canada, New Zealand — decided from 1971 on to do so too. In the 1977 meeting of the Anglican–Orthodox Conversations, some Orthodox members walked out of one session in protest: how could Anglicans continue to claim to be faithful to the apostolic tradition when they were so manifestly abandoning it? The personal responsibility to hold the two sides together fell, above all, upon Runcie, and his accompanying of Archbishop Coggan on a visit to Russia and Armenia late that year was undoubtedly of special importance for him. Coggan's knowledge of the Churches of the East was limited as was his sense of diplomacy. Runcie realized in consequence just how much in this field must depend on him.

Many Anglicans were now caught within a great dilemma: their more liberal sense urged them to go ahead and overcome the charge of sexual discrimination within the Church; their more traditional and cautious sense led them to hold back because for years they had been trying hard to be reconciled with both the Orthodox and the Roman Catholics, both of whom were officially firmly opposed to the ordination of women. Why, just at this point of ecumenical progress, create an awful new obstacle to Church unity? For almost no one was the dilemma personally greater than for Runcie: elements of traditionalism and elements of liberalism jostled within his temperament while he felt himself — perhaps unreasonably — too little of a theologian to be quite confident as to how to resolve them. One thing he did know: he was the Anglican Bishop responsible for good relations with the Orthodox Churches. Their continued good rapport with Anglicanism must, to a very considerable extent, depend upon their continued trust in him. It was necessary that within Anglican councils, he should put their case whatever those councils finally decided. And so he did. As Bishop of St Albans he argued in the Lambeth Conference of 1978 and in the General Synod in 1978 and 1979 both firmly and consistently: 'When the Anglican Church embraces such a fundamental change as to the nature and character of the ordained ministry without sufficient regard for those with whom we proudly aim to share the apostolic ministry, it registers itself as a different sort of Church', he declared at Lambeth. He never declared himself opposed to the ordination of women in principle; he did declare it dangerously inopportune and in Synod he opposed the recognition of women ordained canonically elsewhere. Annoyed as many liberals were that he did not in this go along with the increasing majority view of the English bishops, it is hard to see how in his position at that point he can be faulted. His task within Anglicanism was, for a while, to be the advocate of the continued consensus of Orthodoxy. Even when he became Archbishop he did not quite abandon that role, as is shown by the way he arranged that at his enthronement the creed should be recited without the *Filioque* clause which the Orthodox have always rejected. It was a moving liturgical ecumenical gesture which Pope John Paul himself imitated at Pentecost of the following year. The Orthodox Churches, both in Britain and overseas, have long recognized that he remains a very special friend.

It was to strengthen this role that in 1979 he took a sabbatical, which he had long been hoping for, but devoted it to an extremely energetic tour of the Orthodox world. He began with Istanbul in February, followed by Jerusalem, Damascus, Alexandria and Cyprus.

From there he went to Greece, where the Archbishop of Athens had gathered the Committee of the Holy Synod on Ecumenical Relations to meet him in a lengthy conference. If in England he had, in a way, to be the spokesman of Orthodoxy, here inevitably he had to be the spokesman of Anglicanism — an Anglicanism which had already moved well along the road to women's ordination — and he defended the arguments for that development in a way he had not previously done.

A second half of the tour took him to Hungary, Yugoslavia, Bulgaria, Romania — where he celebrated the Orthodox Easter — and, finally, the Soviet Union, arriving home in the middle of May. As so often in Runcie's life it is the professional thoroughness with which he carried out this tour which impresses one. Surely no other Archbishop of Canterbury has had so extensive a knowledge of the Eastern Churches, to which should be added earlier visits to the Middle East and India, a major concern of his life. It may be balanced by the fact that until 1978 he had never crossed the Atlantic.

On 5 June 1979 Archbishop Coggan announced that he would be retiring on 25 January 1980. Who was to succeed him? In 1975, the see of York became vacant when Coggan moved to Canterbury to succeed Michael Ramsey. It is thought that two bishops were offered the post and refused it. Robert Runcie came third. He too refused it and Stuart Blanch, Bishop of Liverpool, then accepted it. This was the last archiepiscopal appointment under the old regime, dependent essentially on the decision of the Prime Minister, and it shows, in its way, that the system was breaking down internally. It shows too that Runcie was now clearly recognized as a leading bishop. He had, indeed, even been thought of by Michael Ramsey as his own successor at Canterbury.

There was in 1979 no overwhelmingly obvious candidate: Stuart Blanch at York and John Habgood at Durham will have been considered among others. For the first time, the Crown Appointments Commission, consisting of bishops, representatives of General Synod, of the diocese concerned, and even of the Anglican Consultative Council (John Howe, as Secretary of the ACC, was present but without a vote), but chaired by a layman appointed by the Prime Minister, would be functioning formally to choose an Archbishop. Sir Richard O'Brien was the lay chairman, nominated by James Callaghan while still in office. Two names had to be selected for submission to the Prime Minister (who was now, since a couple of months, Mrs Thatcher), and she was expected, though not bound, to choose the first. It gave the Prime Minister's letter of invitation a great new authority. On 19 July such a letter arrived at St Albans and his chaplain handed it to Runcie with the quiet remark, 'Now your troubles begin'. He was deeply reluctant to consent, conscious as ever of his own supposed theological limitations, and it seems likely enough that under the old system, he might well have declined. 'I can't. I can't. I'm a child', he almost sobbed to Eric James in the first period of revulsion. No one was less ambitious or anticipative of the 'top job'. 'But you really have to', James replied, 'or how could you ever again ask any of your clergy to do something really hard?' Slowly he geared himself to the realization that he would have to say yes, but it took time and twice he asked for more, before giving his acceptance. It was an acceptance to the call of the Church, the first such call to Canterbury and, therefore, the first such acceptance genuinely to have happened for many centuries. So he agreed and the news was published in September that Robert Runcie would become the 102nd Archbishop of Canterbury.

Runcie was now 58. What sort of person had he become and how did he compare with his predecessors? In age he was entirely average: younger than Coggan or Lang who had both spent long years as Archbishop of York, a little older than Ramsey or Davidson, exactly the same as Fisher. Archbishops of Canterbury have for centuries all had previous episcopal experience. One has to go back a long way, and to some very outstanding people, to find a non-bishop selected for Canterbury — as was Basil Hume for Westminster. Anselm, Langton, Cranmer, the greatest names of the past, were chosen directly as monks or academics. Perhaps the caution of an Erastian Church has had something to do with the modern system whereby Runcie's seven predecessors had each had two episcopal appointments prior to Canterbury. It had also something to do with the twentieth-century tendency to promote the Archbishop of York. It was a safe system rather than an imaginative one, and one from which the Crown Appointments Commission would need to break away.

Runcie had been bishop of only one diocese and that not one of the most senior. He had also been a bishop for a rather shorter period than any of his twentieth-century predecessors. His was the nearest to a promotion from the ranks since Edward White Benson's appointment in 1883 when Bishop of Truro. There was then a measure of freshness, of institutional unpredictability in the choice from that point of view, though it was less unpredictable than that of his successor, a more genuinely original appointment in terms of education and length of episcopal experience (only three years). Otherwise, Runcie's career had been characteristic of the new leadership style. Archbishops from the middle of the nineteenth century until Geoffrey Fisher had mostly been public school headmasters. None of them had taught in a theo-

PREVIOUS CLERICAL OCCUPATIONS OF 12 ARCHBISHOPS OF CANTERBURY 1862–1991

12 Arch-Bishop	More Junior Appointments						Senior Appointments				
	1 Curate	2 Junior Oxbridge Don	3 Assistant School-Master	4 Chaplain to Arch-Bishop	5 Theological College Staff Member	6 Parish Priest	7 Head-Master	8 Principal Theological College	9 Professor of Theology	10 Dean	11 Bishop
Charles Longley 1862–8 York		*					Harrow				Ripon Durham
Archibald Tait 1868–83	*	*					Rugby			Carlisle	London
Edward Benson 1883–96			*				Wellington				Truro
Frederick Temple 1897–1902		*					Rugby				Exeter
Randall Davidson 1902–28	*			*						Windsor	Rochester Winchester
Cosmo Lang 1928–42 York	*	*				*					Stepney (Suffragan)
William Temple 1942–4 York	*					*	Repton				Man-chester
Geoffrey Fisher 1945–61	*	*					Repton				Chester London
Michael Ramsey 1961–74 York	*				*	*			*		Durham
Donald Coggan 1974–80 York	*				*	*		London College of Divinity			Bradford
Robert Runcie 1980–91	*	*			*	*		Cuddes-don			St Albans
George Carey 1991–	*				*	*		Trinity Bristol			Bath & Wells

logical college (and such colleges only began to exist in the later nineteenth century). On the contrary, from Ramsey onward, no archbishop has taught in a public school while each has taught in a theological college. If Ramsey had not become a university professor of theology, he would probably have become Principal of a theological college, and all his successors up to Carey (as also Habgood of York) have been Principals. Runcie shared with many of his predecessors both the absence of any lengthy period of purely pastoral work in a parish (no one since Lang has had that) and the experience of being a fairly junior Oxbridge don (he was even Junior Proctor). (See Table, p. 29.)

In all these outward ways his career marks both the continuities and the changes in the top clerical leadership of the Church of England. Inwardly, he is more difficult to characterize. Temple had the qualities of a hugely successful public polymath, a national and international figure, who had written, lectured and presided over conferences of every sort and size. Fisher had been a headmaster for eighteen years and an assistant master before that, and he had the traits characteristic of a successful headmaster — considerable pastoral concern but a rather dominating tone. Ramsey was the true theologian and half a monk, the one professor (though Temple could easily have been so too) in the group. Coggan was a distinguished scholar of Oriental languages but still more the evangelical preacher. In their ways all these men are relatively easy to characterize and indeed to caricature, but the outstanding qualities proper to each were obvious enough and were nationally known before their appointment to Canterbury. Runcie was far less widely known than his predecessors at that point, and had no obviously comparable outstanding quality. Behind the manifest intelligence, perfectionism, dedication and charm, he remained something of an enigma, perhaps even to himself: a man without quirks or eccentricities, who had written almost nothing, without almost any ploy of self-projection, conscious or unconscious. Even his breeding of Berkshire pigs had not gone on for very long or taken up much of his time. Actually he was really more knowledgeable about horses — a skill he learnt from his father — though he never bet. 'Everyone thinks I am only interested in pigs', he once remarked plaintively.

Profoundly religious as he was, Runcie in 1980 remained a more secular, ordinary, less clerical, person than most bishops: not just the family man and the cricketer, but the former classics don and tank commander. There was an inner toughness, a clarity of judgement and a spiritual balance which were all important and derived from his education and early experience. His inner soul remained somewhat masked not only by the style required of today's Church of England episcopal leadership, but by an exceptional capacity for friendship and by a sense of humour. His theological diffidence, while possibly felt as a weakness, was really a source of added strength. He had always shown a quite exceptional capacity for adapting himself wholly to his job and its wider framework in such a way that he himself was only noticed by the more perceptive. Unlike his dear friend, Hugh Montefiore, there was nothing of the prima donna in him. Many might have said that he lacked charisma. What was noticed was how successfully each job had been done, whether at Westcott House, at Trinity Hall, at Cuddesdon or at St Albans. What came across was a sense of almost detached professionalism; but detached is really quite the wrong word because undoubtedly Runcie always agonized about his responsibilities and their polished fulfilment. Those closest to him saw at work an iron will and became used to an often repeated and revealing phrase, 'We mustn't be outwitted': the competitive determination to win was very much still there. There was certainly nothing soulless about him and few priests had more numerous and varied friends. Moreover, he shone especially in the very personal relationships of spiritual director and adviser. It seems to have been the ability to link a clear-sighted objectivity with the warmth of human trust which made this possible. A high, rather cool intelligence, the ability to drive himself exceptionally hard and a quality which one can only describe as selflessness combined to bring Runcie to the top of the Church of England — its very first Archbishop actually to be chosen by the Church — and yet to leave him still exceptionally difficult to describe convincingly.

One of Runcie's very favourite texts are some lines of Meister Eckhart, the fourteenth-century German mystic. He frequently quotes them and seems likely to have turned them over in his mind as he set about moving from St Albans to Lambeth. We may repeat them with him at this point, as they seem appropriate:

There is no stopping place in this life. No, nor was there ever one for anyone — no matter how far along the way they've come. This then, above all things: be ready for the gifts of God and always for new ones.

🌿 2 🌿

Cantuar: the evolution of an office

Robert Runcie is the 102nd Archbishop of Canterbury. To say that at once suggests an amazing measure of continuity. Certainly there is no one else in England, not even the Queen, to hold so ancient a title. From the end of the sixth century there has been an unbroken succession of archbishops (apart from the gap during the Civil War and Commonwealth between Laud's execution in 1645 and Juxon's appointment in 1660 after the restoration of Charles II). There has been an English monarchy only from the end of the ninth. When the Archbishop of Canterbury crowns the monarch, he is doing so in terms of a national primacy which preceded the political unity of England.

Each Archbishop of Canterbury has been both Bishop of his diocese, the greater part of Kent, and Primate of the Church throughout England. He has also always had a powerful, if largely undefined, role within the secular political leadership of this country. The episcopal line of descent goes back via Canterbury's first Bishop, the Italian monk, Augustine, to Pope Gregory the Great, thus sharing in the apostolic succession common to the hierarchy of the whole Christian Church. The twelfth-century chair of Augustine in Canterbury Cathedral in which each Archbishop is enthroned is the symbol of this, as of an episcopal authority which, centuries before the Reformation, was already a very special one: it was, certainly, not the authority of a Patriarch. Moreover, Rome claimed the 'Patriarchate of the West' and did not, therefore, allow further patriarchates to develop within its area. Nevertheless, the role of the Archbishop of Canterbury was traditionally not so far off that of a Patriarch. It was a role relating to a whole country, to the two provinces of what had come from the twelfth century to be known as *Ecclesia Anglicana*. It was a role hallowed by the quite particular holiness, learning and general distinction of many of its holders: Theodore of Tarsus, the Greek monk, in the seventh century, Dunstan in the tenth, Lanfranc and Anselm in the eleventh, Thomas Becket in the twelfth, Cardinal Stephen Langton in the thirteenth. Anselm was one of the greatest theologians and philosophers of all time as well as being a very lovable saint. Thomas was a fierce fighter for the rights of the Church and one of the most famous martyrs in Church history. Dunstan, Lanfranc and Langton were all outstanding statesmen as well as being scholars of distinction. There were many other holders of the see of Canterbury little less remarkable. Possibly no other see in the medieval Church was in fact held by so many outstanding men. An office grows through the quality of its holders — in authority, in the weight and respect people accord to it.

It was, of course, always a religious and ecclesiastical office in principle, not a political one. Its first holders and several later ones were personally chosen by the Pope; others by the monks of Canterbury, or by the King. For it was, from very early times, an office of great political importance as well: its holder was the closest adviser of the King and the first of his subjects, the man with the greatest moral authority in the country, and one with much temporal power too, having lands, castles and knights of his own, though this was always a very secondary dimension of his importance. An Archbishop of Canterbury never had the independent or semi-independent secular dominion of many archbishops on the Continent or even of the Bishop of Durham. Nevertheless, Dunstan, Lanfranc and Langton were people of immense public authority: the King's closest colleague or, equally, the King's most feared critic. The political role of an Archbishop of Canterbury, grounded firmly in his non-political role as senior Bishop of the Church in this country, was always in principle double-edged: both counsellor and critic. To collaborate with the Government in strengthening peace and good order, but also on occasion to criticize Government for not doing these things — these tasks are not new. They are certainly not the product of some twentieth-century rethink of political theology; equally they are not the product of 'Establishment', as a creation of the sixteenth-century Reformation (indeed they were to a considerable extent put on ice by that development). They are characteristics of the role of the Archbishop of Canterbury over a far longer period. They are, one can reasonably claim, a part of the unwritten constitution of this country.

However, the role of the Archbishop has never been an unchanging one. It has always had to relate to the diocese of Canterbury, to the Church in England as a whole, to the total Catholic Church and to the state in England, but the form these relationships have taken and the way they have themselves interrelated have varied considerably. At the start, the stress was certainly on Canterbury. Here for centuries the archbishops lived and died. Only in about the twelfth century did they begin to dwell more in London, at Lambeth, than in Canterbury, and in the eighteenth they hardly visited Canterbury at all, no longer having a residence there or even bothering to make the journey to be enthroned. They were enthroned by proxy instead! Lambeth Palace was now their home, with a country estate at Croydon or Addington. This shows well enough how their basic pastoral and diocesan role had declined in face of a primatial, political or simply aristocratic one: an eighteenth-century archbishop often behaved more like a duke than a priest.

A few medieval archbishops were cardinals, and a few were actually chosen by the Pope. All accepted that they were part of a single visible communion of the Catholic Church, whose Councils they would attend, whose laws they would enforce. The Archbishop of Canterbury was brother to the great archbishops of the Continent — of Paris, Cologne, Vienna, Milan, Lyons — and if he was in some conflict with the King, as could often happen, he would count on sympathy and support from Rome and more widely from the Continental Church. However, in the later Middle Ages, the role of the Archbishop of Canterbury became increasingly domesticated within English national political life. In practice it became the King who chose him, though in most cases he would certainly endeavour to choose someone of good repute and spiritual stature. Despite the formalities which continued to require Roman as well as royal appointment, the shape of a too governmentally controlled Church was becoming clear. The Act of Parliament of Henry VIII which abolished papal authority in England and made the King instead 'head' (later, 'supreme governor') of the Church was theoretically revolutionary. In practice it did little more than ratify the way things were.

The Great Charter of 1215 had declared in the first of all its clauses that the *Ecclesia Anglicana* — that is to say, the whole Christian Church in England, constituted by the provinces of Canterbury and York — should be 'free'. That freedom was never properly spelt out or applied. It remained a high medieval ideal. After the Reformation it was hardly an ideal any more. The ideal, instead, was one of a national Church dependent upon Crown and parliament, the spiritual side of the nation, but with no measure of independence from political control and no continued sacramental and institutional links with either Rome or any other part of the world Church. 'The Church of England' had arrived. Those English Christians who could not accept that arrangement became in due course, despite all the efforts of the State, 'free' Christians outside the established Church, some Roman Catholic, some Protestant. Their refusal to conform prevented the established Church from ever being fully the national Church, but until the nineteenth century these minorities remained quite small. In the nineteenth century, however, under the impact of Methodism, Irish immigration and other factors, the established 'Church of England', while always claiming national status and frequently demonstrating a genuinely national care, came to represent not much more than half the nation. Indeed, as the 'nation' now meant the United Kingdom, including Scotland, Wales and Ireland, all sharing a single parliament, that parliament was no longer by any means a 'Church of England' assembly as it had been by the very principle of the Reformation settlement in the sixteenth and seventeenth centuries. Nation and parliament had been pluralized and secularized. Yet the Bishops of the Church of England remained in the House of Lords and were chosen by the Prime Minister. The Church had no separate organ of government whatsoever. The Convocations did have some independent existence until the early eighteenth century, and were revived in the late nineteenth.

The position, as it had developed by the late nineteenth century, had lost any sort of logic. First in Ireland and then in Wales, the Church had actually to be disestablished. In England there were millions of Nonconformists and Roman Catholics. Yet, if the proportion of Anglicans within the state had decreased, their number had increased with the vast total increase of the nineteenth-century population. The Church of England, unreformed, corrupt, almost moribund as it could have seemed at the start of the nineteenth century, had by the end of the century built thousands of new churches with some help from the state. It had created new dioceses, especially in industrial areas, but also in the south-east, St Albans among them (an Act of Parliament being required for each one). It had taken in hand the training of its clergy by the establishment of theological colleges and it had sent missionaries to many other parts of the world.

The 'Anglican' or 'Episcopalian' Church in Scotland, small as it was and is, has an importance for Anglican history which we should now note. If in England the Established Church after the conflicts of the seventeenth century remained an episcopalian one, in Scotland it did not. The established Church of Scotland is Presbyterian, but — just as in England there were Presbyterians who refused to conform to the Establishment and survived as a 'free' Church — there were Scots who determined to remain Episcopalian, though for a time they were persecuted for doing so. In consequence, there was always, from the late seventeenth century on, a branch of Anglicanism which was not 'established', a little embarrassing as that was to some more establishment-minded English Anglicans. The first bishop for the Church in the United States of America after the War of Independence, a non-established Church in a rebel land, found a British bishop willing to consecrate him, not in England but in Scotland.

As the nineteenth century wore on, a network of Anglican dioceses spread and spread throughout the world, both in the British Empire and outside it. When the first 'Lambeth Conference' of its bishops met in 1867, on a Canadian suggestion, this already considerable 'communion' of dioceses was 'established' only in England and Wales (once the Church of Ireland was disestablished the following year). Archbishop Longley, who presided over it, had been at first timidly reluctant to agree to its assembling. Thomson, the Archbishop of York, was utterly opposed to such a 'synod', doubted its legality and refused to attend — it would after all, be meeting solely on the invitation of the Archbishop of Canterbury, not on that of the Government. The Dean of Westminster Abbey would not allow its 76 bishops to hold their closing service within the Abbey's walls, so this took place in Lambeth parish church instead. Nevertheless the Anglican Communion and the Lambeth Conference had arrived. Some of the bishops present even suggested that the Archbishop of Canterbury be chosen as Patriarch of this new international Communion. The title would certainly have embarrassed Longley. Others thought it would be illegal. But the Lambeth Conference at ten-yearly intervals was here to stay with the Archbishop of Canterbury as its convenor and President: a major international ecclesiastical gathering. And next time round even the Archbishop of York attended it.

At this juncture, when the old national establishmentarianism was still rather uncomprehendingly struggling against the emergence of a new, far larger and more vital unit — a non-established, world-wide Anglican Communion — it had been fortunate that Archbishop Longley was able, if rather cautiously, to take the lead in what was new. He would be succeeded by a number of outstandingly able archbishops, almost all of them equally cautious by nature, who would all the same pragmatically pioneer a greatly changing role for the Archbishop of Canterbury. It was inevitable that, as the British Empire grew, the political status of the established Church of England and its leadership would change. From one point of view, its importance had to diminish: the British government, being responsible for the ruling of many countries with quite different religious complexions from that of England, could no longer afford to extend to the Church of England privileges which would offend others. From another point of view, however, it would increase — if the Queen or King of England was sovereign over an empire on which the sun never set, the man who crowned the sovereign must have an enormously enlarged field of spiritual influence. And so it happened. Privilege declined, but the opportunity for service greatly expanded.

If one considers the ministry of Randall Davidson, Archbishop of Canterbury from 1903 to 1928, one sees a role enormously enlarged and very much more spiritual and Christlike than the very Erastian, worldly and rather limited office of a late eighteenth-century archbishop: the old duties remained — a sort of high chaplaincy to the Crown, an affable relationship with the chief ministers, a regular attendance in the House of Lords — but so much else had revived or developed: much more regular attention to the Cathedral and diocese of Canterbury; far closer participation in the appointment of English bishops; from 1920 on, presidency of the new Church Assembly in which the laity had been added to the old Convocations of clergy; but, beyond all this, a far wider and continually demanding care for Churches outside England. This care might be one of direct responsibility in the case of many missionary dioceses, or simply one of consultation and advice in regard to independent Anglican provinces, or again of wider help and support in regard to many non-Anglican Churches in difficulties and appealing for assistance to the most important ecclesiastic within the British Empire. His tour of the United States in 1904 was the first ever made by an Archbishop of Canterbury to one of the more distant provinces of the Communion. For Davidson, the Lambeth Conference, far from being a slight embarrassment, became almost the cornerstone of his episcopal career. While verbally he repudiated any idea of a Patriarchate of Canterbury (a phrase which was anathema to all the American bishops in particular), in reality the wider functions he regularly exercised outside his own province can really best be thought of in patriarchal terms — a patriarchate, not of law but of pastoral responsibility.

Inside England, too, the role of the Archbishop was changing. Consider the matter of the appointment of English bishops. By the first part of the nineteenth century, it had become a part of the Prime Minister's patronage, exercised largely with political considerations in mind. But a higher sense of moral seriousness in regard to the Church on the part of many lay political leaders had begun to change that even before Queen Victoria was able to exercise her influence. In an age of Reform, the old-style selection of bishops looked increasingly scandalous and Prime Ministers, like the Duke of Wellington, Robert Peel and, still more, Gladstone and Salisbury, came instead to look hard for the best man for the job in pastoral terms. But how could the Prime Minister know who would be best? Queen Victoria began to insist that he must at least consult the Archbishop of Canterbury before making a nomination. Her personal influence on appointments was also considerable. It was a highly moral one. The new system ensured, for the most part, outstandingly good choices. When Queen Victoria, William Gladstone and Archbishop Tait, for example, put their heads together, it is hardly surprising that it should have done so.

The evolution of the system did not stop there. In the twentieth century, as more dioceses were created and the number of bishops multiplied, it was agreed that not all of them would have seats in the House of Lords. Moreover, as the number of peers multiplied too, the proportionate weight of episcopal votes in the Lords declined. In other ways, as well, bishops now mattered less politically, while Prime Ministers cared less about the Church. For Gladstone an episcopal appointment was a very important matter. For Lloyd George, Neville Chamberlain or Winston Churchill it was not. Moreover, no sovereign entered very actively into the business of episcopal selection after Victoria. In consequence, in practice the Archbishop of Canterbury increasingly took over. He did not always get his own way, but by the period following the Second World War, he generally did so, though he continued to be limited in his choice by the Prime Minister's Patronage Secretary, a conscientious senior civil servant, who might hold the post for many years and exercise considerable, if discreet, control over the selection of names in accordance with his own views as to who might be suitable. Once more, in practice, this system worked more or less satisfactorily. It certainly added much to the Archbishop of Canterbury's responsibilities, but it was no more ideal for the Archbishop to choose all the English Anglican bishops than it was for the Pope to choose all the Catholic ones. That the selection of bishops over fifteen years should practically depend upon Geoffrey Fisher, for instance, was surely not very desirable. It was still less ideal to have the interference of a civil servant whom almost no one had ever heard of but who was able to exercise something of a veto over appointments — probably of a mildly radical kind — which he might judge improper. Moreover, while effectively the choice of bishops was thus being handed back to the Church, which was right, theoretically that was not the case: the choice continued to appear to be that of the Prime Minister only. Of course, if the Prime Minister was Harold Macmillan, who had some personal interest in the matter especially in the case of the most important appointments and of Canterbury, the choice still really was his.

Canterbury remained a special case. An Archbishop of Canterbury can hardly be permitted to select his successor, but in the curious vacuum to which the Church of England had effectively arrived in regard to episcopal appointments by the middle of this century, there was no very respectable alternative. The outgoing Archbishop was indeed expected to give his advice to the Prime Minister. What other advice could the latter easily seek? Hardly that of the Archbishop of York who might well be the person chosen. In an appointment to Canterbury the Patronage Secretary was hardly important enough to advise. There was little alternative but for a conscientious Prime Minister to consult the Sovereign and any other wise person he could think of and then continue as in the past to choose as he thought fit. William Temple died suddenly when in office so his advice was not available. Churchill's selection of Geoffrey Fisher, the Bishop of London, has often been criticized, but it was at the least a defensible one of an exceptionally able man. The most obvious alternatives were Bell of Chichester (too radical and a critic of Government policy, unacceptable in an Archbishop in Churchill's eyes) and Garbett of York (rather too old). When Fisher retired, he did not want Ramsey of York to succeed him and said so to the Prime Minister, Macmillan, but the Prime Minister thought Ramsey incomparably the most distinguished person and rightly selected him. When Ramsey retired, he suggested John Howe, but the Prime Minister, Wilson, preferred Coggan of York, a much better known person. One consequence of the increasing vacuum at the centre of the selection process was the strong temptation for the Prime Minister to play safe and move the Archbishop of York one up to Canterbury: in this century, Lang, Temple, Ramsey and Coggan were all Archbishops of York first. This is not a very imaginative way to do things and, while it has not worked badly in practice, it has been one more sign of a system needing a pretty radical overhaul. The State was quietly opting out of a control of the Church it had seized in the sixteenth century, and things were falling more and more by default into the hands of Canterbury.

The point that needs stressing is that the pressures on the Archbishop were steadily increasing from the age of Longley to the age of Ramsey in this area as in many others. The growth of the ecumenical movement added still more: new gatherings to address or preside over, new relationships to be regularly oiled. A late nineteenth-century archbishop did not expect to see much of any Free Church leader — he might well never have met even the most distinguished. From the time of Davidson that was no longer possible. From the time of Lang in the 1930s, regular contacts were established too with the Roman

Catholic Archbishop of Westminster and with Eastern Orthodox leaders. In the 1940s the British Council of Churches was created and Archbishop Temple became its first President. Fisher or Ramsey had now to preside not only over the Lambeth Conference, the convocations of Canterbury and the six-monthly meetings of English bishops, but over the Church Assembly and the British Council of Churches as well as regularly attending the House of Lords. Davidson and Lang were assiduous as regards to the latter, but, as other duties have multiplied, the relative importance of presence in the Lords has inevitably declined. Nevertheless, it is still a major element in every Archbishop's round of work. It remains one way in which his pastoral duty is fulfilled in regard to issues of large public importance.

Geoffrey Fisher presided over two meetings of the Lambeth Conference, those of 1948 and 1958. He was also the first Archbishop to tour the Anglican Communion world-wide. It was in his time that the new, quickly growing, provinces of black Africa were given autonomy and that black bishops began to multiply. He consecrated some of them on his tours. The patriarchal role of the Archbishop, already proposed in the time of Longley and increasingly obvious in the long years of Davidson, was becoming even more of a reality. But it was a 'patriarchate' in which each province emerged to maturity, powers were shed and only the role of guidance and encouragement, a presidency of maturity and affection, remained. Legally, the Archbishop has no authority over the world-wide Anglican Communion, but the time and thought he needs to give to it may not be the less for that.

The role of the Archbishop of Canterbury has considerably changed then since late Victorian times. Its secular pomp has continued to decline. Lambeth Palace, a very splendid building combining medieval towers and early nineteenth-century state rooms, remains his principal home. Standing by the Thames, just across the river from Westminster, it was obviously well placed for the first subject of the Crown: the archbishop could be rowed in high solemnity to parliament. But the solemnity has passed. While the Archbishop still really lived in the state rooms of the palace in the first half of this century, recent archbishops have lived in an upper-floor flat. The fine library and archive has grown and grown, requiring an ever greater amount of space. Much else has become an administrative centre. The state rooms are still used for frequent receptions — indeed probably a good deal more than was formerly the case. It remains very pleasant to have your office and your home in such a splendid building, but an archbishop today does not live in a palace in the way his predecessors did, any more than someone residing in a grace and favour flat in Hampton

40

Court can be said to occupy a palace. Historic buildings need to be preserved in a living condition. Lambeth Palace is a very historic building and its present uses carry on the tradition of the past, but are not the same as those of the past. Like the archiepiscopate itself, it has survived by evolving.

Michael Ramsey was Archbishop of Canterbury from 1961 to 1974. One reason why his predecessor, Fisher, thought he would be unsuitable at Canterbury was that Ramsey was a distinguished theologian and scholar, an immensely spiritual man, but one rather bored with administration. He seemed too unworldly. A successful Archbishop of Canterbury needed — thought Fisher, out of the long years of his experience — a good deal of hard worldliness. Macmillan appointed Ramsey all the same because Ramsey was so clearly head and shoulders above any obvious alternative. What neither of them will have foreseen was that Ramsey would turn out to be one of the great revolutionary archbishops in Anglican history. If the role had been changing little by little, decade by decade, throughout the century, the change had largely been covert. It was Ramsey who brought it out into the open, saw the way things were going and reshaped them publicly along new lines. A bit like Pope John XXIII, he was able to sit lightly to major administrative changes — in a way Fisher was not — just because his mind was so surely set, not on administration, but on another world of truth and love.

The Church of England was not disestablished in the archiepiscopate of Michael Ramsey, but it did move a long way on the road to effective disestablishment, to creating a new institutional freedom for itself from the State, even if the later stages of the Ramsey revolution took place not in his time but in that of his successor, Donald Coggan. Ever since the revised Prayer Book approved by the General Assembly of the Church had been rejected by the House of Commons in 1928, it was clear in principle that something needed to be done. Michael Ramsey, a student at the time, had felt it to be intolerable. And so did many other people. The majority of practising Anglicans in the House of Commons had voted for it, but a majority of the House, whipped up by all sorts of prejudices, fears of Rome, simplistic and anachronistic notions about what the Church of England stood for at the Reformation and whatever, voted against. Yet for 40 years nothing much was done. To demand disestablishment in order to be free to revise the Prayer Book without the veto of a medley of parliamentarians seemed an over-reaction, irritating and confusing as the veto was. As, anyway, almost no one is able to say what 'Establishment' now really consists in or what 'Disestablishment' would amount to either, it is hardly surprising that few people, archbishops especially, were very keen to follow a road so vaguely marked out. Surely the 'national' character of the Church should not lightly be thrown away — so it was widely felt. To give the impression that the English State was somehow repudiating Christianity would be painful and, possibly, pointless. In the nineteenth century, when the Church of England still had many privileges, many non-Anglicans were eager for disestablishment. As the privileges were whittled away, so was that eagerness. In the twentieth century it has mostly been Anglicans, not non-Anglicans, who have argued for disestablishment, believing that they have been left with none of the perks and all the problems, with a vague aura of being a Government Church in an age in which Government Churches are quite anachronistic. Yet the number of people who feel strongly about this are probably quite few — radicals, enthusiastic theorists — or so archbishops have tended to think. In consequence nothing was done.

In the 1960s the mood had changed. Establishment or disestablishment, the Church needed a greater measure of freedom — real freedom and visible freedom to rule itself, to reform its liturgy, to outline its doctrine, to choose its leaders. All this was largely accomplished through the Ramsey revolution. First of all, the Church Assembly was transformed by Act of Parliament into a General Synod in which bishops, priests and laity would mostly sit and work together and would have far greater national authority and be concerned with a wider range of matters than the old Assembly. It came into existence in 1970. Next, Synod claimed and needed authority to produce new liturgies. For some the required freedom had to include the right to abolish the use of the Book of Common Prayer if it wished to do so. Ramsey saw that to claim such a right would horrify many good old-fashioned Church people and might well never get through parliament. It was wiser not to go so far. The Worship and Doctrine Measure establishing the effective autonomy of the Church in both areas passed General Synod in February 1974 and the House of Lords the November of the same year, Ramsey's seventieth birthday and his last day as Archbishop of Canterbury: 'If it is suggested that I am an old man in a hurry, I would recall that at my enthronement in Canterbury thirteen years ago, I pleaded for the necessity of a measure on these lines, and it has taken until the last few hours of my primacy for its introduction to come about'. William Temple appealed for the Church's freedom in the Life and Liberty movement of 1917. It was his devoted disciple, Michael Ramsey, who actually brought it about 57 years later.

Besides worship and doctrine there was the matter of the appointment of bishops. In 1968 he set up the latest in a long series of Archbishop's Church and State Commissions to consider every aspect of the relationship. It was chaired by Owen Chadwick and its report, submitted in 1970, lay behind both the Worship and Doctrine Measure and proposals to create new machinery for the selection of bishops. As we have seen such machinery was needed: not because unsuitable bishops were being foisted by the Government on a suffering Church, bishops being in fact now chiefly selected by the archbishops; but because the appearance of uncontrolled appointments by the Prime Minister survived and was disedifying, because the reality of a system whereby the two archbishops were largely able to select whom they liked without any wider participation by Church representatives was not in the long-term best interests of the Church, and because the existing system was weak at handling the selection of an Archbishop of Canterbury.

It was in 1977 in the archiepiscopate of Donald Coggan and the prime ministership of James Callaghan that the main conclusions of the Chadwick Report in this area were realized. A new Crown Appointments Commission was established to include the two archbishops, representatives of the Synod and of the diocese concerned. It would return two names to the Prime Minister, with the expectation that the first of the two would normally be accepted for appointment. A minority in the Church and State Commission, and many other people, felt that this still did not go far enough. There is really no reason why any selection at all should be left to the Prime Minister. In the established Church of Scotland the government exercises no control whatsoever over appointments. It is not clear why it should do so in England constitutionally or of what gain it is to the Church. Nevertheless, it is clear how large a change this did bring about. Whether the Crown Appointments Commission has been given quite the best shape it could have, one may question. (The presence, for instance, of the two archbishops and not necessarily of any other bishop for all appointments in both provinces seems a pity.) What is certain is that the Church now knows for the first time how bishops are selected and that the selection is its own. It is theologically right that this should be so and it must add to the authority of the bishop and the confidence of the Church.

Nevertheless, it adds further to the burdens of the Archbishop. It was one thing to think hard about the best nomination for a particular see and write to the Prime Minister about it. It is another to have to preside over endless meetings of the Crown Appointments Commis-

43

sion, listening to the arguments between diocesan and synod representatives, high and low, clerical and lay, and to have to read through all the confidential paper work involved. It is not surprising that with the new system the delay in making appointments has grown.

In other ways, too, the archiepiscopate of Ramsey brought an increase in the business of presiding. Not only is there now a General Synod. Each diocese also has a Diocesan Synod. General Synod meets three times a year. The Archbishop must normally attend all three sessions. The Diocesan Synod meets at least twice. Again, he is expected to preside over that of the diocese of Canterbury. At the other end of the range of his duties, the Lambeth Conference of 1968 decided that the one meeting in ten years was not sufficient to keep the Communion in touch, so it set up a smaller Anglican Consultative Council to meet every two years. The 1978 Conference added a meeting of Primates. Inevitably, the Archbishop of Canterbury is expected to preside over both, ineffective and lightweight as the meetings of the Consultative Council tend to be (they suffer from having, just like the Lambeth Conference, only a consultative status, while lacking the atmosphere of pageantry or a certain sense of moral significance which Lambeth generally achieves).

So Ramsey, who was bored by meetings and seldom spoke in them unless something he judged of real importance was at stake (which was not often), had managed to add very considerably to the range of meetings his successors had to preside over. The full list of the more important by the end of Coggan's archiepiscopate was as follows: Diocesan Synod, General Synod, Crown Appointments Commission, British Council of Churches, Anglican Consultative Council, Primates' Meeting and Lambeth Conference. No wonder archbishops found less time than previously either for the House of Lords or for a holiday!

Finally, there was a wider range of international ecumenical visits which from the Ramsey era had become *de rigueur* for an Archbishop of Canterbury. Here, Fisher, at the end of his life, and responding to the new atmosphere of the pontificate of Pope John XXIII, had commenced the new model. From Fisher on, every Archbishop has been to Rome as well as to Istanbul and to visit other Orthodox Patriarchs. Each, too, is expected to visit the World Council of Churches in Geneva and to go to its lengthy General Assembly every seven years. Archbishops before Temple had almost no institutional ecclesiastical relationship with anything non-Anglican. Since Temple such relationships have multiplied, involving very varied degrees of formality. So the leadership of the Church of England has not only readjusted itself to be only a minority portion of Anglican leadership, the leadership of the Anglican Communion has also now continually to adjust to a far wider unformulated working collegiality as one portion of the leadership of the Christian community as a whole. Within that community it has been most particularly concerned to re-establish as close a relationship as possible with the papacy and the Catholic communion world-wide in the wake of the Second Vatican Council. Policy-wise, that is quite probably the most significant legacy left to his successors by Michael Ramsey, the Archbishop who lived and died with the episcopal ring on his finger which had been personally placed there by Pope Paul VI in 1966. The office of the successor of St Augustine was always deeply affected by the circumstances in which it began — the 'Italian mission' of a monk sent from Rome with detailed instructions from one of the greatest of Popes. That sense of a certain historic dependence, and of a fraternal communion of Churches and sees, long turned sour, was greatly revitalized by this new symbolism of the Petrine and Pauline ring placed upon the finger of the most mystical of Canterbury's modern Archbishops.

All these responsibilities have simply accumulated. There is no book of rules to tell an Archbishop of Canterbury how much time and energy he should give to his diocese, how much to the ecclesiastical affairs of this country, how much to its political affairs, how much to the Anglican Communion as a whole, how much to the wider leadership of the world Christian community. Inevitably, each Archbishop will have his own priorities. What is certain is that the burden has become almost impossibly heavy for one man with a quite small staff, and that there are inherent tensions within the office as it has now developed — tensions especially between England and the world. Anglicanism is extremely weak in a theology of the authority of anything above the bishop; equally the Church of England has been extremely reluctant to admit any sort of legal ecclesiastical authority wider than its own frontiers. This may be paralleled by the present British gut reaction against any loss of 'sovereignty' to the EEC. In consequence, the Anglican Communion has developed on a model of the autonomy of its parts and of a merely consultative role for the Lambeth Conference, the Anglican Consultative Council, the Primate's Meeting and any other such overarching authority. The Archbishop of Canterbury may preside but he certainly does not rule, legally. The refusal to envisage in theory any circumstances in which the principle of autonomy is not enough is one factor behind the quite exceptional and probably unnecessary strains produced by the issue of the ordination of women to the priesthood.

Roland Walls, an old friend, called on Michael Ramsey shortly after his move to Canterbury. 'Roland', he asked him, 'before going into all your business just answer me a question about mine; have I to become a Pope or just be a Bishop of Canterbury?' Walls asked him why he asked. 'Because if you look over there on that table, you will find that I am now in the position of Pope Leo I — requests for counsel, decisions and my opinions on this and that. They come in from all quarters of the globe.' 'Off the cuff, Father', replied Walls, 'I would recommend you to be Bishop of Canterbury.' 'Yes', said Ramsey, 'that's my opinion too, but it wasn't my predecessor's.'

In practice, Ramsey had to follow his predecessor, and his successors have had to follow him. Late in Coggan's archiepiscopate a senior priest wrote in the correspondence column of the *Church Times* that the international role of the Primate of All England 'has increased, is increasing, and ought to be diminished'. Coggan did not believe in diminishing it, was not at all good at delegating and drove himself quite impossibly hard. He was only at Canterbury for five years and survived, but no successor could do the same. However much, since the time of Longley, the option of a patriarchate has been repudiated in theory, in practice and in unchartered form, it has steadily developed. And rightly. There must be some authority and pastoral symbol of unity in the Church above that of bishop, province and nation: a truly international one. A major problem in modern Anglicanism has been some recognition of that in practice, its emphatic denial in theory.

Such was the ministry entrusted to Robert Runcie in 1980. For it he had been prepared with excellent diocesan experience at St Albans and his wider contacts with Orthodoxy. Otherwise his international preparation in ecclesiastical terms was somewhat limited. He lacked the reputation or the range of achievement of a Temple or a Ramsey, but he had one quite special asset: he had been chosen by the Church. While Lang was chosen by Baldwin, Temple and Fisher by Churchill, Ramsey by Macmillan and Coggan by Wilson, Runcie had not been chosen by Mrs Thatcher but by a Commission of the Church, including several of his fellow bishops. Mrs Thatcher had merely accepted their choice, by no means the same thing.

🌿 3 🌿

Ten years at Lambeth

Modern Archbishops of Canterbury retain two residences, Lambeth
Palace in London and the Old Palace, beside the cathedral in
Canterbury. For many centuries Archbishops have spent far more
time in London than in Canterbury. They still do so. Lambeth, not the
Old Palace, has, unquestionably, been the Runcies' home, and this
already says much about the shape of the Archbishop's
responsibilities. Ramsey might, as we saw, have preferred to be, above
all, Bishop of Canterbury, but it was a romantic rather than a realistic
preference. Runcie too would have liked to go on being the pastoral
bishop of his own diocese. Once in Canterbury he even ventured to
remark, a little tongue in cheek, that 'an argument could be mounted
to demonstrate that all the achievements of twentieth-century
archbishops can be traced to the thinking, reading and conversations
in Canterbury and all their mistakes to spending too little time there'
(October 1984). He was glad that the Lambeth Conference moved to
Canterbury in 1978 and retained it there in 1988; he would like
General Synod, too, to meet in Canterbury, not London. But he
recognized from the start that Lambeth, not Canterbury, must be the
base for most of his work as Primate of All England and President of
the Anglican Communion, and his strategic conception of his office
gave these duties ultimate priority.

A few months after his enthronement in 1980 Runcie vested Richard Third, the new Suffragan Bishop of Dover, with full responsibilities for the day-to-day management and care of the diocese, including
parochial appointments. The diocesan administration ceased to be
divided between an office in Lambeth and another in Canterbury.
They were reunited in Canterbury. This indicated a quick and significant decision intended to leave Runcie free for his primatial responsibilities without making the diocesan administrative timetable
debilitatingly subsidiary to his national and international commit-
ments. The Bishop of Dover is expected to function effectively as
Bishop of the diocese of Canterbury. This strategic administrative
arrangement did not, however, indicate that Runcie was uninterested
in Canterbury or seldom had time to go there. On the contrary. Both
his sermons in the cathedral at Christmas, Easter and Whitsun, and

his presidential addresses to the Canterbury Diocesan Synod are among his most important and pondered utterances. He spends nearly half the weekends of the year in Canterbury and also finds time for quite a number of pastoral engagements, for ordinations and some attendance at diocesan staff meetings. The right balance between Canterbury and Lambeth remains one of the most subtle of issues within an Archbishop's life and sense of priorities.

It is in Canterbury that the Archbishop appears as priest and bishop: as pastor of his own clergy surrounding him in the morning Mass on Maundy Thursday, as the ordainer of new priests, as the cathedral's principal preacher, not only at the great feasts but responding to public crises such as the Zeebrugge ferry disaster or the IRA bomb atrocity in the barracks at Deal. The liturgy of Canterbury Cathedral today combines Anglican tradition with almost all that is best and richest in Catholic worship as reformed after Vatican II, and it might be hard to find any Catholic cathedral on the Continent in which the liturgy is celebrated more impressively than it is at Canterbury. This has, of course, depended upon the deans rather than the archbishops. Runcie is not particularly interested in liturgical detail and rather prided himself on never having spoken in Synod in a liturgical debate in the 1970s, the age of Anglican liturgical change — one of the very few bishops at that time not to have done so. But he loves the rich symbolism of services which draw on the fullness of tradition and the cathedral's liturgy today certainly provides a context entirely congenial to his own religious and pastoral sense.

At Lambeth the appearance is less of the priest than of the statesman. There is a lovely thirteenth-century chapel, but prayer here is much more private. It is the Archbishop's study and the offices of his staff that matter in practice, while the public symbolism is not one of prayer at all, but of power. Lambeth Palace is still today in appearance an impressive castle in the heart of London confronting the Palace of Westminster across the river Thames. The reality is, of course, very different. That sort of power, never very great anyway, has long passed away.

Up to the Second World War Archbishops of Canterbury continued to live in Lambeth Palace in some style. It was then badly bombed and, though it was carefully restored, an army of servants could no longer be retained in an age of austerity. Archbishops began to live in a flat at the top, the state rooms being used for public occasions, but there developed a certain air of abandonment. Part of the building became a hostel for visitors. The splendid library and archive, which even in the nineteenth century had expanded to take over the Great

Hall, remained the most viable part of the Palace's current use, an almost independent unit but with inadequately modernized accommodation. In the 1970s the Bishop of London abandoned Fulham Palace, his almost equally grand and historic stately home a mile to the west. It may well have appeared likely that the Archbishop of Canterbury would shortly do the same. Living in a palace, even an uncomfortable palace or in a pretty ordinary flat within it, could easily be judged unsuitable for a Church leader in the modern world.

By the time the Runcies arrived at Lambeth there was, then, a certain sense of run-downness. The gardens in particular had almost gone to ruin but the chapel too had never really recovered from its wartime devastation, the library had too little space, while the expense of upkeep was inevitably considerable — an expense borne, of course, by the Church Commissioners. Yet to abandon Lambeth Palace, as had actually been mooted in Ramsey's time, would be to abandon both a colossal chunk of religious and national history and a potentially very usable asset — once you got the new mode of usage right. In fact the staff of the Archbishop was expanding and needed more working space, the Church required suitable rooms for welcoming important guests and holding all sorts of meetings hosted by the Archbishop, the library — a major depository for national and ecclesiastical history — had too small a reading room. One of the most endearing qualities of the Coggans was their note of austerity, but it was not the best quality for making imaginative use of a palace. And they only had a bare five years there anyway. Lambeth Palace was, in consequence, one of the problems the Runcies had to face and, if it was truly to be their home for over ten years, it was very much Lindy's problem, for she is a natural home-maker if ever there was one. She was, understandably, hardly keen to take on the job. Someone who becomes intensely devoted to the place she is living in, she has never wanted to move. Brought up in Cambridge, she hated the idea of moving to Cuddesdon but came to cherish Cuddesdon with a quite special love so that she was then extremely reluctant to move to St Albans. Her devotion to St Albans in due course became so great that she was quoted in the press as saying she would only go if carried out feet first. After that, to have to move to a house the size of Lambeth Palace was first distressing and then challenging.

Together they revitalized it. His increased staff ate up the ground floor rooms. Lindy's artistic sense provided the right note for the refurbishment of the state rooms, while her standards as a caterer ensured that Lambeth Palace fare became a pleasure, not a penance, to share. Whenever there was a reception, she was up at five to buy the flowers. But it was the library, the chapel and the garden which were most profoundly transformed: the new Runcie Reading Room in the library is just the right size for its specialist purposes, while the redecoration of the chapel and especially the painting of its roof and rearrangement of the stalls has — as the Archbishop has claimed — given it back 'its mystery and its memory'. Lambeth Palace today is not only a historic monument but also a busy, fully used, yet still rather calm place, every part of which can well be justified. This could not have been achieved without the support of numerous generous Friends of Lambeth Palace and Library, who have contributed to the renewal of each side of it.

The garden especially has been Lindy's responsibility. In Ramsey's time the Church Commissioners actually suggested building their offices in it. It is a considerable area, though over a century ago Archbishop Tait already cut off a large section and presented it to Lambeth Council for the provision of local recreational facilities. With the disappearance of the pre-war army of gardeners and any great will to rescue it, it had fallen on sorry times. In 1985 Lindy could stand it no more and, with her characteristic vigour, set about raising funds for its restoration in a thoroughly imaginative way. Today it is once more a beautiful central London garden, open to the public several times a year and available for a variety of entertainments. It is functional, yet with no more than one full-time gardener to keep it so. In the midst of it stands a charmingly vibrant bronze of a young woman and child, paid for with money given by a popular newspaper in compensation for libelling Mrs Runcie. She wanted the money and made sure that she got it — not for herself but for her beloved garden.

The Archbishop of Canterbury is the head of a large, highly international Church, with wider ecclesiastical and political influence than any other churchman in the world, except for the Pope. Lambeth Palace enables him to entertain the steady flow of distinguished foreign visitors, and it provides a visual symbol in the heart of London for his this-worldly significance. Perhaps it is rather an ambiguous symbol but it is both historic and practical and it makes sense enough for someone who has frequently, by the nature of his job, to relate to the Queen, to the Prime Minister, to the Pope, even to foreign governments.

Queen Elizabeth II, Margaret Thatcher and John Paul II, were all in place before Runcie became Archbishop and only one—by two months—left before him. For the Queen he is her fourth Archbishop as Alexander Tait was Victoria's fourth. Her advantage in her relationship with Archbishops as with Prime Ministers is that she has seen a lot of them. She knows what to expect. She had Fisher for ten years, Ramsey for thirteen and then Coggan for five. There is a pattern of things set, much of it from the far past, to which Runcie, himself no natural revolutionary, could hardly fail to conform — a pattern which can take up quite a lot of his time. The Archbishop is expected to minister at royal weddings and baptisms, to attend a great many royal banquets, to be a family friend, adviser and chaplain extraordinary. Runcie never had the greatest royal duty to perform — to crown the sovereign. That was last done by Fisher. Lang crowned George VI, Davidson George V, Frederick Temple Edward VII. But Runcie has married both the Prince of Wales and the Duke of York. He has baptized Prince William and several other princes and princesses. As the Queen's first subject the Archbishop of Canterbury takes precedence over everyone else, is the first person to be introduced to foreign Heads of State and Runcie has sat beside many of them at banquets in Buckingham Palace.

He has been the guest at numerous other banquets held by the Lord Mayor of London, the Warden of All Souls College, Oxford (the Archbishop is ex-officio Visitor of All Souls) and elsewhere. He has attended still more numerous sessions of the House of Lords, speaking about twice a year, at times on matters of great importance. He is traditionally expected to participate in the debates of the Lords and certainly not merely on occasions when they discuss some religious or ecclesiastical topic. In practice, he does this rather more than his immediate predecessor but considerably less than Archbishops of Victorian and Edwardian times. He would, however, most certainly be failing in his duty, according to the traditions of the country, if he did not, in the Lords, enter actively into the discussion of 'political' issues. England at least, with its established Church, has wisely never recognized a clear division between the religious and the political.

All these things are expected of an Archbishop of Canterbury and Runcie has certainly given himself to them without reservation. There is a socially vivacious man-of-the-world side of his character which enjoys a banquet whether in Buckingham Palace or in Cambridge. He is an excellent and witty after-dinner speaker, so his presence will have been more than ordinarily appreciated on many such occasions. Yet all this remains a rather small, conventional segment of his work, an accumulated inheritance of English history, and at times little more than a rather tiring necessity taking up time needed for far more difficult creative and pastoral roles.

With Margaret Thatcher the relationship has been less conventional. She had only been Prime Minister a couple of months when she forwarded his name to the Queen for appointment as Archbishop. She has little sense of history and no one to compare him with, while he has a great sense of history and considerable powers of comparison. He has probably irritated her far more than she has irritated him because she cannot stand disagreement within the establishment while he takes it for granted. Their styles are different. There is a story that someone asked Douglas Hurd, 'It's such a pity that the Archbishop of Canterbury and the Prime Minister don't get on, why do you think it is?' To which Hurd replied, 'Well, the Archbishop is a witty man and humour does not rank high in Mrs Thatcher's scale of values, and the Archbishop is a master of the throw-away line while Margaret has never thrown away a line in her life.' Nevertheless no Archbishop in this century can have had easier access to the Prime Minister. They have had to co-operate continually over the appointment of bishops and, perhaps still more closely, of deans. They have done so without significant disagreement, despite the fact that Mrs Thatcher paid a lot of attention to the appointment of bishops, in which she personally took great interest. She has not always accepted the Crown Appointments Commission's first name, and she has sometimes made her own enquiries about proposed candidates. She is wary of theologians, but she has always played fair according to the new rules. Runcie's archiepiscopate has, nevertheless, been more profoundly affected by a single Prime Minister than any before him. Her sense of the Church and religion as a force for the reinforcement of personal morality is rather different from his. His conviction of having a political responsibility, and his frequent participation within what can be called the public secular field in a non-Thatcherite way have been in consequence the underlying cause for much of the vituperation he has suffered. To that we will return. We note here simply that a relationship with 10 Downing Street is an integral part of the work of an Archbishop of Canterbury and that the career and views of Mrs Thatcher have deeply coloured this side of Runcie's ministry.

To John Paul II we will return. The Pope was elected in 1978, so here too his period of office began only shortly before Runcie's. Previous Archbishops had to relate to the upheaval in the Catholic Church brought on by Pope John XXIII and the Second Vatican Council and then to the rather enigmatic figure of Paul VI. Runcie, himself profoundly influenced by the Council, had instead to relate to the very different and far more forthright figure of John Paul II. In some ways the Pope corresponds only too well to Margaret Thatcher — each represents the mood of the 1980s determined to overturn part at least of the more liberal legacy of the 1960s. As Runcie did not share that mood to any great extent, much of his work may be seen as an attempt to restrain, resist or play down the endeavours of his more powerful contemporaries.

Even a workaholic like Runcie could easily find it quite impossible to cope creatively with the duties of his job — the public political duties, the diocesan duties, the strictly Church of England duties, the Anglican Communion duties, and the still wider duties of a religious leader on the world scene: all these rolled into one. Being an efficient man, he realized this from the start; much of the early advice he received was also largely about how to cope with so vast a range of responsibility. There had in fact been a meeting of the top five Anglican bishops held at Leeds Castle in Coggan's final months to consider exactly this problem. Runcie is a good delegator of inessentials, but quite unwilling finally to delegate what he sees as important. He enlarged the Lambeth staff and endeavoured to make sure the shape it took was right. The most startling development was the appointment of a bishop, no longer as the kind of senior Chaplain that Geoffrey Tiarks had been to Archbishop Ramsey, but to head the Lambeth curia and be a sort of mini secretary-of-state. Bishop Hook came from Bradford to be the first 'Bishop at Lambeth'. He was succeeded in 1984 by Bishop Gordon from Portsmouth. A head of staff of this seniority is able to take a great deal of weight off the Archbishop's shoulders. The 'Bishop at Lambeth' parallels the Bishop of Dover at Canterbury within the Runcie administrative system. Equally important was the selection of staff members including a number of lay people. Runcie's eye is a keen one for quality, and he is not daunted by unusual opinions or a streak of idiosyncrasy. At each stage in his life he has been good at spotting the exceptional person and in taking some risks with the special appointments. Mark Santer for the staff of Cuddesdon, Eric James as Canon Missioner for St Albans, Richard Chartres as his chaplain both at St Albans and in the first four years at Lambeth are just some of the examples. Mark he spotted already as an exceptional classics student at Cambridge, Eric had been notorious as a 1960s reformer, Richard was a highly intelligent but quite strongly opinionated and prickly young man who had been a student at Cuddesdon, left unordained, but later finished his ordination training at Lincoln. In each case the Runcie eye rightly detected alpha quality and that is what he wanted.

Terry Waite is the most striking case of all — a new sort of appointment for Lambeth staff. Officially named 'Assistant for Anglican Communion Affairs' he was intended to keep the Archbishop in touch with whatever was going on internationally in the Anglican Communion. Trained as a Church Army captain and experienced as a director of lay training in the diocese of Bristol, he had gone on to work for three years in Uganda, organizing Church leadership courses and learning the problems of a murderous regime in the shape of Idi Amin's government. From there he went to Rome, still an Anglican, to work full time for seven years for a large international Catholic order of nuns. This brought him much travelling throughout the world and was at least as unusual a job as that which followed at Lambeth. Terry, a gentle giant, six foot six in height, combined the qualities of an adventurer — quick judgement, the ability to laugh at himself, delight in speed, danger and the hardest of challenges on uncharted roads — with that of a profound religious, if unconventional, commitment and a great sense of the Church's real frontiers as they are today. Only an Archbishop willing to take some risks would have been likely to employ him.

The most ceaseless occupation of an Archbishop of Canterbury today is the giving of addresses — sermons, speeches, lectures, words of welcome and the rest. Most of them must either be highly repetitive or they must largely be prepared by others. Runcie was the first Archbishop to opt for the latter course, following the example of the Pope, the Prime Minister, and all senior modern leaders. Without a large team at Lambeth, this regularly means farming out the initial preparation to friends and experts at a distance. Runcie is himself not an easy writer. He frequently rings up those he trusts, chats about this or that, and asks for a draft on such and such a subject. The drafts he receives he works over a great deal, adding, subtracting, making sure they really express what he wants, sometimes rejecting a piece entirely because it does not suit him.

There is a shared quality about the final productions which is the best guarantee that they do really represent the Archbishop's own approach: there is a lot of history in them, mostly Church history, an anecdotal familiarity with the past — perhaps surprisingly this is largely the medieval and post-medieval past. Despite Runcie's classical education, there is little allusion to the ancient world. There is a repeated affirmation of the central Christian truths, of Incarnation, Cross and Resurrection, and a concern to see all the problems and possibilities of the world today in their light. There is a notable absence of ideology, formal philosophy or systematic theology, a fairly old-fashioned adherence to biblical truth perceived in its main historical and symbolic lines, but a marked dislike of fundamentalism. There is an ever-present anxiety to be effective without being simplistic, and to respect the freedom of others as much as he possibly can while not abandoning the attempt to provide as large a measure of comprehensible and authoritative teaching as he can manage.

In consequence of this method, he has given an extraordinarily large number of well-prepared and varied addresses, relating very closely to the subject and audience of the moment. They certainly represent his own mind and technique, but they also represent the mind of a group of people around him. Historically, an Archbishop of Canterbury always has had his *familia* — the younger clerics who formed his household staff and shared his mind. It is largely from the writings of Thomas Becket's *familia*, for example, that we know so much about him and his death. Thomas — like Runcie — was not a man to write greatly himself. In this, Runcie has been truly an Archbishop of tradition, more so than Ramsey or Coggan, for whom personal authorship was much more decisive, the role of the household far less so. They stand more on their personality, publications and career, quite apart from their archiepiscopate. Not so Runcie. As ever a chameleon, he rose to the requirements of one of the greatest ecclesiastical offices in the world, taking on its appropriate hue to such an extent that he remains only with difficulty distinguishable from his office. As Archbishop he has stood surrounded by a group of people from whom he expects a very great deal in hard and rapid work and from whom he receives a quite exceptional loyalty.

It is not possible to survey the whole range of his activities, but three deserve particular consideration at this point — his world travel, the appointment of bishops, the functioning of General Synod; others will be the subject of the following chapters.

There was nothing new in an Archbishop travelling abroad, visiting other provinces of the Anglican Communion. Davidson began the practice by visiting the United States almost ninety years ago, but it was Fisher who much developed it, responding in the 1950s to the new possibilities of the age of long-distance air travel. Ramsey and Coggan continued it but, as Bishop Michael Marshall has observed, 'All three put together would not equal' Runcie. For him it became a regular, almost systematic part of his duty to keep in touch with every part of the Communion. His visits have paralleled (and even coincided with) those of John Paul II and while the Archbishop's relationship to other provinces of the Anglican Communion is in no way the same as that of the Pope's — it is one of a primacy of love and of influence, but in no way of legal power and control — it has become all the same an expression of a kind of Canterbury patriarchate which Runcie secretly believes is needed and has, in the least dominating of ways, helped to develop.

In May 1980, six weeks after enthronement, he flew to Ghana on his first visit to black Africa and on the way to Zaire for the inauguration of the new French-speaking Anglican province of Burundi, Rwanda and Zaire and the enthronement in Bukavu of its first Archbishop, Bezaleri Ndahura. Runcie had ordained him only five years before in Luton. The establishment of this province — in origin a missionary extension of the Church of Uganda — is symbolic of what is going on in Africa, a huge growth of the Christian Church in all sorts of unexpected ways. In this case, breaking out of the English-language part of Africa into a French-speaking part: a breakthrough Anglicanism could achieve in Africa far more easily than in Europe! It was highly appropriate that Ndahura's enthronement should be Runcie's first major liturgical engagement after his own. It was also an oddly appropriate decision that on the way to it, in Ghana, Runcie should meet John Paul II for the first time. Both were on their first African visits. That they should meet in Accra, still one of the great place names in the history of African independence, put their first encounter in a new and exciting context. For both Communions it is Africa that in the coming years may matter most. It is fitting that their relationship should increasingly be placed in the context, not of Europe with its historic ecclesiastical separations and modern religious decline, but of Africa with its twentieth-century growth and current opportunities. It is not at all that everything looks fine in Africa, for the Churches or anyone else. On the contrary, its problems are gigantic. But they are real problems — growth problems, life and death problems many of them, problems of the interpretation of the Christian faith within new cultures: these probably represent Christianity's most exciting and serious challenges in the late twentieth century, so it was appropriate somehow to relocate the Rome–Canterbury relationship within this context.

This was only the first of Runcie's African visits. Seven more were to follow: to Nigeria in April 1982, to Kenya in October 1983, to Uganda in February and to Nigeria again in July, 1984, to South Africa in September 1986, to Egypt in September 1987, to Malawi, Botswana, Zambia and Zimbabwe in June 1989 and to Ethiopia in January 1990. This considerable series is matched by a first long visit to Asia — Burma, Hong Kong, China and Sri Lanka — in January 1982, to Hong Kong and China again in December 1983, to India in February 1986, to Malaysia, Singapore and Japan in May 1987, to Pakistan and Bangladesh in February 1990 and to Sabah and Korea in September 1990. Add in again visits to the Caribbean in March–April 1984, and several Latin American countries in May–June, 1990, to Australia in

February 1985 and 1988, to Hawaii and New Zealand in March–April 1983, to Canada in July 1983 and September 1985, plus a whole series to the United States from a first long one in April and May 1981 followed by others almost every year. All that still leaves out Europe. Runcie's frequent visits to Europe are something of a novelty for an Archbishop of Canterbury — at least since the thirteenth century. As the relationships of Britain to Europe alter, as Britain, if at times apparently rather reluctantly, recognizes that it is primarily a part of the European community, so the Church of England needs greatly to increase its degree of European awareness. The Hague, Utrecht, Dublin, Brussels, Geneva, Dresden, Leipzig, Lyons, Paris, Bonn, Berlin (East and West respectively), Lausanne, Zurich and Strasbourg — quite apart from Rome — have all listened to lectures and sermons from the Archbishop in these years, but he has also visited Bulgaria and Romania in 1982, Yugoslavia in 1984, Hungary in 1987 and the Soviet Union in 1988, for the millennium of Russian Christianity. His special personal interest in the Orthodox Churches has made him want to insist very emphatically over many years that 'Europe is not the same thing as Western Europe'. So he told the Jean Monnet Institute of Strasbourg in 1986 that 'a central part' of the witness of the Church in Western Europe must be 'to find ways of affirming friendship and fellowship' with the peoples and Churches of the Soviet Union and Eastern Europe.

Strange as it seems to say, the relationship with Africa appears more or less unambiguous (perhaps deceptively) but that with Europe seems at present far more difficult to get right, if only because there are so few Anglicans on the European Continent and English people often find European Protestantism in particular difficult to understand. Some English dioceses do, it is true, have valuable links with European ones. Thus Canterbury itself is linked with Arras, just across the Channel. English Anglicans and French and Belgian Roman Catholics have long felt they had special affinities. There are also some German connections though far too few. One feels that in the last few years Runcie has put a lot of work into strengthening such connections and they certainly need strengthening, if the Church of England is to be able to pull its weight as a fully European Church integrally involved within the Continental dialogue of European Christianity. He has put much effort into Anglican–German Protestant relations. He has also devoted a great deal of time to developing a working relationship with the French House of Bishops and one of his last major engagements at Canterbury was to welcome there Cardinal Decourtray, the Archbishop of Lyons and President of the French Bishops' Conference.

57

Runcie's awareness of the challenge Europe presents to the identity and future character of the Church of England has been steadily growing and he could remark uninhibitedly to a conference of North American Deans in Washington in April 1990: 'Frankly I feel that I have come full circle in the last ten years. I have been through my Anglican Communion years, and very enjoyable they have been. Now I am coming back to give attention to my old European friends.' He wants Anglicans to 'Europeanize Canterbury', to use a provocative phrase, yet certainly without opting out of their Anglican Communion obligations. With 1992 so close, the challenge is clear enough, yet the Church would seem to lack clergy qualified to meet that challenge. It should at least, as was pointed out in his final General Synod at York, mean that more Anglican priests should learn to speak the languages of the Continent. An insular national Church is in some danger of being beached in the Europe of the future.

Add all these visits together and it comes to a very great deal: two to three major expeditions outside Europe every year, each of which involves a lot of preparation and follow-up. Lambeth lacks anything at all comparable in staff and income to the Vatican, but a well organized archiepiscopal visit abroad, while it will be less triumphalistic, may not be noticeably less demanding than a papal one. An activity which began as a relatively marginal addition to the work of an Archbishop in the time of Fisher and even Ramsey, had become for Coggan, and still more for Runcie, one of the most important sides of the Archbishop's work. This is indicative of the way the 'patriarchal' dimension has been quickly growing of late.

That does not mean that the home dimension has been diminishing, or that its cares are less burdensome. Nevertheless, here again there has been a subtle reshaping of structure in process. The relationship between the Archbishop of York and the Archbishop of Canterbury has often been a difficult one and in the Middle Ages there was a long period of extraordinary bickering. If Canterbury is 'Primate of all England', York managed to obtain somewhat oddly the title of 'Primate of England'. Each has always needed to be careful not to tread on the other's toes. The modern relationship between the two deserves more study than it has received. When for twenty years Davidson was at Canterbury and Lang at York, there developed a hitherto unparalleled closeness of sharing of archiepiscopal responsibility between them; there was, again, a very interesting balance in the 1930s when Lang was at Canterbury and Temple at York. Any such relationship seems rather to have faded after the war with Fisher's more monopolistic approach to primacy. Again, for the fourteen years that

Ramsey was at Canterbury and Coggan at York, one sees little evidence of a symbiotic relationship. It is this which, in the last eight years, would seem to have been restored between Runcie at Canterbury and Habgood at York. The two Archbishops are both Presidents of General Synod and both are members and chairmen of the Crown Appointments Commission, so they have anyway to work very closely together indeed to make the new structures work. Beyond this, however, the impression given is that as Canterbury's international responsibilities have grown, so has there been a sort of implicit redivision of labour with some delegation of a larger part of the home primacy to York. Thus Habgood has chaired all the discussions leading up to the establishment of the new Ecumenical Instrument. The existence of the archbishopric of York and its traditional title of 'Primate of England' seems ideally suited to fill the gap which would otherwise be left as more and more of the time of the 'Primate of All England' is taken up by the presidency of the Anglican Communion. The Archbishop of York has also taken on the World Council of Churches role formerly the responsibility of Fisher and Ramsey when they were Archbishops of Canterbury.

This development has owed a great deal to the personal relationship between the two men. Runcie and Habgood share a common Oxbridge education and links with Cuddesdon and Westcott — Habgood was a student at the former and succeeded Runcie as Vice-Principal at the latter. Both were Principals of theological colleges in the late 1960s. Habgood moved from Queen's College, Birmingham, to the see of Durham three years after Runcie went to St Albans. His promotion in 1983 to York was entirely to be expected. He is more of an intellectual and a writer than Runcie, just a little less adroit as a diplomatist, with a scientific instead of a classical background, and a PhD in physiology. Neither has a first degree in theology. Their collaboration has been excellent yet the crucial point is less their personal rapport than the significance for the development of the international role of Canterbury of this degree of structural back-up at York. Without it there could be grievous problems.

None of this, however, means that the Archbishop of Canterbury has not heavy and continuous national responsibilities within England. On the contrary. It may be best to approach them through the greatest single tragedy of Runcie's archiepiscopate — the case of Gareth Bennett and the Crockford Preface in 1987. It was a custom that *Crockford's Clerical Directory* of the Church of England be prefaced by a long, anonymous article by some well-informed priest commenting, often acidly, but perceptively, upon aspects of the current life of the Church. David Edwards, the Provost of Southwark, wrote them for several years. Responsibility for Crockford had recently been taken over from Oxford University Press by the Church Commissioners and the Church's Central Board of Finance, so the Preface might claim even greater 'authority' than it had in earlier years. Gary Bennett, a distinguished priest-historian and Fellow of New College, Oxford, was invited by Derek Pattinson, Secretary-General of Synod, to write the 1987/88 Preface. He completed it in July and it was published in early December.

Bennett was 58 years old, read history at Cambridge and obtained his PhD with a study of an eighteenth-century Bishop of Peterborough, White Kennett. As a lecturer in history at King's College, London, he was ordained in 1956. Perhaps unfortunately, he never had a full theological college training, beyond spending the three Long Vacation terms at Westcott House, where he had appreciated the help of Runcie. In 1959, he was elected Fellow and Chaplain of New College, Oxford, and remained there until his death. He published a major study of Bishop Atterbury in 1975. His historical interests did not move far outside the eighteenth century and while he wrote some more theological pieces, they were of minor significance. Bennett was a self-conscious Anglo-Catholic, not excessively rigid, with a sharp, clear, irritable mind, a man who did not find it too easy to be either pious or kindly, but tried quite hard to be both. His experience was excessively one-sided: the unmarried priest, almost thirty years Fellow of an Oxford College, he had never been full time in a parish and had had no proper theological or pastoral course of training.

Bennett's one major outlet was ecclesiastical politics. Since 1975 he had been the University Proctor in General Synod and had given a great deal of his time to Synod activity. He was not only a frequent Synod speaker, he also became a member of the Doctrine Commission, the Faith and Order Advisory Group and the Board for Mission and Unity. More recently, he had been elected to the Standing Committee of Synod and joined its Policy Sub-Committee. Finally, just after writing the Crockford Preface, he was elected to the Crown Appointments Commission. Collectively, at least, these were major responsibilities and certainly placed him among the most influential members of the Church of England. Indeed, if he had not been so placed, he would not have been asked to write Crockford's Preface. That is the role of an insider, and he could not have written it as he did without deep inside knowledge. The one-sidedness of his experience and the quirks of his temperament made it impossible — at least in the judgement of an outsider who never met him — for him to receive senior pastoral promotion. The Regius Chair of Ecclesiastical History in the University of Oxford has been frozen for some years. Gary Bennett would have filled it well and appropriately. As it was, and understandably, he felt some frustration after his long years at New College and part of that frustration seems to have fired the distinctly one-sided and even cruel criticism of the Church of England he vented in his Preface.

The tradition of an anonymous, insider's commentary of this sort appears to this author an irresponsible and, indeed, sub-moral one, especially when it was held to include close comment upon named individuals. There is always a rather naughty feel about this sort of slightly indiscreet peep-show offered to every Tom, Dick or Harry by some member of the inner circle of a great establishment. While appearing responsible it is in reality essentially irresponsible. Of course, the comment was often wise enough and the secret frontier of what could be said about individuals without causing too great offence was mostly well observed. The comments, for instance, upon David Jenkins in the 1985/86 edition could be used for comparison: they almost crossed the frontier but not quite. Those responsible were, I would personally judge, to blame for creating and maintaining this tradition and the air of bogus authority anonymous remarks at the head of the Church's Clerical Directory must obtain. Yet general Anglican opinion held it acceptable and, I suppose, pleasurable too.

Unfortunately, Bennett overstepped the secret frontiers. Much in his commentary, over which he had undoubtedly thought hard, was perceptive enough. I suspect that the first third, covering general issues of the nature of Anglicanism and authority, together with the failure of Lambeth 1978 to address the issues, reflected pretty closely Runcie's own views in the run-up to Lambeth 1988. He then turned to Runcie himself and despite the Archbishop's charitable subsequent refusal to accept that this section really constituted an 'attack' upon himself, it clearly went far beyond the line tolerable in an anonymous piece — perhaps, indeed, even in a signed piece. Some of the things he said about Runcie, both positive and negative, were true. What was totally unacceptable was the repeated attack on Runcie's moral character, the assertion that he was a mere pragmatist, a person without principle. It would be good to be assured, declared Bennett, that Runcie 'actually knew what he was doing and had a clear basis for his policies, other than taking the line of least resistance on each issue... he has the disadvantage of the intelligent pragmatist. . . . His clear preference is for men of liberal disposition with a moderately Catholic style which is not taken to the point of having firm principles. . . . Dr

Runcie and his closest associates are men who have nothing to prevent them following what they think is the wish of the majority of the moment.' Bennett provided no evidence for these extremely serious charges. He then went on to analyse and criticise the functioning of General Synod (as powerless) and the appointment of bishops as reflecting no more than the liberal preferences of the two Archbishops. To these two matters we will return but, while in part unbalanced, the comment upon them did not as grossly overstep the secret frontier as had the preceding remarks. It is regrettable that the Secretary-General of Synod did not refuse to publish the above lines and require Bennett to rewrite them, but he lacked the experience of the publisher and disastrously under-estimated the likely press reaction.

The publication date was Thursday 3 December. That day, the Preface was front page news in every national paper except for the *Daily Mirror*. Perhaps unfortunately, but quite inevitably, Church leaders went at once to the defence of the Archbishop and condemnation of the Preface. Bishop Taylor of St Albans called it 'a cowardly and disgraceful attack by a writer who has abused the privilege of anonymity which was accorded to him'. Inevitably, too, the press were out at once to uncover the author. Few people could conceivably have combined his intimate knowledge and particular viewpoint, and the guess that it was Bennett spread only too quickly. He was asked and, correctly but dangerously, denied authorship. If he had been a more experienced person, he would have guessed in advance how impossible a position he might be getting himself into. The pressure of the press, including considerable offers of money if he would write on the subject, and the almost universal criticism from Church and press directed at the still unknown author, proved too much. On the afternoon of Saturday 5 December he killed himself.

For Runcie, the public challenge was insignificant, the private grief considerable. Bennett had been his student at Westcott thirty years earlier and had remained a friend and collaborator. He had actually, by chance, received his last communion from the Archbishop's hand at Pusey House the previous Sunday. Runcie valued Bennett's skills as an historian and his clarity of mind, and had supported his appointment to the Crown Appointments Commission. He made no public comment whatever upon the Preface and would, doubtless, have been relatively little affected by it. Certainly, the comments were cutting and unfair and he could have no way to reply to them, but people in authority get used to such things and Runcie has not been short of criticism — though not previously from someone so close. Bennett's death added quite a different dimension. It turned an awkwardly bizarre episode into a tragic one, an ecclesiastical fiasco of the first order, as well as a personal sorrow for Runcie, who had done so much to help Bennett over the years.

The whole episode and the criticism contained in the Preface were, however, too important to be left unconsidered here, painful as it remains for all concerned. The more extended sections of critical analysis, written by a scholar of note, were probably very largely accepted by journalists and other observers as reliable. Some of it is, but much also is not. The two main areas Bennett raised in the latter part of the Preface were the appointment of bishops and the functioning of General Synod. These are, without doubt, central areas in regard to Runcie's responsibilities as Primate of All England and it is now time to turn to them. They represent a large core area within the year-in-year-out work of an archbishop and, as things now stand, the wider healthy functioning of the Church must largely depend upon them. It is only across the bench of bishops and across Synod that a Primate can hope to influence the Church as a whole. The attempt to do so on a direct face-to-face, teaching basis will impress the few who attend services in Canterbury Cathedral or read the Archbishop's books or even watch his televised New Year message, but the core of effective leadership is bound to be more indirect and structural.

In 1987 the new Crown Appointments Commission had been functioning for ten years and it was reasonable enough to examine its methods of working and its fruits. Unfortunately, this could not be done in the bitter, almost sneering manner adopted in the Preface. The Commission, chaired by two Archbishops, serviced by the Archbishop's Patronage Secretary and the Prime Minister's Patronage Secretary and consisting of six permanent members elected by Synod and four persons chosen for a particular appointment by the Vacancy-in-See Committee of the diocese concerned, meets from time to time for a two-day session. Bennett's account of its functioning (which he had never attended at the time he wrote) need not concern us but the fact of the Commission's existence is important. Prior to 1977 episcopal appointments in practice depended almost wholly upon the Archbishop and the Prime Minister's Patronage Secretary. Appointments in Runcie's time would never be as wholly Runcie's as appointments a decade earlier were Ramsey's. In commenting upon the report of the group reviewing the first seven years of the Crown Appointments Commission Runcie remarked that however hard he looked in the mirror he could not see a man whose biography would include a chapter entitled 'Bishop Maker'. No diocese ever used to have anything like the say in the choice of its bishop that every diocese now has. Nevertheless it need not be doubted that Runcie's influence remains very great, especially given his own highly diplomatic way of managing things. If appointments have been poor or of one hue alone, he can hardly escape a great deal of the blame.

Have they? The Crockford Preface accused Runcie and Habgood of having

> worked closely together to create a new kind of episcopate. The result has been a virtual exclusion of Anglo-Catholics from episcopal office and a serious under representation of Evangelicals. . . . The present discrimination is sometimes explained as a policy of appointing 'central' candidates, rather than 'party' men but it must be a matter of legitimate doubt whether Liberals are so central to the life and spirituality of the Church of England or whether they are foremost in its mission. One thing cannot be doubted: the personal connection of so many appointed with the Archbishop of Canterbury himself. . . . Though one may accept that an archbishop should have an influence on appointments, it is clearly unacceptable that so many are the protégés of one man and reflect his own ecclesiastical outlook. . . . A sign of the times is the increasing isolation of the diminishing number of Anglo-Catholic bishops. . . . More precarious is the position of the group of Evangelical bishops.

The facts, however, suggest a very different picture.

Of 42 English dioceses other than Canterbury, six have, at the time of writing, bishops appointed before 1980 (Chichester, Gloucester, Leicester, Liverpool, Manchester and Ripon) and one other (Hereford) is vacant. Of the 35 others, five have bishops who were already diocesans before 1980 but elsewhere in England (Habgood, Durham–York; Leonard, Truro–London; James, Wakefield–Winchester; Bowlby, Newcastle–Southwark; Waine, St Edmundsbury–Chelmsford). Of these, Habgood is a fairly quintessential Liberal, Leonard and James Anglo-Catholics, Waine a moderate Evangelical. Certainly the transfer of Leonard to London and James to Winchester, two of the five senior sees in the Church, hardly suggests an anti-Anglo-Catholic bias. But let us leave these aside and concentrate on the 30 new diocesan appointments since 1980 still holding office in 1990.

For decades, the large majority of bishops have been men trained at Cuddesdon or Westcott House, the two theological colleges with which Runcie has himself been associated. Selection from these stables is nothing new. It has naturally continued to happen. Nevertheless, the 1980s have witnessed an increasing number of appointments of men who studied elsewhere. The current bench includes men from all the following colleges: Lincoln, Ridley, Oak Hill, London College of Divinity, Wycliff Hall, St John's Durham, Ely, St Stephen's House, Mirfield, Wells and Clifton. One wonders whether at any earlier time the spread would have been as wide. In respect to their main previous work and expertise, the greater number in the less prestigious sees have, as one might expect, had straight parochial experience, while a considerable minority have taught for a while in a theological college and five were Principals of theological colleges: Carey (Trinity, Bristol), Santer (Westcott House), Hope (St Stephen's House), Sutton (Ridley) and Graham (Lincoln). Two of these colleges are emphatically Evangelical, one emphatically Anglo-Catholic, two moderate Anglo-Catholic — again, a fair mix. We may remember that both Runcie and Habgood were Principals of theological colleges (Cuddesdon and Queen's, Birmingham) when appointed to the episcopate, as was Coggan (London College of Divinity), and note that this is now a principal avenue for senior episcopal leadership, including Runcie's successor at Canterbury. Of senior university academics, there are probably fewer than formerly: at present only Jenkins of Durham, and Sykes of Ely. This remains, however, an important group entrusted with more 'academic' dioceses (Ely includes Cambridge), as well as normally a wider theological responsibility within the episcopate; but it may be a group difficult to maintain even at the present numbers with the decline in senior ordained Anglican theologians in the universities.

One of the major characteristics of the Anglican episcopate as at present constituted is the very considerable number of diocesan bishops who were formerly suffragan bishops, probably almost half at any one time. In the past, fewer suffragan bishops were later given dioceses of their own. Now this is becoming almost normal and it stresses the pastoral character of the appointment. There is often the complaint that a bishop is not trained but this is hardly true in regard to those who spend four or five years as a suffragan; equally it is not quite true for others who were archdeacons prior to their appointment. Here again, considerable episcopal-type experience was gained prior to diocesan appointment. In the present group there are also two men who were bishops abroad (Bavin of Portsmouth, formerly Bishop of Johannesburg, and Harris of Southwell, formerly Bishop of Northern Argentina) as well as some others who had other overseas experience (Sutton in Uganda, Barrington-Ward in Nigeria). The fact that many of the diocesan appointments of the Runcie years were already suffragan bishops in the 1970s certainly reduces any possibility that he could have decisively shaped the episcopate over a decade. The pro-

65

cess of habitual transfer from suffragan bishoprics to dioceses, and even from junior dioceses to more senior ones means that the shaping of the episcopate takes a very long time. If one thinks of Colin James, appointed Suffragan Bishop of Basingstoke in Ramsey's time, Bishop of Wakefield in Coggan's and Bishop of Winchester in Runcie's, the sense of a selective, on-going, rather lengthy process of episcopal upgrading becomes evident. For the most part, only the academics and the theological college Principals are left out of this. Durham, though the fourth most senior see, is normally given to an intellectual, and David Jenkins went there straight from a Chair in Leeds and with hardly a minimum of normal pastoral experience. The same can be said for Stephen Sykes, promoted from the Regius Chair of Divinity in Cambridge to Ely. But these are exceptional and while there is always room for exceptions — and a great need to have some theologians on the bench — the normative pastoral structuring behind the episcopate and its selection is well established.

In relation to the past, one of the most noticeable current characteristics of the House of Bishops is probably the significant minority who have not been to Oxford or Cambridge Universities or to a theological college in or near Oxford or Cambridge. This includes several leading Evangelicals, among them George Carey of Bath and Wells, Michael Baughen of Chester and Robert Williamson of Bradford — a particularly interesting group as it includes the 103rd Archbishop of Canterbury. One has to go far back into the Middle Ages to find another non-Oxbridge Cantuar. Carey is also the first Archbishop of Canterbury (perhaps the first bishop too?) to have been at a secondary modern school. In this he certainly outflanks the relatively humble origins of Runcie. It is worth stressing then that he was very much a Runcie appointment, already selected by the Archbishop before his episcopal appointment to succeed the Bishop of Chichester as Chairman of General Synod's Faith and Unity Advisory Group. In Carey Runcie had recognized the alpha quality but he could not look less like someone reflecting Runcie's own viewpoint or background. Nor could Williamson, a Northern Irish Protestant, trained at Oak Hill, with no degree but a most effective and impressive bishop in the exceptionally difficult circumstances of Bradford.

This analysis has been a lengthy one, but it was worth doing because it illustrates a major side of Runcie's care for the Church of England as a whole. It would be hopeless to try and sort out 'Evangelicals', 'Anglo-Catholics' and 'Liberals' among these men. The terms are just too simple. They characterize the young but seldom the mature. Good bishops outgrow such labellings. Yet it seems clear that Evangelicals have not been under-represented while 'Anglo-Catholics', apart from a rigid, but unrepresentative wing, are so central to the Church of England today (Cuddesdon and Westcott have both still to be labelled Anglo-Catholic, if labels have to be attached) that it would be absurd to claim they are being somehow left out. It is hard to think of able men who have been simply passed over. It may well be that the over-all intellectual calibre of the bench is lower than it was thirty or sixty years ago. If so, it is because the Church as a whole and its ministry is drawing fewer people of exceptional intellectual ability, but within such constraints the evidence suggests that the Crown Appointments Commission and Runcie as its principal Chairman have done their work well in this period. It would be surprising if it were not so because, if Runcie has an exceptional gift, it is for spotting talent and insisting upon the best. The very fact that he is not a party man means that he is likely to have sought his bishops in every possible quarter and he certainly seems to have done so. This is all the more understandable in the light of the fact that, faced with a legacy of synodical government which has proved far better at resisting things than achieving them, he has stressed, for some years, the need for stronger leadership from the House of Bishops.

To General Synod we must now turn. It was inaugurated in 1970. The members of its clerical and lay houses are re-elected once in five years. Runcie's archiepiscopate has coincided almost exactly with the third and fourth General Synods. While it replaced the Church Assembly it carried on many of the latter's practices so that it can be said that its Standing Orders were substantially drafted by Hugh Cecil who died many years before it came into existence. The laity who were most influential in the first twenty years of General Synod had mostly learnt the business of being a good Synod man or woman in the Church Assembly. But General Synod has wider powers and responsibilities and is less divided into separate Houses in its regular working than were its predecessors into Bishops, Clergy and Laity—although voting is still by House. The old Provincial Convocations of Canterbury and York have in practice met only very rarely in separate session. In consequence, the introduction of Synod actually simplified Church government.

The rationale behind the establishment of synodical government was twofold. On the one side it was to decrease parliamentary control of the Church for the benefit of both the Church and an over-worked parliament; on the other it was to ensure that the Church's freedom did not result simply in episcopal government but in a balanced system in which bishops, clergy and laity had all to participate. Noth-

ing can be decided positively without the agreement of a majority of
the bishops, and the bishops have a special role in all matters doctrinal
and liturgical, but equally nothing can be decided without the agreement of a majority of the representatives of clergy and laity. This has,
of course, for long been the practice of all other non-established
Churches within the Anglican Communion. In this matter, the
Church of England in 1970 was simply catching up with its daughter
Churches. The General Synod meets three times a year, twice non-
residentially at Westminster, and once, residentially, at York. These
three meetings are meant to cover in all not more than nine days but
this limit has seldom been kept to. Its membership of 560 includes a
very considerable number of women — far more than in parliament.
The reason for this is in part an unhappy one, indeed one of Synod's
principal troubles: the length of its meetings is too great for anyone
in normal full-time employment to be a member. The middle-class
wife without a job, perhaps a priest's wife, is occupationally the ideal
Synod candidate.

When Runcie moved to Lambeth, General Synod had almost completed ten years of work. One of the fruits of what we have called the
Ramsey revolution, it was now an established institution. It had
carried through major liturgical changes, another aspect of that revolution. It had begun to operate the new system of selecting bishops, a
third aspect. It had also shown its proneness to conservative decisions
by rejecting both union with Methodism and the ordination of
women, despite in each case the advice of the Archbishop of Canterbury of the time. These rejections were the consequence of a system
requiring a two-thirds majority in each House on major issues — in
principle a sensible protection against change by a small majority. But
a two-thirds majority in three separate groups is something hard to
obtain and among the clergy, in particular, it has proved almost
impossible.

Runcie's first synodical experience as Archbishop was to say fare-
well to the second Synod. It was a good moment to begin. The era of
liturgical and institutional revolution was over. The *Alternative Service Book*, the product of 25 years' work, was to be published that
November. He ended his Presidential Address pretty emphatically,

Finally, and I really mean it, we stand at a point where the heroic
age of constitutional and liturgical change is over, and at least for
a while there will be a pause in the tide of measures, canons and
liturgies. The style of the Synod during this past era has been
necessarily complex. It has involved detailed legislation, ex-

tended patterns of consultation, and administrative elabora-
tion. . . . Dare one hope that this style will not become a continuing way of life? . . . Can we now seek the grace of Christian
simplicity and give priority to a renewal of the Gospel message, a
deepening of the spiritual life, and a new concern for, and dialogue
with, those of our fellow citizens who do not yet feel the lure and
the attraction of Christ?

There is no doubt that this wish was heartfelt from someone whose
soul has never been turned on by 'constitutional and liturgical
change'. The trouble is, a Synod is shaped to cope with such things but
how really can it help with 'a deepening of the spiritual life'? One
might well argue that if 'the heroic age' was over, the Synod's meetings
should at once have been greatly reduced in length and simplified in
form. It could be claimed that General Synod in the 1980s has achieved
very little, blocked important developments, and engendered a great
deal of unnecessary frustration. It rejected the Covenanting Scheme
in 1982. It has ensured that the 1990s have begun with no women
ordained as priests in England, and no women ordained abroad allowed
to celebrate in this country. It has even prevented the rationalization
of the Church's Central Administration by the sale of Church House
and the removal of Synod staff to join the Church Commmissioners
at Millbank (a scheme which it earlier approved and which would have
saved the Church a great deal of money).

It has become increasingly clear that the Church of England has not
yet effectively resolved the inherent tension between a synodical and
an episcopal form of government. In administrative terms, is the
Church's central cabinet the Standing Committee of Synod or the
House of Bishops? Of course, there is overlap between the two and
good arguments either way. The defence of the synodical model is that
it deeply involves the laity and makes clear that the Church is not
ruled by the clergy: if the laity in parliament are no longer to have
much say then they must clearly do so somewhere else. The worry is
that synodically-involved laity are inherently unrepresentative, in
that they have few, if any, pastoral responsibilities to temper and
weigh against their synodical opinions, and that they are collectively
almost unknown to the wider Church and the nation. The wider world
can easily know who the Bishop of Oxford is and it knows more or less
what he is; after forty years of superbly dedicated service to General
Synod, Mr Oswald Clark remains an unknown figure beyond an inner
circle of the well-informed. The Hewitt Report of 1988 proposed an
increase in the general powers of the Standing Committee and its

accessory bodies. Would it have the prestige necessary to rule the Church to this extent, Runcie diplomatically enquired.

There is an inherent tendency for a large body like Synod, and especially for capable people within it who have found in this the major personal interest of their lives, to push for ever increased powers. It was natural that when synodical government began, the bishops as a House took a rather 'low profile' in order not to seem to challenge this new authority. During the later 1980s with the encouragement of Runcie, the House of Bishops made something of a come back while very wide-ranging criticism of Synod has mounted. In 1986 a group of conservatives produced a stinging critique of General Synod entitled *The Synod of Westminster: Do We Need it?*, edited by Peter Moore, Runcie's old Dean of St Albans, and including Graham Leonard, the Bishop of London. People complain that it has confused the legislative role of legislating on things which the Church needs to decide for itself with a deliberative role, perceived as the discussion of endless problems of the modern world about which it can do next to nothing and on which it is little better informed than anyone else; that its groups produce too many reports for discussion which lead nowhere; that it pays singularly little attention to what goes on in Diocesan Synods; that its procedures over issues that really matter to it are too adversarial; that the length of its sessions excludes the possibility of membership for most lay people with a full time job; that it is far too large; that it costs a very great deal of the Church's money which could be better spent in other ways.

Gary Bennett, who was an insider, declared that 'the ineffectiveness of the Synod is shown at every level of its operation'. Despite his bitter tone, his analysis should not be ignored on account of the tragedy of his death. His Preface was here at its best informed. And yet the Synod has not been wholly ineffective. It has, after all, for years blocked many important things which would certainly have happened if they had been left to the Archbishop of Canterbury and the House of Bishops.

How has Runcie related to the Synod and its problems? The first thing to say is that he behaves as a natural Synod animal, even if at times he must be excruciatingly bored by its proceedings and he has consistently defended both the principle and the practice of synodical government when it has come under attack. While Ramsey too often simply looked bored (it is noticeable that his biographer has not found it necessary to include General Synod in his index) and while Coggan preached, Runcie truly presides. He has influenced it a great deal by the care he has given to it, his loyalty to its decisions, his lack of partisanship and willingness (perhaps over-willingness) to admit that while he will vote one way, he has considerable sympathy for the other point of view too. He is not a man who personally believes in structural revolutions — that is one of the reasons why he has managed to have so little enthusiasm for the ordination of women. He has something of the cynicism of the amused historian about all claims that this or that change will make all the difference. He works with changes when they come to make the best of them. Once approval was given for the ordination of women to the diaconate, he ordained a large number of women deacons at Canterbury with a considerable flourish.

So Runcie has worked to make the Synod a success but thought rather little about how to change it. There can be little doubt that the first five years of his successor, the period of the fifth General Synod, will be a time when the nettle has firmly to be grasped. There is to be a Synodical Government Review Commission and, doubtless, there will be a great deal of argument, heart-searching and indeed, the clash of deeply contrasting views about the appropriate form of the Church's leadership. The outside observer can only wonder whether General Synod needs to be quite as big as it is — not much smaller in numbers than the House of Commons. A maximum of nine days of meeting a year ensures that most members can never take a very active part.

Archbishop Runcie has, more than once, made one major suggestion. His own 'dream' he has called it. It is generally agreed that the residential meeting at York achieves a happier note than those at Westminster. Cut the number of meetings a year from three to two, and have one in York and one in Canterbury, both residential. He has told Synod that he is sure it will come about sooner or later. Probably it will. The Lambeth Conference benefited by being moved by Archbishop Coggan from London to Canterbury. Let General Synod do the same thing. It is a sensible suggestion which could greatly improve the whole atmosphere of the central leadership of the Church but it is characteristic of Runcie that it is not something he has battled for. He is not himself a great reformer, only a subtle presider over the schemes, struggles and structures of others.

General Synod has at least remained for Runcie a relatively painless matter. He is probably grateful for that. He has experienced a number of extremely painful moments in his archiepiscopate. The first was the violently abusive attack on him in March 1982 in the Liverpool Church of St Nicholas by 'Protestant' demonstrators, with placards such as 'Rome Rules Runcie', 'Thirty pieces of silver — how many for Runcie?', who prevented him with boos and hisses from preaching or even praying. The second was the kidnapping of Terry Waite in 1987

in Lebanon while negotiating the release of hostages, and the continuous strain and sense of responsibility he felt for Waite over the
following years. Terry Waite was first appointed at Lambeth with very
different aims in the Archbishop's mind. His role as a hostage rescuer
came accidentally. It began with Iran in 1982 but the hostages involved were mostly Church people and Waite, in going to Tehran as
the Archbishop's envoy, was going to Khomeini, a religious person-
age. Next came Libya. Here at least he was still the Archbishop's
envoy to someone explicit — President Gaddafi. But the more he
became personally committed to this kind of work and the more the
press took it up, the more he became a sort of folk hero, and the more
the terms of the initial appointment effectively faded. In Lebanon, he
was not the Archbishop's envoy to anyone in particular. The Archbishop was, moreover, increasingly worried, but for Waite it was now
his life's work and only a formal instruction could have stopped him.
They both knew the dangers involved and it was Waite, not Runcie,
who was determined to keep on despite warnings from the Foreign
Office. Nevertheless, Terry Waite remained 'the Archbishop of
Canterbury's envoy'. It was hoped that would protect him, but it
meant too that Runcie had the final responsibility. Had a humanitarian desire to free people, which had earlier produced results, got out
of control? Had Runcie's judgement slipped up and should he have
been firmer with Waite? It is easy to ask such questions with hind-
sight. It is certain that the Archbishop agonized over them. The third
was Gary Bennett's attack on him in Crockford, and, much more,
Bennett's subsequent suicide.

Those were the worst occasions, but nearly as bad were the attacks
on him for lack of patriotism because he prayed for Argentinians in
the Falklands War service, for being a communist because he appointed a commission to report on inner city deprivation (a commission chaired by the former Chairman of the Manpower Services
Commission and personal assistant to Field Marshal Montgomery),
and for being a papist in disguise because he declared publicly in Rome
as elsewhere that he could accept an ecumenical (but not jurisdic-
tional) Roman primacy for the sake of Christian unity — a position
well inside the main line of Anglican tradition. Previous archbishops
have frequently been attacked, especially Michael Ramsey, whenever
they fulfilled their office and said anything significant which offended
the interests or susceptibilities of some sectional group in the country.
But Runcie is the first to feel the full nastiness of the press in its
current state of partial degeneration, a nastiness which has overflowed on to his wife.

She too has been so much attacked that it is necessary to say something about her role at Lambeth. Lindy is a pianist, not one of the world's greatest — as she is the first to remark — but good enough to have raised over half a million pounds in concerts for charities, from Dr Barnardo's Homes down, during her years at Lambeth. She is an exceptionally warm, vital person, determined to live her own life, and filled with an infectious enthusiasm for her music, her charities, her garden and her grandchild. Bach, Beethoven and Brahms are the other men in her life, she remarks humorously, but there is no shadow of a doubt who the first man is. She has never been a typical clergy wife. Ecclesiastical affairs quickly bore her and she is very willing to admit to that boredom. She does not see the point in following her husband round to every sermon he preaches. She judges it more sensible and really supportive of him to raise money for charities, restore the Palace garden, or just keep her own independent spirit fresh with a day a week teaching music in St Albans. But she has accompanied him on a number of his overseas tours and is very often present at important functions. The Palace has been her home and she its hostess.

I am by no means an old or intimate family friend, but I have watched her selling postcards at a stall to all and sundry at a garden party for the Church Urban Fund with the most charming enthusiasm, I have watched her receive the kiss of peace from her husband at the Easter Eucharist in Canterbury Cathedral and afterwards accompany the cathedral organist on the piano at the drinks party in the Old Palace, I have seen the look in her eyes as she tried to persuade her husband, when not at all well, to leave a public reception. Her greatest strength is not the sheer vitality, delightful as it is, though on occasion disconcerting in the uninhibited character of her comment on events — it may have upset more conventional Church people and it has fuelled the nasty attacks sections of the press have made on her. It is rather her special combination of total loyalty to her husband with the individuality and developed interests of a very modern woman. The profound affection between them is not in doubt. A close friend has remarked that marriage was the only thing Bob Runcie ever found difficult to get right, and that it has been good for him that this was so. It has doubtless been, on occasion, an explosive relationship but it is hard for the observer to doubt that they have got it right, a 'union of duty with delight' — a phrase of Austin Farrer which Runcie is fond of quoting. To suggest otherwise is simply malicious.

The role of an archbishop, the inherent problems of theology and ecclesiastical relations, the sheer tension involved in endeavouring to be both Christ-like and reasonably on the wave length of the late twentieth century, are all things about which most journalists know very little. A simplistic attack on him for not giving a moral lead about something they care not two hoots for themselves, and would probably attack him for if he did give a lead, is the easiest of journalistic ploys — amusing enough to write, but still painful enough for him to read.

Lord Halifax, most devout and ecumenical of lay Anglo-Catholic leaders of the early part of this century, once remarked rather fiercely: 'Nothing but the martyrdom of an archbishop can save the Church of England'. Of course, the martyrdom of archbishops always has been a rather special Canterbury theme. Already in the eleventh century Archbishop Alphege was murdered by the Danes. In the seventeenth century William Laud was executed on an Act of Attainder by the Long Parliament. Most poignant of all, Cranmer, an often hesitant man whom Runcie deeply admires and sometimes compares himself to, was burnt to death outside Balliol College, Oxford, for his Protestant faith, in 1556. But the central symbolism of Canterbury was for centuries dominated by the murder within its cathedral walls of Thomas Becket in 1170 in one of the greatest Church–State rows of the Middle Ages. The pilgrimage to Thomas's shrine at Canterbury became a central motif of late medieval religious and social life and, in Chaucer's classic, of its literature as well. Henry VIII smashed the shrine and flung out Becket's bones, correctly recognizing that what Becket stood for was highly incompatible with his own supreme headship over the Church. Thus for a time was crushed part of the special historic identity of the church of Canterbury and its symbolic politico-religious role in English life. A State-controlled Church in which all the bishops were appointed by the Crown eliminated in principle (though not always in practice) the relationship of healthy dualism between Church and State which may at a time of crisis lead even to martyrdom. Yet the cult of Thomas of Canterbury has nonetheless survived and revived. T. S. Eliot's *Murder in the Cathedral*, written in the 1930s for production in Canterbury Cathedral, is a powerful witness of its renewed vitality. It is noticeable how frequently Runcie refers to it. But the twelfth-century martyr has to some extent to give way to twentieth-century ones. In Idi Amin's Uganda, Janani Luwum, the Anglican Archbishop, was arrested and murdered in 1977; Oscar Romero, the Catholic Archbishop of San Salvador, was murdered while celebrating Mass by a right-wing death squad the very day before Archbishop Runcie was enthroned in Canterbury Cathedral and was specially remembered in prayer and sermon the following day. A chapel of twentieth-century martyrs has become a very important shrine in the cathedral and to it, in 1982, Runcie led Pope John Paul II, who himself had been nearly assassinated the year before.

When Lord Halifax uttered his rather cryptic remark in what was still a highly Erastian Church most of this had not happened. But all of it has undoubtedly entered into Runcie's consciousness. His photograph and that of Oscar Romero appeared together on the first page of the newspapers on the day of his enthronement and in his enthronement sermon he referred to his martyred brother archbishop. It is not impossible to imagine that not only the Church of El Salvador but that of England too might indeed in some way be 'saved' by the courageous witness of Romero and many other Christian martyrs of the twentieth century.

Personally, Runcie appears conscious of the theme of the martyr-archbishop, whether it be Becket, Luwum or Romero, to a degree that his predecessors were not. His very fondness for Eliot has contributed to this. Martyrdom, however, can come in many forms — the martyrdom of blood being traditionally only one of them — and a Methodist, contemplating these themes at the time of Runcie's enthronement, sent him the following poem entitled *An Archbishop at His Enthronement (with apologies to T. S. Eliot)*:

This is not all what I had in mind at all
When I was seized by the ear, as you might say,
And hauled out of my safety into a life
Which I imagined would be somewhat different.
I thought of some sort of martyrdom perhaps,
Ecstasy possibly, the Poor my blood brothers—
And total self-abnegation; now here I am
Coped, mitred, and croziered, like a totem.
On a throne; inter pares, yes, but certainly Primus.
Multitudinous activities, all through official channels,
Multifarious meetings with representatives,
An heartfelt spontaneity seized by the Media,
Examined, interpreted, twisted, falsified.
One could be tempted to self pity.
That would be betrayal — tribes need a scapegoat.
Mitre, Cope, Palace, Chauffeur, and all.
Is it possible that this is the martyrdom you had in mind?

We have here, once more, the intimation of martyrdom — not, understandably, by some group of Tory thugs dispatched from Downing Street after the Archbishop's Falklands sermon or the *Faith in the*

City report: the swords of the four knights are to be found these days in the pages of *Mail*, *Star*, *Express* or *Sun*. 'Examined, interpreted, twisted, falsified.' The great temptation for a Church leader would be self-pity or, still worse, some attempt to satisfy the cravings of the popular press or the instant moral answer brigade in or outside the Church. Instead today, as in 1170 or 1556, a brave archbishop may have simply to steel himself for 'some sort of martyrdom'. It may well be that in the twentieth century no Archbishop of Canterbury before Runcie could reasonably be said to have needed to do so. In this the Methodist poem writer appears remarkably prescient. But it should be stressed too that this dimension of Runcie's experience has been only an English one. His relationship with the wider Anglican Communion has had its problems but nothing to approach the often venomous treatment a highly sensitive and conscientious man has been accorded by some of his fellow countrymen both inside and outside the Church.

Most central, however, to an experience of martyrdom has probably been the inner tension between a unique responsibility, moral and doctrinal, upon the one hand and the personal uncertainties and intellectual complexities of an exceptionally subtle and well trained, but also humble, modern mind upon the other. Intellectually Runcie remains the Oxford classics scholar deeply affected by the lessons of 1940s Logical Positivism. Surrounded by Billy Graham and David Jenkins, John Habgood, John Paul II and Mary Whitehouse, let alone Margaret Thatcher and Arthur Scargill, Runcie probably has considerably less natural confidence in his own way of formulating the truth, liberal or conservative, than any of them. He recognizes most deeply both his own limitations and, across them, the inherent limitations of understanding and certainty all humans are subject to. Yet he still occupies a chair from which an authoritative lead and pronouncements are ceaselessly called for. He knows, too, how much ordinary people really need and want leadership. In facing this dilemma, as much a personal as an institutional one, he is far more like Paul VI than John Paul II. Unlike all his twentieth-century predecessors who would seem, even Ramsey, to have wanted the move to Canterbury, Runcie was profoundly reluctant to occupy that chair at all. He accepted it as a duty he could not refuse but not at all as something he had expected as his deserts, much less desired. He may be the only Archbishop of Canterbury in history to have earlier refused the archbishopric of York. His deepest martyrdom has been to sense better than anyone else the demands of the job, attempt ceaselessly to meet them, but to remain intensely conscious all the time of his own supposed inadequacy for doing so. This, it must be stressed, is the judgement of the author. It is not his. There is no evidence to suggest that Runcie himself has ever seriously seen his predicament in terms of the martyr, despite the toll taken by the degree of mindless abuse unparalleled in the modern history of Archbishops of Canterbury, to which he and his wife have been subjected. With a certain donnish self-deflation he would probably not wish to take himself so seriously. It is only the historian who may do so.

❧ 4 ❧

At Mansion House

Every year in November it is a function of the Archbishop to propose the toast to the Lord Mayor and the Court of Aldermen at the Lord Mayor's Banquet in Mansion House. It is the final speech the Lord Mayor will hear in his term of office and since, as Runcie explains, it follows the Prime Minister's substantial review of the state of the nation, 'it has to be a skilfully blended combination of comic relief and measured tribute'. Runcie has always excelled since his school days at providing comic relief and it seems right to show at least a little of this side of him. 'I stand as usual poised rather uneasily between the cliché and the indiscretion', he remarked at a lunch for American journalists, not discontentedly. A mimic, a joker, delighting in parallels which both enlighten and deflate — often at his own expense — or in phrases which were meant seriously, perhaps uttered pompously, but which now sound deliciously silly, Runcie uses his humour both to make a serious point and to break through into social groups where he might otherwise seem alien. It is a pastoral skill as well as a sheer gift for entertainment.

At Mansion House banquets, through the jokes and the words which follow, he encourages the City in the need for high moral standards within its job of wealth creation, he praises the Lord Mayor for all his charitable work and he keeps the bridge open and friendly between Church and big business. He does all this more lightly and, therefore, more effectively than most Church leaders and many of his predecessors could have managed.

Humour has its own problems. It breaks down some barriers but it can create others. Cultural worlds of humour differ profoundly. Probably the greatest débâcle of Runcie's archiepiscopate was caused in 1981 by trying to be amusing about the religious role of women at an international ecumenical conference at Sheffield. The wavelength was just wrong and a snide Oxbridge note almost had him booed off the platform. But it is exceedingly seldom that he misses the right mode of conversation in that way.

With the 'Fathers' of the City of London Runcie need never worry that he is not at home linguistically. That is a help. It may, however, be to the point to stress that the Archbishop's relationship with the

City is not just a personal but an institutional one. That may seem odd. London has, after all, its own bishop but the Archbishop of Canterbury, as Primate of All England, relates directly to its capital. If a service of national importance is to be held in St Paul's Cathedral, it is the Archbishop, not the Bishop of London, who will normally preside. He has in fact three great churches to which he relates not just as an honoured guest but by the very requirements of his office: Canterbury Cathedral, Westminster Abbey and St Paul's Cathedral. Indeed he officially became Archbishop of Canterbury at the moment his election by the Canterbury Chapter was confirmed in the crypt of St Paul's Cathedral in the presence of the Lord Mayor and Sheriff of London: a strange arrangement to a mind unfamiliar with the inner ways of the English State. After it was over he was taken straight to luncheon by the Lord Mayor at Mansion House. The Archbishop's expected relationship with 'the City' could not be clearer. For better or worse it makes him part of 'The Establishment'. It is part, too, of the background to *Faith in the City*.

Humour is also a difficult quality to report at second hand. So much depends on tone of voice, gesture and the right atmosphere. Yet the following extracts from speeches in the City, and elsewhere, but especially at Mansion House, may give some idea of Runcie's way.

* * *

My Lord Mayor, etc. . . .

A couple of weeks ago I was present at a civic occasion in Moscow. It was more unpredictable than this festivity. As we walked into the Kremlin Great Hall an official voice hissed in my ear, 'Mr Gromyko will speak first, the Patriarch of Rumania will speak for the Orthodox, Cardinal Casaroli will speak for the Catholics, and you, you will speak for all the rest'.

Flattering for the Anglican Communion, daunting for the speaker.
(1988)

It is a very great pleasure for me to propose this toast. After a year of more eating and drinking than anyone else in the kingdom, the Lord Mayor finds himself faced at the last by the Archbishop of Canterbury.

The sense that what follows will be the last rites must be almost irresistible.

Irresistible perhaps, but fortunately inappropriate. For all the buf-fetings of office I am delighted to see that Sir Allan still retains that alert and even hungry look that seems to characterize the best of chartered accountants. In his presence I carefully avoid all statistics, but I cannot refrain from mentioning that with his departure I shall have proposed the toast for just over 1 per cent of all the Lord Mayors there have ever been.   (1986)

When I was legally confirmed in the crypt of St Paul's and identified as indeed Robert Runcie, I was invited to lunch at the Mansion House. It was my first meeting with Sir Christopher who was Sheriff and accompanied by Lady Leaver. My wife was also there in animated and uninhibited mood. Sir Christopher turned to my Chaplain saying how much he had enjoyed Mrs Runcie's company but observed also that such were the pressures of life in the public eye she would, alas, be ironed out into a dull conformity within six months. A small sum was wagered on whether this would in fact happen. I understand that, as a gentleman, my Lord Mayor, you have already paid up.   (1982)

The American press has been very helpful and even kind ever since my enthronement. I particularly cherish the headline in the *Washington Post* which went 'easy moving, over six feet tall, husky, pig-keeping, war veteran, gets top job!'   (1981)

The Archbishop of Canterbury has a seat in the House of Lords. To tell you the truth I sit on the only bench in the House of Lords which has arms, because one of my eighteenth-century predecessors was so consistently drunk that he was in the habit of rolling off the end of his bench onto the floor. Even in the heavy-drinking Age of Enlightenment and Reason this was considered unedifying — hence the arms.   (1981)

It is unusual to have a sense of relief before delivering a speech and not after it. I am very pleased that the Resolution that I should be made Freeman of the City has been passed so decisively. This means that I will not now have to put my contingency plans into effect.

I was also rather mindful of the story of the vicar who was on holiday for his 50th birthday. A telegram arrived that morning which read, 'At their meeting last night the PCC passed the following Resolution. We wish the vicar a happy birthday. There voted for the motion 12, against the motion 11.'

(Speech in response to being granted the Freedom of the City in Canterbury, 1984)

This evening is not only welcome for its splendour and generosity but also as one of those occasions when the secular ministers to the spiritual — and not vice versa — civic balm cools ecclesiastical fever.

As you know we have just had a gruelling time in Synod where the occasional good humour and tolerance of that body was stretched to its limit on the ordination of women. A summer debate on the subject is becoming like Wimbledon, Ascot, Trooping the Colour. (1988)

The Lord Mayor has received national leaders — from Mexico, China and India. He has entertained countless small delegations with the same degree of thoughtfulness, welcoming them, I am told, with a few sentences in their own language. I am not sure how he managed when the Metropolitan Police Special Dog section was received at the Mansion House. (1985)

'First the man, then the priest.' Do you know the story of Frederick Temple? When he was a Bishop of Exeter I suppose, or it could have been during his time in London, he used to examine those seeking ordination by throwing himself on a couch and saying, 'Pay me a sick visit'. And so they did to the best of their ability. But one day a young ordinand responded to the challenge by striding into the room, slapping the bishop on the back and saying, 'What, Frederick, drunk again!' Temple jumped up, 'You'll do', he said, 'you'll do'.

It was to an inner city school just along the road from us in Lambeth that I went last week. I was dressed for the occasion in purple cassock and wanting to put an easy question to connect with the infants I said, 'Do you know where I live?' A hand shot up and one wide-eyed child immediately replied, 'Up in the sky'. The headmaster whispered to me, 'Is that the first time you've been confused with your employer?' (1988)

You yourself have broken new ground by becoming the first woman to be Lord Mayor in the 792 years of that office. Therefore I feel a little defensive at being the 102nd male incumbent of an office which has existed 1,387 years. Perhaps it is the City rather than the clergy who should be assailed nowadays as dangerous radicals. (1984)

The bishops have had a year of theology. It was the world-weary Lord Melbourne who commented to Queen Victoria that 'much mischief has been done by theological bishops'. If that is so then I am afraid, my Lord Mayor, that you are entertaining a houseful of unrepentant mischief-makers. (1986)

Last year I was in Korea. They had already completed the Olympic Stadium and they wanted to display its impeccable efficiency to me. They wanted to welcome me with words on the electronic scoreboard. As I walked into the stadium the words were flashed on, 'Welcome to you Archbishop Lunchie'. (1988)

Archbishops might be thought to have a special interest both in the original and metaphorical sense in wool. Sheep are reckoned to be our professional concern—perhaps I can remind you of the schoolboy who wrote home after a visit of the Bishop, 'Now I know what a real crook looks like': while the elusive qualities of theological speech and the more high flown rhetoric of ecclesiastics are dismissed by practical men of affairs as woolly.

I might have pleaded my own modesty and interest in the breeding of Black Berkshire pigs to have shifted the image in a more earthy direction. But this has not always stood me in good stead. Recently I was visiting the more remote areas of Romney Marsh and thought I would call on one of my clergy.

My Chaplain thought it would only be fair to warn him and on ringing up received the response, 'Is he coming as swineherd or shepherd?'

In European culture shepherds are languid figures with jerkins and ukuleles and rather a trivial line in love lyrics. They are benign. But biblical shepherds and early Archbishops of Canterbury have not always dwelt in such pastoral peace.

One of the saints of Canterbury was Archbishop Alphege who was pounded to death by mutton bones, but I don't think that he is a line worth following though I sometimes muse upon his fate when I think that I am being pounded to death by the media.

(To the Woolmen's Company, 1986)

You have listened so well that you deserve a new story to conclude my speech. It has a moral. Two nights ago I went to Heathrow Airport in order to welcome Bishop Desmond Tutu and to congratulate him on being awarded the Nobel Prize for Peace. It seemed that all the television and radio and press of Europe were crowded round the exit from Concorde on which he had landed from New York for a break before he took the plane to Johannesburg.

I was placed at the top of the tunnel from which the passengers were to emerge and behind me there were cameras, arc lights and television crews, a great battery of them. We waited expectantly and there emerged first not Bishop Tutu and his family but an American and his wife. They seemed somewhat dazzled by the lights and the cameras and my assistant, Terry Waite (who is here tonight to vouch for the story and is a kind of Scarlet Pimpernel of the Anglican Communion who manages to get by with a strong sense of humour). He stepped forward and said to the Americans, 'It is a special facility of Concorde that each passenger is welcomed in the country personally by the Archbishop of Canterbury'. The reply was 'Oh, really'. It was a mixture of amazement and suspicion!

(Speech in Canterbury on being granted the Freedom of the City. October **1984**)

❧ 5 ❧

Church and society

The principal traditional way in which an Archbishop of Canterbury and, in lesser measure, other bishops played a role in the general political life of the country was as members of the House of Lords, a body in which they have strict priority, consisting as it does of 'Lords Spiritual and Temporal'. It was William Temple who, as in many other things, began a shift in the life of the Church. He had an enormous concern for secular issues of all sorts, but rather little interest in the House of Lords. While whatever impact his predecessors, Davidson and Lang, made on social issues of every sort was almost entirely through the Lords and through their confidential relations with members of the Government, Temple acted far more through public meetings, the chairing of conferences, the commissioning of reports (including a very important one in the 1930s on unemployment entitled *Men Without Work*, published by Pilgrim Trust), and the writing of books such as *Christianity and Social Order*, a Penguin Special.

The reasons for this shift are clear enough. On the one side, the House of Lords had greatly declined in importance. Up to 1910 it was a chamber of nearly equal weight to the Commons. Its powers were then cut down by the Parliament Act and, still more, in 1945 by the Attlee Government. As its importance in government was reduced, it became less appropriate for the Church's voice to the nation to be heard principally within its walls. Still more important, however, was that speeches by individual bishops in the House of Lords are heard by few people and not so many more read *Hansard* or even the fairly detailed summaries which used to appear in *The Times*. If the Church's voice to the nation was to be heard, if it was to be a genuinely corporate voice, if it was, furthermore, actually to galvanize the Church into doing something for the nation, then things needed to be shaped rather differently. Lang represented the old order, Temple the new. In the post-war period, however, Geoffrey Fisher only partly followed the Temple lead, his own interest in social issues being very much more limited. Moreover, at a time when the Government was itself endeavouring to establish the Welfare State along lines which Temple and others had helped to sketch out, the Church's leaders could easily feel that they had no need to say very much. In the 1960s Michael Ramsey, in this as in much else the heir of Temple, whom he greatly admired, took a remarkable lead on a number of issues — the alteration of the law on homosexuality, the abolition of capital punishment, race relations, and white Rhodesia's UDI, among others. While he certainly gave less time to the House of Lords than Davidson or Lang, he probably used his time there more effectively than any archbishop in this century. Nevertheless, his public leadership was by no means confined to what he did in the Lords. On the contrary, he was, for instance, appointed by Harold Wilson as Chairman of the new National Committee for Commonwealth Immigrants — a remarkably imaginative move on Wilson's part.

When Runcie went to Lambeth, a suitable political role for the Archbishop, in relation to contemporary society and its problems, had been largely staked out by Ramsey following in the steps of Temple. Runcie simply carried on very much in the Ramsey way. He has made a number of major speeches in the House of Lords and has used his presence there to keep communication open between Church and State but, undoubtedly, what he has done elsewhere has been very much more important. Lambeth Palace arranges a rota of bishops to say prayers in the Lords and tries to ensure that individual bishops are present to speak on matters about which they are knowledgeable, but the general episcopal presence is undoubtedly often rather thin — busy diocesan bishops can hardly find the time to spare from their dioceses to be in London for lengthy debates, especially when the agenda for debate is usually known only a week or two beforehand. When in June 1983 the Duke of Norfolk proposed the Motion for the Loyal Address in response to the Queen's Speech at the beginning of the new parliament, Runcie supported him on behalf of the Lords Spiritual and continued a little jokingly, 'Governments may come and governments may go, but the Lords Spiritual always sit in the same place'. He said it because he was only too aware that they sat there rather too seldom.

Whitelaw had just become a Viscount and Leader of the House. He had been Runcie's old commander in the war and naturally that had to be referred to: 'As someone who many years ago learned most of what he knows about leadership from serving under the noble Viscount during the war, I am particularly pleased once again to soldier under him as Leader of the House. I hope that I can bring other Members of the Lords Spiritual into the same frame of obedience on this matter.' He promised the Government the prayers of Christian people, 'as we, the Lords Spiritual, sit with not uncritical solidarity with them on these Benches'. To which Whitelaw replied, 'It is a great thing to think that at one stage of one's life one actually commanded the Archbishop of Canterbury'. Certainly, the relationship between the Archbishop and the Leader of the House was likely to be eased by their wartime relationship and continuing friendship, and that easing could be needed when he came under often quite unjustified attacks from some Conservatives. At this point, as at many other lesser ones, Runcie's wartime contacts were worth their weight in gold.

Relations with Labour were no less important, but where the bishops came under fire from Tory ranks for being too outspoken on social issues, they could be accused by Labour of not being critical enough.

Thus a couple of years earlier, in January 1981, Lord Wells-Pestell, formerly a Labour Minister, complained that the bishops were not doing nearly enough to challenge the Government's bad social record:

> We have not had from the Bishops Bench in the last Session of Parliament all the help that this House has a right to expect. . . . There were about three contributions on unemployment; there were several on education; there were two on housing, and I think there were two on immigration. I really do not think that is good enough. If I may say so with very great respect, I think this House can look to the bishops to provide a knowledge which is denied to a good many people in your Lordship's House. . . . I believe as a Christian Socialist that the Church has a voice which is of supreme importance in these matters. I think we need to know what the Church is thinking more often than we do.

Runcie thought the criticism unfair, but the concern entirely right. If he had an old friendship with Whitelaw on one side of the House, deep down in his soul he shared with Wells-Pestell on the other side the feeling that he was a 'Christian Socialist'. That was how he had developed at school and, after passing through a Tory phase in the army and back at Oxford, it was the way in late maturity in which he could again characterize himself, if a little nostalgically.

Apart from brief formal speeches, supporting a loyal address to the Queen Mother or the Prince of Wales, lamenting the assassination of Mrs Gandhi, or paying tribute to the late Lord Stockton (Harold Macmillan) — whom he had once conducted round Greece on a Swan Hellenic Cruise — and apart from two or three interventions of some length on specifically ecclesiastical matters, Runcie made major speeches on the International Year of Disabled People and the Nationality Bill (both in 1981), on the Brixton riots and the problems of the inner city (1982 and 1987), the Falkland Islands (1982), crimes of violence (1983), the fortieth anniversary of the United Nations (1985) and foreign policy (1988, in the debate on the Address). These are all lengthy and exceptionally well prepared speeches. In general, they all reflect Runcie's convictions, that almost every issue of significance has a 'moral' dimension and that

> the Church has a special concern to speak for the vulnerable, the inarticulate, those who are weak in bargaining power — for all those in our country who are at the bottom of the heap. It also has a concern for justice. This will mean that on, for example, racial questions, and on many matters of economic and social concern, it should have special things to say. If it fails to say them, it is not being true to its beliefs. (Address to the Cross-Bench Peers, June 1982)

His most forceful intervention in the House of Lords came in 1981, on the British Nationality Bill. All the Churches strongly criticized it and the Archbishop in the House of Lords was able to speak from a position of wide ecclesiastical consensus. Thus, in his second speech on the subject, in October, he could declare,

> I want, once again, to place on record our deep concern that on so fundamental a matter as nationality, we seem about to pass into law a measure which, in the view of the leaders of all our Churches — and we are increasingly working together in these matters — is questionable when judged on moral principles and the effects of which will be to sow doubts in an area where reassurance is desperately needed.
>
> This is an occasion when I speak not for a single denomination. The Bishops' assertions have not been academic, theoretical or party political; nor do we claim any monopoly of moral sensitivity; but they arise from our deep pastoral concern and extensive local knowledge. History, I suspect, will judge that this was a great opportunity missed. This is a Bill of which future generations will not be proud.

Despite some improvements which had been made by the Government as a result of criticisms on the Second Reading, Runcie insisted that it was a 'bad Bill then and it is a bad Bill now'. Bishops do not generally criticize Government policy as sharply as that in the Lords, nor do they generally take part in the actual voting. In this case, Runcie spoke on the Second Reading when seven other bishops were also present. During the seven Committee days, bishops spoke on ten occasions. A major amendment was tabled in the name of the Arch-

87

bishop and three other bishops to clause 1, which, if accepted, would greatly have improved and simplified the Bill. At the Report stage, which took three days, bishops voted on almost every amendment, Runcie spoke again at the Third Reading and he, with five other bishops, then voted for the amendment tabled by Lord Elwyn-Jones declaring that the Bill 'will exacerbate racial tension'. It was a record of very serious endeavour to protect the interests of some of the most under-privileged groups in our society. As Runcie reported sadly to Synod, 'The final result did not, unfortunately, reflect the power of our arguments, but I would like nevertheless to record my thanks to all who batted so nobly through two Readings, seven Committee Days and three Report Days'. At least it was made clear what the Church thought and perhaps, too, the presence of the bishops in the Lords was pragmatically justified in the eyes of some people, who, in theory, saw no point to it.

This was the only case in which the Archbishop came near to acting as leader of the opposition. He did so because he believed that basic characteristics of a Christian and liberal society were at stake and because of the exceptionally strong feelings within the Churches on this matter, evidence at least of the great concern of Church people to be helpful to the immigrant population. In his other speeches there was no comparable degree of confrontation, even though he was doubtless often pressing a somewhat different line from that of the Government. On the Falklands, however, he fully supported British military action, if no other way of freeing the islands from Argentinian control was possible, on the two grounds of the overwhelming importance of maintaining international law and the right to self-determination, even of a small people. He said this both before the British Task Force was sent and after it: 'I believe that within the complexities of an imperfect world, self-defence and the use of limited force in defence of clear principles can sometimes be justified'. In this opinion, of course, many Christians did not agree with him, and he incurred a good deal of abuse in consequence from that side. In 1983, well after the war was over, he gave a lecture at Chatham House on 'Just and Unjust Wars' in which he examined and defended the traditional theory of the Just War and concluded once more that the British action over the Falklands fell within its limits. In the immediate aftermath of the war, however, he had a different role: to preside over and preach at the national Falkland Islands service in St Paul's Cathedral in the presence of veterans of the war, many members of the royal family and the Prime Minister. The sermon is given in full in Chapter 9. It was a very carefully measured piece, a combination of thanksgiving, mourning, a lament for the evil of war, and a plea for reconciliation. Twice he spoke of the Argentinians:

> In our prayers we shall quite rightly remember those who are bereaved in our own country and the relations of the young Argentinian soldiers who were killed. Common sorrow could do something to re-unite those who were engaged in this struggle. A shared anguish can be a bridge of reconciliation. Our neighbours are indeed like us.

There was nothing at all triumphalistic or militant in the sermon, no trace of jingoism, of a 'God on our side' mentality. For this he was much abused by some. The Prime Minister was said to be displeased. How little people learn! How sick-making was the religious jingoism of the early period of the First World War! Most Church people of the next generation were deeply resolved not to repeat that and, on the whole, in the Second World War, it was not repeated. Runcie had been through the Second World War and if anything had convinced him of its justice, it was what he saw in the concentration camp of Belsen. He was not a pacifist, but still less a jingoist. It was the best of the Second World War Christian spirit — the attitudes inculcated through Oldham's *Christian Newsletter*, for instance, which he had regularly read — that Runcie carried across to the Falklands War, a spirit perhaps forgotten by some of a younger generation whose experience of war was nil.

When preaching a couple of years later to commemorate the fortieth anniversary of D-Day, he recalled how he had listened to Archbishop Temple preaching in Canterbury Cathedral at a service of preparation for the invasion of Europe:

> I did not know then that he had written in his diary his vision of a Victory Service which should begin with an act of penitence for our share in the sins of the whole world out of which came the calamities which afflict mankind and that this, along with an act of dedication, should be the final expression of thanksgiving. He had shared these thoughts with Churchill who was silent for a while and then said, 'Yes, I understand that'.

It was perhaps with that in mind that Runcie had endeavoured to provide the true note for the Falkland Islands service and if he incurred a great deal of odium for not preaching a 'victory' sermon of the old sort, some at least were able to recognize the point and say, 'Yes, I understand that'. After the sermon a Falklands widow wrote to him, as did a very senior Marine commander involved in the conflict: they thanked him for saying what he had about the Argentinian widows.

Runcie's views on social and political issues can be defined as neither those of the Right nor of the Left, in terms of their spirit, but in terms of what he actually held on most matters, they probably put him at the wettest end of the Conservative Party or the most moderate wing of Labour. If that is so, then he undoubtedly stood where the majority of ordinary English people stand. Thus when Synod's working group on nuclear warfare produced, in 1983, its very fine report, *The Church and the Bomb*, with its unilateralist recommendations, Runcie argued against their acceptance: British unilateralism would not serve the cause of peace effectively. On the contrary, it could make the world more dangerous. He refused to admit that it was 'a debate between faith and principle on the unilateralist side and pragmatism on the side of the multilateralists'. On the contrary, the latter had an equal moral seriousness. 'Principle is not the exclusive possession of those who are attracted to larger gestures. . . . Principle also belongs to those whose moral sense expresses itself in the painstaking precision and care about detail which I have found among some of those actually involved in disarmament negotiations.' The point here is not whether he was right or wrong. The point is that he considered each issue very carefully in its own right in Christian and moral terms, and that his conclusions were certainly not unfailingly radical. A multilateralist who emphatically supported the Falklands War but also the Brandt Report and who opposed the new Immigration Bill tooth and nail — that is hardly the picture of an ecclesiastical revolutionary.

A notable development in the last twenty years has been the great growth of new forms of care in the voluntary sector, for the handicapped, the aged, the terminally ill, dropouts, the underprivileged of every sort. On one side, this development, which is in part a consequence of the manifest and growing inadequacies of the Welfare State, may be linked with, and seen as, a critique of Thatcherite policies which have moved away from the provision of adequate State care for those in need. But, equally, they represent a positive response to the Thatcherite stress upon the necessity and rightness of a greatly enlarged voluntary sector. In several addresses Runcie has taken the latter view: humanity and the Churches need to share freely, locally and in as individual a way as possible in the care of those who require special assistance. He is far more deeply a suitably responsive Primate for a Thatcherite Britain than a critic of Thatcher's policies. President of Help the Aged and the National Association of Victim Support Schemes among much else, his addresses to these two bodies, as to the Abbeyfield Society, the Churches' Council for Health and Healing, the Birmingham Community Relations Council, Helen House, the National Society, the Building and Social Housing Foundation, and his Prison Reform Trust Lecture, as well as more commemorative addresses celebrating the survival and contemporary significance of earlier initiatives such as the Peckham Settlement and the Thomas Coram Foundation in the City, all stress the importance of imaginative concern for 'minute particulars' in regard to human need. For Runcie this is most suitably a voluntary activity. We may here note too, in regard to the larger horizon, addresses to Oxfam, the Global Forum of Spiritual and Parliamentary Leaders on Human Survival, the Court of Human Rights and the European Parliament, as also speeches in the Synod on the Brandt Report, minority ethnic groups, youth work and many other topics. Together these addresses add up to a very considerable corpus of teaching.

In speaking to Oxfam, Runcie confessed to being 'a slightly perplexed Archbishop, who finds most of the problems of the world crossing his desk'. As he went on, 'Today, I am at Oxfam. Tomorrow I shall be at the Bank of England.' What should be his priorities? Preserving old buildings, helping the most needy in Britain, giving everything away for those in Ethiopia dying of hunger? It seems heartless to spend any money on old buildings when millions are dying of hunger, and yet he wants, 'passionately to keep our great buildings because they contribute something unique to the nation'. How again to divide our attention between the priority of Blake's requirement that 'he who would do good must do it by minute particulars' and the recognition that global problems require a global response? One needs to think on a large scale but act locally, that is the Archbishop's basic conclusion.

It was a conclusion demonstrated above all in what was to become the most important venture of his whole archiepiscopate, the enterprise in which he affected the most people, was most attacked and most justified, the venture for which he is in the long run likely to be most remembered, *Faith in the City*. In February 1982, the House of Lords debated Lord Scarman's Report on factors behind the Brixton riots of the previous April. In his speech welcoming the Report the Archbishop spoke of 'the creative role' which was needed in regard to 'the future of the inner city'. This was his first public reference to what was developing in his own mind and in the Church. Soon after the riots (27 May 1981) *The Times* had published a letter from Eric James on 'the relation of the Church of England to the vast inner city areas of our land'. He added that he would 'like to see the immediate appointment of an Archbishop's Commission'. He sent a copy to Runcie and pressed for a reply in regard to his suggestion. Runcie referred the matter to the group of urban bishops — David Sheppard of Liverpool, Stanley Booth-Clibborn of Manchester and others — and plans were slowly knocked into shape in the course of 1982. Runcie gave his approval to the proposals in January 1983 and a suitably high-powered membership and chairman for the Commission had then to be found, together with adequate funding and a secretariat. The terms of reference were as follows:

> To examine the strengths, insights, problems and needs of the church's life and mission in Urban Priority Areas and, as a result, to reflect on the challenge which God may be making to Church and Nation: and to make recommendations to appropriate bodies.

Sir Richard O'Brien, formerly Chairman of the Manpower Services Commission, agreed to chair the Archbishop's Commission. David Sheppard (the Commission's Vice-Chairman) was the only episcopal member until Wilfred Wood was made Bishop of Croydon. The academic world was represented by Professor Halsey, a Fellow of Nuffield College, Oxford, Professor Pahl, a sociologist from the University of Kent, and Professor Pickering, from the Institute of Science and Technology of the University of Manchester. Dr Anthony Harvey, a Canon of Westminster, was the Commission's chief theologian, Robina Rafferty was the Assistant Director of the Catholic Housing Aid Society, Mary Sugden the Principal of the National Institute for Social Work, John Burn, the headmaster of a school in Tyneside, Ron Keating, the Assistant General Secretary of the National Union of Public Employees. There were other representatives of clergy and laity. Several of the members were black, including Wilfred Wood. It was an extraordinarily strong and well-balanced group with no particular political leanings, certainly no great political radicalism. In no case were its members chosen for their political views, but only for their relevant expertise. Its secretary, John Pearson, was a senior civil servant seconded for two years from the Department of the Environment.

Runcie's contribution to *Faith in the City* was, above all, a contribution to the calibre of its membership. If the job was going to be done, it had to be done exceedingly well. All his sense of the necessity for perfectionism was here at work to ensure that in what he had come to recognize was a vitally important project, but one which could easily misfire, 'we must not be outwitted'.

The Commission was announced in June 1983 and it had two years in which to do its work. It had an extremely experienced chairman, its members had quite exceptional collective expertise, and they worked enormously hard. Runcie had set it up. He had nothing what-soever to do with its functioning or its conclusions. When the Report was completed, he recognized at once that it was a thoroughly serious and coherent document, but a pretty contentious one too. Having commissioned it, he was loyal to it and never flinched from 'owning' it and implementing it vigorously. It became 'my' Report.

Faith in the City declared that

It is our considered view that the nation is confronted by a grave and fundamental injustice in the Urban Priority Areas. . . . One of the most distressing features of the communities we visited was a profound sense of alienation, experienced by so many residents, not least the young. . . . The underlying factors are the same everywhere — unemployment, decaying housing, sub-standard educational and medical provision, and social disintegration.

For all the members of the Commission — and the Report was unanimous — it was true that

Somewhere along the road which we have travelled in the past two years, each of us has faced a personal challenge to our lives and life styles: a call to change our thinking and action in such a way as to help us to stand more closely alongside the risen Christ with those who are poor and powerless. We have found faith in the City.

The greater part of the recommendations were addressed directly to the Church of England (38 in all) including number 25:

A Church Urban Fund should be established to strengthen the Church's presence and promote the christian witness in the urban priority areas.

Twenty-three further recommendations were addressed to Govern-ment and nation. They mostly concerned job creation, child benefit and housing. The 400-page Report was due for publication in Decem-ber 1985. Immediately before its publication, newspapers were said to have been informed by Downing Street that a Cabinet Minister had called it 'a Marxist document', something containing 'pure Marxist theology'. The Conservative MP for Luton North, John Carlisle, de-clared that 'the Church of England seems now to be run by a load of Communist clerics', while Peter Bruinvels, the MP for Leicester East and a member of General Synod, said that by publishing such a report the Church was 'stabbing its own loyal flock in the back. . . . It is blatant Marxist theory.' Paul Johnson in the *Mail* described it as 'a flawed gospel. . . intellectually beneath contempt', while the *Daily Telegraph* in an editorial called it 'Savourless Salt' on account of its 'lack of specifically Christian theology' and its 'intellectual inadequacy'. The popular press in general denounced it as the work of a group of misguided clerics led by the Archbishop.

In fact, of course, the membership of the Commission was predominantly lay and heavily professional, while Runcie was personally responsible for not a single word of it. Not one member of the Commission could conceivably be described as a Marxist. The theological chapter was extremely Christian and of a particularly careful and moderate character. The Government and press almost entirely overlooked the fact that the Commission both in its original intentions and in the bulk of its recommendations was directed towards the Church, its responsibilities and opportunities. It may well be that it was a weakness of the general analysis to consider too little how the current urban situation has developed historically and to put too little blame on unimaginative policies and housing patterns in the pre-1980s. It was obviously impossible for a Commission with a time limit of two years to do everything. Its focus had rightly to be on the current state of things and present responsibilities, not on history. There is certainly no reason to think that if policies had been more libertarian in the 1960s and 1970s, the outcome would have been better. In almost no case was there any evidence that the wild criticisms of the Report, the attempt to rubbish it even before publication, derived from any serious reading of it at all. It was the gut reaction of a sort of unintelligent Toryism, furious that the Church should dare to suggest that all was not well after six years of Conservative rule.

The reaction was counter-productive. It gave greatly increased publicity to the Report. It ensured that 17,000 copies were sold in the first few months, followed by over 66,000 copies of the abridged version, and translations were made into some European languages. The manifest unfairness of the reaction soon forced ministers to back-track fairly noticeably. On the Report's official publication after days of vituperation, Runcie insisted that it was 'a Christian critique with, no doubt, political implications'. It was in no way a party political matter, still less had it the slightest 'Marxist' character, unless of course, as the *Mirror* remarked, 'it is Marxist to treat human beings with dignity, to care about poverty, to warn of the dangers of a divided nation'.

The best immediate press comment upon the Report was given in an editorial in the *Financial Times* entitled 'A church not very militant'. It is still worth re-reading:

The Lady's spokesmen do protest too much. For the second time in recent months, ministers have tried to confront criticism by rubbishing it before it is actually published. The Institute for Employment simply enjoyed more publicity than its rather over-simplified attack on the Government's economic policy would otherwise have enjoyed. The attack on the Church of England report on the problems of inner cities, which will be officially published later today, is likely to be more damaging — to ministers. It is so intemperate that it simply gives the impression that they are rattled.

The first fact that may surprise those who will have heard the row, but are unlikely to read the report itself, is that its prime target is the Church itself. The overwhelmingly middle-class clergy of the Church of England are ill-equipped by upbringing or training to tackle the problems of deprived minorities in Toxteth or Tottenham and the report bitterly acknowledges the fact. It would be impertinent for us to comment on the many remedial steps which are suggested.

The only one which could raise any political hackles is that the clergy should speak out more on political and social questions where they feel that Christian values are involved. What priests with direct experience of social deprivation have to say may be uncomfortable, but is hardly a threat to the separation of Church and State or the Bishop of Liverpool would already be regarded as a threat to the constitution. Most people, even non-believers, surely expect religious leaders to be outspoken on moral issues.

(*Financial Times*, 3 December **1985**)

A year later there was a further debate in the House of Lords on inner city problems (12 February 1987) initiated by Lord Scarman in which he took occasion to refer to *Faith in the City*:

Whether or not one agrees with its proposals, or with all or any of them, it is the finest face-to-face analysis and description of the problems of the inner city and of the other urban priority areas where those problems exist that we have yet seen. In the long run, it will take its place, I believe, as a classic description of one of the most serious troubles in British society.

Coming from the author of the Scarman Report, that is surely sufficient vindication.

There can be little doubt that *Faith in the City* considerably stimulated Government concern with inner city problems, so clearly manifest in its general election campaign of 1987. In 1990 a sister report, and no less substantial, *Faith in the Countryside* was published, produced by a second Archbishop's Commission, chaired this time by Lord Prior. It is too early to analyse its impact, but here again what is important to note is the quality of membership and functioning of a project set up by Runcie to examine and advise upon an area of major concern, ecclesiastical and national. It was a traditional characteristic of our society to have weighty Royal Commissions to examine major and wide-ranging problems from time to time in a manner genuinely independent of Government policy, but such as to impose a certain obligation upon the Government subsequently to respond to their conclusions. The appointment of such commissions has been notably lacking in the last ten years. It is quite remarkable that the Archbishop of Canterbury should have, somehow, been able to step into the gap and commission two reports which certainly far exceed in thoroughness and public importance anything the Church has produced in the past. From this point of view, the Church's participation within the secular world has been more, not less, significant in this decade compared with earlier periods.

Nevertheless, the primary intention of *Faith in the City* was to stimulate the Church itself to rethink its whole strategy for areas in which the ecclesiastical decline had been as noticeable as the secular. It is vital to recognize that *Faith in the City* was not an isolated document, published in style and then left to gather dust on the shelves of Church offices. It was a programme for action and it has, most certainly, been acted upon. There were important follow-up reports produced in a number of large cities — Birmingham, Manchester, Leeds. There was also the rapid establishment of the Church Urban Fund with the aim of raising 18 million pounds to be spent on inner city projects over a period of twenty years. The Archbishop himself has chaired it with Sir Richard O'Brien as Vice-Chairman, and it has, quite remarkably, kept to its target. The money has come from business, from charitable trusts and from the Church. Rural dioceses have responded with enthusiasm to the needs of the inner city. Her Majesty the Queen has shown herself particularly interested in its progress by becoming its Patron. A full-time Church officer for Urban Priority Areas was appointed, an on-going advisory group and link officers for every diocese. There can be no possible doubt that the effect of all this on the life of the Church has been very considerable and very salutary. It has provided hope in areas of deep decline by offering a coherent strategy for renewal and service, which people can recognize and take part in.

The Archbishop has totally supported the Report, the Church Urban Fund and everything else that has come out of it. It is perhaps the finest example of his style of leadership: nudged by others, he recognized a major problem, he consulted quite cautiously before agreeing to take it on board, but he then ensured that it was tackled in a thoroughly professional way. He left those he had appointed completely free to come to their own conclusions, but when they had done so, he backed them through thick and thin. That, perhaps, was the sort of leadership he had learnt about in the army. In September 1990, at one of his last large public meetings with his own diocese of Canterbury — one of the more rural of dioceses — he was able to comment on the result:

When *Faith in the City* was launched there were many faint hearts who thought that the creation of the Church Urban Fund was beyond our capacity to manage. They thought of the infrastructure needed to create from scratch one of the largest charities in England. Yet it has been done with a tiny central staff. That's because the structure is already in place — it is to be found in the parishes of England, in the clergy and congregations in every locality. In the parishes there has been a will to do something to help the church and people in our inner cities. That is where faith, confidence and loyalty are found. And I am delighted tonight to announce that this diocese has passed its target for the Church Urban Fund. Congratulations to all of you who have helped in whatever way.

Faith in the City is likely to stand as the greatest single achievement of his primacy and a very characteristic one, for which he was both most responsible and least — in regard to details — closely involved.

Archbishop Runcie's political role has been in no way different from that of many of his predecessors in its underlying principles, nor has it differed from that for which Archbishop Romero was murdered in El Salvador the day before Runcie's enthronement, or that of Archbishop Tutu in South Africa. It is the historic role of the Christian bishop *vis à vis* society and its government. It is a role which, as President of the Anglican Communion, he has a duty to inculcate in Anglican bishops the world over. So we may end this chapter with part of the instruction Runcie gave to a young Korean bishop whom he consecrated in Taejan in 1987, Paul Yoon:

A bishop is inescapably a public figure, and he has a unique responsibility to prevent the Church becoming an exclusive club concerned only for its own spiritual welfare. He must see the wider scene, identify the major moral issues of the day, and be ready to speak the unpopular word of warning. He may well be called to be the voice of the voiceless and a spokesman for the weak. He will know that the God with whom Christians have to do is the God who inspired the prophets, and demanded social justice for his people. That is a dimension of the Gospel that rests in the hands of the Church's leaders, and the Church is therefore bound to do whatever it can to uphold and advance the cause of justice. Prophetic witness in a world with nuclear weapons, in a world with racism, in a world which ignores human dignity, or exploits human labour, must be passionate but it must also be constructive. The urgency of the needs can make the Church's voice shrill and distorted: passion must lead to wise and thoughtful proposals, so that the Church can make its own distinctive contribution to society, and be a voice of reconciliation as well as justice.

❧ 6 ❧

Between women priests and
John Paul II

Runcie's form of Anglicanism may be best described as an open-ended Anglo-Catholicism of the post Michael Ramsey generation. In Ramsey's younger days, there was still a bit of a battle to establish that being Anglo-Catholic was not, at least slightly, to be disloyal to Anglicanism. For an earlier generation the battle was more severe and Queen Victoria objected to the presence of any Anglo-Catholics among the bishops, though that barrier had been broken well before her death. Yet it was one reason why Geoffrey Fisher thought Ramsey would be an unsuitable successor to him at Canterbury: Ramsey was a full-blooded Anglo-Catholic theologian, or so he seemed, while Fisher — in so far as he had any theology — was a representative of an older style of the Church of England, more decidedly Protestant. But, in reality, Ramsey was not only easily the most distinguished Anglican of his generation, he was also as near as anyone to what seemed its contemporary centre. The long shift produced by Tractarianism had across a century of influence — mostly a quiet influence — not only reached the centre (it had done that with Lang, if a little uneasily), it had coalesced with the centre so completely as to be no longer, except in its more 'spiky' forms, independently recognizable. It had done this in and with Michael Ramsey.

When Runcie was ordained deacon, Ramsey was Regius Professor of Divinity in the University of Cambridge. For most of Runcie's life as a priest and a bishop, Ramsey was an archbishop, first at York then at Canterbury, and incomparably the Church of England's principal public theologian. It was Ramsey who consecrated him Bishop of St Albans in 1970. Runcie was Ramsey's junior by seventeen years, just the right gap for him to be able to take for granted the full impact of Ramsey upon the Church. He could also take over from Ramsey, as indeed Coggan too had taken over, the great new priority which Ramsey, the Second Vatican Council and the wider revolution of attitudes in the Roman Catholic Church and the circumstances of the 1960s had provided for the Church of England — reunion with Rome. This had always been a sort of secret priority, implicit in the whole

99

history of the Church of England from the reign of Elizabeth I and its refusal to adopt a full Protestant stance. It was by name, by common repute, and by deep conviction, a Protestant Church, a Church which had emphatically and rightly rejected many aspects of late medieval religion. At the same time, in its bishops, its Book of Common Prayer, the worship of its cathedrals and even the theology of its best divines, it had retained a more markedly 'Catholic' under-side than the Protestant Churches of the Continent. The Tractarian movement of the nineteenth century appealed to and reasserted this 'Catholic' dimension which involved both a more positive appraisal of patristic, and even medieval, Christianity than was usual within a Protestant ethos and a willingness to admire and to learn even from contemporary Roman Catholicism. Anglican Catholics, nevertheless, and in this Michael Ramsey was quite characteristic of them, while feeling a very strong sense of identity with all the on-going riches of the Roman Catholic tradition — mystical, liturgical, theological — could seldom abide the legal, centralized rigidity of the modern Church of Rome and its claims to a universal direct jurisdiction and to verbal infallibility. In this they were fully Protestants. Such a position had within it an almost unformulated 'If'. If Rome were to change, were to recognize that at least in some important matters the Reformers really had been right; if Rome were to be willing to live with other Christian traditions in a communion of Churches, within a genuine pattern of 'Uniatism' instead of endeavouring to impose a Roman and ultramontane order of Church law and government, of liturgy and theology, upon everyone in communion with it; if Rome should once more show a true respect for reason, freedom, biblical scholarship; if this should once happen then the Church of England must surely at once respond with enthusiasm to seek the restoration of ancient bonds not only with Rome but with Paris and Vienna, Milan and Cologne, while not forgetting, of course, Constantinople, Athens and Moscow.

In the 1960s it was this, suddenly, that seemed to happen — or almost to happen. The coming of Pope John altered everything. His personal warmth and sincerity coupled with the teaching of the Second Vatican Council, which went amazingly far along the road sought by Catholic-minded Anglicans and even Protestant-minded Anglicans, unlocked the doors as never before in four hundred years. Geoffrey Fisher, in whom there was not the slightest trace of Anglo-Catholicism, was moved in consequence to go to Rome to visit the Pope (the first Archbishop of Canterbury to do so since before the Reformation). The appointment of Michael Ramsey in 1961, just before the Council actually met, put into the Primacy the ideal person to meet the new situation: a great theologian, a devout and generous Anglo-Catholic but not at all someone with any weakness for the drearier side of modern Roman Catholicism. No one was less papalist. No one was more Catholic. His great visit to Pope Paul, once the Council was over, in March 1966 proved a symbolic occasion of very great power — with Pope and Archbishop worshipping together in public in St Paul's-without-the Walls. When the Pope incredibly slipped off from his own finger the episcopal ring given him by his diocese of Milan and placed it in Ramsey's hand, he staggered even Ramsey. He wore it ever after and, when he died, his widow gave it to Archbishop Runcie to become the permanent possession of the See of Canterbury, a sort of supra-theological symbol of archiepiscopal recognition. This visit began an on-going theological dialogue between the two Communions which started the following January, when a joint commission comprising five bishops and five theologians from each side met together at Gazzada in the Alps. Out of this, ARCIC, the Anglican–Roman Catholic International Commission, developed.

No one could go back on the significance of these meetings. The stated intention behind them was to achieve full visible ecclesial unity between Roman Catholics and Anglicans and especially the unity of freely sharing together in the Eucharist; but the intention was also to recognize how large a measure of unity already existed (something often denied in the past). Because of the unity already there, because of the goodwill manifestly revealed, because of the obvious value and significance for Christians and for the world if the Anglican Communion and the Roman Communion could once more fully accept each other within the unity of the Church, neither the one nor the other crushed in esteem or obliterated in identity, it was essential to push ahead. It is very striking how clearly this was recognized by Donald Coggan, Ramsey's Evangelical successor. Coggan came from no Anglo-Catholic stable, but he was really as determined to pursue the goal of unity with Rome and made a very memorable appeal in Rome for intercommunion. More cautious ecumenists thought it undiplomatic, and it certainly embarrassed its hearers; yet it was also prophetic and fundamentally correct. Coggan's concern to arrive at a visible and sacramental unity shows very well how reunion with Rome had become quite simply an Anglican priority. When Runcie became Archbishop, he too accepted it as such.

Hitherto, he had not in point of fact been closely involved in Roman relations. On the contrary, he had been entrusted instead with responsiblity for relations with Eastern Orthodoxy, which was also his own special personal interest. Nevertheless, once Archbishop, and with the clarity of his strategic sense fully operative, he realized at once that it was absolutely incumbent upon him to carry forward, so far as in him lay, the Roman enterprise. All the more was this necessary in that already there were signs that Rome's own mood was faltering. In early 1980, the complexities of John Paul II's exceptionally powerful character and intentions were not fully evident, but one could already sense the likelihood that Rome's real ecumenical enthusiasm was increasingly tempered by reluctance to come to any very substantive agreement. More than ten years before, its refusal to accept or officially publish the Malta Report of the Anglican–Roman Catholic International Preparatory Commission, completed in 1968, had been a sign of much that was to come. The setting up of ARCIC I was a partial response to this report, which was eventually published by ARCIC. The growth of a common mind among a group of theologians in ARCIC remained one thing, the resolve to endorse or implement its conclusions or find any other effective way forward was another.

Runcie's acute diplomatic sense will have taken these things in but not dashed his determination, inherited from his predecessors and from the deep logic of Anglican history, to press as far as he responsibly could. He had undoubtedly been prepared for this by important Roman Catholic contacts at Cuddesdon and St Albans, especially with Robert Murray at the former and Bishop Christopher Butler at the latter. Butler lived at St Edmund's, Ware, some twelve miles from St Albans. He was Auxiliary Bishop and then Area Bishop for Hertfordshire within the archdiocese of Westminster throughout Runcie's ten years at St Albans. He had welcomed him at his enthronement and, thereafter, they co-operated even more closely. They had had much in common: an Anglo-Catholic background, classics at Oxford, Hugh Last had taught them both Roman history, they had shared a rearing on Plato and Thucydides, but they had never met until 1970. Butler had the confidence both as scripture scholar and as theologian which Runcie lacked. He had attended the Vatican Council as Abbot of Downside and one of the Council's most influential theologian members. His views had considerably mellowed ecumenically from the earlier, more controversial years subsequent to his conversion as an Anglican deacon to Roman Catholicism.

It is clear that the two men warmed to each other quite exceptionally, and that Runcie both learnt a lot from Butler and was able diplomatically to draw Butler a little further forward than others could manage. When appointed by Basil Hume as Area Bishop of

Hertfordshire, he was actually installed as Bishop in the Cathedral/Abbey church of St Albans. This was not only highly appropriate for a monk bishop who had formerly been an abbot but it was appropriate personally because of the quite exceptional relationship of friendship and co-operation he and Runcie had established. As Runcie remarked after his death, 'the present Dean and I always regarded him as one of our bishops'. Probably no previous relationship between a Catholic and an Anglican bishop had ever been so close. But as Butler was not only a bishop but also a theologian, concerned especially with Anglican–Catholic relations, their friendship could also be seminal theologically. If Lambert Beauduin's vision, expressed in a paper for the Malines Conversations in the 1920s, of a Church of England 'reunited but not absorbed' turns up in the 1980s in Runcie's programme for the future, it is hardly an accident that it had been a decade earlier one of Butler's chosen themes. The friendship with Butler also helped Runcie establish a quick and close rapport, once he moved to Canterbury, with Cardinal Hume, another former Benedictine abbot. The fact that no less than five cardinals participated in his enthronement certainly says something about how far Roman Catholic–Anglican relations and the spiritual and practical reincorporation of Canterbury within the Catholic collegial episcopate had already developed.

The *élan* within Runcie's Roman diplomacy is striking. Hardly six weeks after his enthronement at Canterbury he had met Pope John Paul II in Accra on 9 May 1980 and invited him to visit England and Canterbury. 'We have a martyr there who would appeal to you.' No Pope had ever been to either before. It was an extremely bold and generous move. John Paul likes both qualities. He knew extremely little about Anglicanism, even less than about Protestantism, but he was glad to say yes and so, in principle, one of the most powerful symbolic moments in Catholic–Anglican relations was agreed to well inside Runcie's first hundred days.

All this was no mere matter of conforming to current ecumenical good manners. It represented rather the attempt to move towards the realization of Runcie's ecclesiological thinking. In this area, his theological thinking had now achieved considerable firmness and consistency, to be repeated again and again. One can find it, for instance, in a lecture in Croydon on Anglican–Roman Catholic relations in March 1982, in another in France to an Anglican–Roman Catholic 'Groupe Mixte' in December 1984, in an address to General Synod in November 1986 on ARCIC and authority, and finally in his Cardinal Heenan Lecture on ecumenism delivered at Heythrop College in December

1989. The understanding of the Church which Runcie consistently presented in these and other lectures is that of a eucharistic communion of diverse local Churches, held together by the episcopate. Returning to the question posed by Dom Lambert Beauduin in his paper, 'L'Eglise Anglicane unie non absorbée', he asks whether Rome could possibly accept a principle of decentralization, very far as it is from the actual practice of the Curia. The affirmative answer Runcie consistently offers is, he claims, at once 'the answer of Vatican II, of classical Anglicanism, and of ARCIC'.

ARCIC I was the successor to the Anglican–Roman Catholic International Preparatory Commission which first met after Ramsey's Rome visit of 1966 and produced the Malta Report in 1968. ARCIC was the child of that Report and began work in 1970. Early in 1982 it submitted its Final Report on Eucharist, Ministry and Authority. Its membership had included a wide range of Anglican and Catholic bishops and theologians, including on the Anglican side the distinguished patristic scholar, Henry Chadwick, and the Evangelical theologian, Julian Charley, and on the Catholic side Bishop Butler and the French Dominican, Jean Tillard.

The Archbishop of Canterbury with whom Runcie may feel the deepest affinity is William Wake, who had been Anglican chaplain in Paris from 1682 to 1684 before becoming Archbishop in 1717. Both in Paris and at Canterbury he corresponded with French Catholic theologians. 'We do with all our hearts desire a union with the Church of Rome', he was able to write — but not, of course, with an ultramontane Rome. A sound Anglican, he sensed how much he had in common with Gallican Catholics. Runcie cultivated the same sort of Gallican links and has claimed emphatically and repeatedly that Anglican theologians have, in the past, been willing to accept a Roman primacy so long as it is the right sort of primacy — one, indeed, not too unlike the sort of primacy he himself exercises within the Anglican Communion. While he probably feels this is still too weak, even for an Archbishop of Canterbury, an acceptable Roman primacy would certainly have to be a lot nearer to that than to the present universal jurisdiction claimed for the papacy by the First Vatican Council in 1870 and practised in the pontificate of John Paul II with greater insistence upon centralization of control than almost ever before. 'I believe the fabric of Anglican theology and ecclesiology is fundamentally open to the idea of a ministry of unity for the whole Church — open to an episcopal office for the service of the unity of the universal communion of local churches.' 'A universal spokesman . . . to articulate the universal faith of Christians' after due collegial consultation is one thing, but 'day to day detailed dictation of the affairs of a particular church from a centralized ecclesiastical bureaucracy' is quite another.

In speaking like this, Runcie can claim to be formulating the view of numerous Roman Catholic theologians as well as Anglican, and not only those who are members of ARCIC, and indeed to be doing little more than trying to put some teeth into Vatican II's doctrine of collegiality and of the communion of Churches. When Vatican II states, both in its decree on ecumenism and in that on the Eastern Catholic Churches, 'this Sacred Synod solemnly declares that the Churches of the East as much as those of the West have the right and duty to rule themselves', it is impossible to comment other than that something is here being solemnly taught by the Council (and the Council nowhere else used the almost technical word 'solemnly' in all its sixteen documents) which has not been applied for many centuries within the Roman Communion either before or after the Council. The Vatican Council was making an 'Anglican' assertion which Rome continues in practice wholly to ignore. So when Runcie questions 'whether a proper balance has yet been achieved between Episcopal Conferences and the Synod of Bishops, on the one hand, and the Roman Curia, on the other', he is acting as spokesman as much for Vatican II-minded Roman Catholics as for Catholic-minded Anglicans.

Impressive as the ARCIC common statement on authority certainly is, it does not quite face up to Vatican I's solemn assertion of the universal ordinary jurisdiction of the papacy. No Anglican-minded Anglican will ever accept that. Unless and until Rome is prepared to abandon it, and there is no sign at all that papal Rome is even slightly considering that possibility, the ARCIC line cannot bear fruit. In practice, in the age of John Paul II, Runcie realizes this as much as anyone; what is remarkable is how firmly, yet still diplomatically, he has kept the dialogue going by appropriating the common ground, making the ARCIC position his own, and offering to accept a papal primacy in a way none of his modern predecessors have quite done. By doing this he has placed the ball politely, but firmly, in the Pope's ground. Undoubtedly the Anglican participants in ARCIC and Runcie himself have had to move a considerable distance to get to this point, but, by doing so, they have placed themselves on impregnable ground, Catholic as much as Anglican, and have in fact made a major contribution to the common ecumenical future. They have also become thereby true contemporary spokesmen of the Vatican II vision at a time when, at least episcopally, it has become increasingly difficult to find such spokesmen within the Roman Catholic hierarchy itself. To this we will return.

All this needs to be borne in mind as part of the hidden agenda behind the quite stunning experience of the Pope's visit to Canterbury Cathedral in May 1982. His coming to Britain was billed officially as a pastoral visit to the Catholic Church. It was crucial that British Roman Catholics should in no way feel themselves upstaged by Anglicans at this point. It was both the very clear rapport in England between Runcie and Hume, and Runcie's diplomatic success directly with Rome through his special envoy Henry Chadwick, which ensured that this did not happen. That was already something of a diplomatic achievement and for Hume quite as much as for Runcie. But then the visit, planned long in advance, in fact coincided with the British–Argentine war over the Falklands. Up to a short time before, the visit remained in doubt and a great deal more diplomacy was needed, including a special 'Mass for Peace' concelebrated in Rome by the Pope, Hume and three Argentinian cardinals. He came. He saw the Queen. He spoke of peace at Coventry. He ordained Catholic priests in Westminster Cathedral.

Undoubtedly the one quite unprecedented part of the papal tour was the visit to Canterbury. The words were still cautious enough but the deeds were either a hoax, which is inconceivable, or an act of mutual recognition between two Christian Churches: 'Sister Churches' as Paul VI had already called them, not in full communion but in a large measure of partial communion. Cardinal Hume and all the English bishops were with the Pope, all the bishops of the Church of England, the members of General Synod and a number of the Primates of the Anglican Communion were with Archbishop Runcie as were also the Moderator of the Free Church Federal Council and all its members and the Prince of Wales. All exchanged the kiss of peace. Pope and Archbishop sat side by side with the ancient Canterbury Book of the Gospels, brought to England by Augustine, enthroned between them.

In theory, Rome has still not accepted the validity of Anglican orders. The 1896 declaration that they are 'utterly void' has never been rescinded or amended. If that is true, Runcie and his fellow bishops remain but a group of schismatic laymen of goodwill. Forty years ago, Roman behaviour was consistent with such an opinion. It has steadily ceased to be so, but never more so than at Canterbury in 1982. A new ecclesiology upon the Roman side, implicit already within the documents of Vatican II, blossomed forth especially at the visit of Michael Ramsey to Paul VI and in the episcopal ring which changed from one hand to the other at that point in 1966. John Paul II's visit to Canterbury sixteen years later solemnized the new relationship in a far wider framework and gave a degree of corporate institutional and ecclesial recognition to the Anglican Communion on the part of Rome which could not existentially be managed in Rome. Canterbury was the place for that. Here and now, probably beyond the intentions of anyone, a new theology was symbolically recognized as valid — the theology of ARCIC, but the theology, too, of Robert Runcie.

* * *

Meanwhile for many other Anglicans a quite different issue claimed a far higher priority: the ordination of women to the priesthood. Since apostolic times, the Christian Church had only ordained men to the presbyteral ministry though women — mostly celibate women — had at different times held various offices: deacons, abbesses, nuns of various kinds. Both in East and West and in all the minor Christian traditions, until the nineteenth century, the practice of a uniquely male ordained ministry or priesthood (and, *a fortiori*, episcopate) was unchallenged. It was generally taken that this was something laid down by Christ and so unchangeable. But the same assumption was made in one part or another of the Church in regard to many matters which we now know developed relatively late and in only one part of the Church (such as general auricular confession, the separation of confirmation from baptism, and even the distinction between presbyterate and episcopate).

The Church's institutional, and even sacramental, structure has largely developed — we can now see — in dialogue with the wider culture of society over the centuries. This must mean that what is suitable for one culture is not necessarily suitable for another. The shape of the Church was not laid down from the start in a changeless manner as almost everyone used to believe (so that controversy between Catholic and Protestant was largely over *which* form was original and therefore obligatory). While it does indeed possess a core which goes back to apostolic times (Eucharist, baptism, the acceptance of apostolic authority, a very simple creed affirming God-in-Christ), the Church has developed its characteristic doctrine and structure, including the full shape of the ministry (which traditionally in the West included three major orders and four minor orders, apart from the episcopate), across the processes of history. This does not, of course, mean that the process could not be Providential. Doubtless it largely was, though at times the process looks more like a succumbing to the less desirable aspects of contemporary culture and power politics. But what it does suggest is that if it was thus, then when culture changes, so can and should the institutions of the Church.

Few people today with any sense of history at all would dispute this overall analysis. Nevertheless, while it does suggest that much more is simply changeable in terms of an appropriate pastoral strategy for contemporary society than in the past Christians recognized, it does not mean that everything can or should be changed in terms of immediate pastoral convenience. The biblical exclusion of women from the ordained ministry, despite the undoubted activity of many women among the early Christians, cannot simply be dismissed as unworthy of consideration. Is the exclusion of women from ordination something which belongs to the very heart of the Church's life and is therefore unchangeable, or is it instead something which simply reflected the social structure of antiquity and the religious culture of the non-Christian world? If the answer given to the first question is 'Yes', then one naturally asks 'Why is this so? And does it really fit in as a principle with the Christian revelation as a whole?' If, on the contrary, the answer given to the second question is 'Yes', then one naturally asks 'Why has God allowed his Church to leave women out for so long from the ministry? Is a woman priest really compatible with the essentials of the Christian revelation?'

In the first half of the twentieth century, nearly all Roman Catholics, Eastern Orthodox and High Church Anglicans as well as most conservative Evangelicals would have given an emphatic 'Yes' to the first question. To the question 'Why?' they would have replied that this reflected the order both of creation and of redemption. The Pauline concept of the dependence of woman on man, the fatherhood of God and the maleness of Christ all require, it would have been said, that men alone preside over the Church and the Eucharist and represent the Father and Christ. However, in the same period, many Protestants were increasingly questioning and rejecting these traditional views, and instead answering 'Yes' to the second question. The exclusion of women from the ordained ministry, they believed, had been a reflection of the generally subordinate position of women in society in the ancient world. It was not a reflection of the heart of the gospel. On the contrary, Paul's great words, 'Neither Jew nor Greek, neither slave nor free, neither male nor female, you are all one in Christ Jesus' (Galatians 3.28) must be applied to the ministry as well as to the life of grace. Why not? God is not male, the Word became 'flesh' or became 'human' (*homo* in Latin, a non-sexed word), became that which is common to men and women. A woman can fittingly represent both. She can also represent the Church, which has anyway always, like

Israel, been given a feminine symbolization. As the century advanced, more and more Protestant churches ordained women, just as parliaments, universities and other institutions opened their doors to them — if, often enough, somewhat grudgingly.

In this, as in much else, the Anglican Communion was torn between its 'Catholic' character and its 'Protestant' character. Nevertheless it seems surprising that pressure to ordain women within it did not arise much earlier. The reason probably lay less in a commitment to Catholic theology than in social conservatism: the Church of England in particular had remained, in social terms, a profoundly traditional body. When the diocese of South China proposed to ordain women and the Lambeth Conference of 1948 was asked whether such an action would be 'in accordance with Anglican tradition and order', a Committee of the Conference chaired by the Bishop of Durham gave a decided 'No', even though the Chinese members of the Committee maintained that it fell within the tradition of the autonomy of national Churches and 'should be regarded as a proper exercise of autonomy not entailing any breach of fellowship'.

Though the Anglican Group for the Ordination of Women had been founded in the 1930s, it was really the new 1960s wave of feminism and the wider contemporary Western stress upon equality between the sexes at that time which finally tipped Anglicanism in the direction of change, though still much less in England than elsewhere. The Lambeth Conference of 1968 considered the matter and its Report on Renewal of the Church in Ministry appears to move mildly in the direction of accepting the ordination of women and preparing the Churches for it. Its only resolutions, however, were to declare the theological arguments for and against inconclusive and to request national and regional Churches to study the matter and report their findings to the Anglican Consultative Council. It also recommended that no decision be taken to ordain women to the priesthood before the advice of the Anglican Consultative Council had been sought and carefully considered. Much of the trouble of the next twenty years can be laid at the door of the inconclusiveness of Lambeth 1968.

Hong Kong once more moved first. Indeed, the first woman ever to be ordained in the Anglican Communion had been Florence Li, ordained as a matter of emergency during the Second World War by R. O. Hall, the Bishop of Hong Kong, to minister as a priest in Macao. When the emergency was over, and Lambeth 1948 unhelpful, she was persuaded to withdraw quietly into lay life, though she has since then returned to active priestly ministry. The Diocesan Council of Hong Kong decided to return to the fray and, in consequence, the issue came before the very first meeting of the Anglican Consultative Council at Limuru (Kenya) in 1971, with a formal question. If a province decided it wished to ordain women, would the ACC approve? Archbishop Ramsey was present and spoke against the resolution. It was nevertheless passed by 24 to 22 votes with Ramsey and the Nigerian chairman, Louis Mbanefo, in the minority. The ACC is a merely consultative body and not a particularly weighty one. It passed this resolution by the slimmest of majorities and against the advice of the Archbishop of Canterbury. Nevertheless, it proved enough to open the way for the ordination of women.

Hong Kong ordained two woman priests, Joyce Bennett and Jane Hwang, the same year. In 1972 the Bishops of the Church in the United States resolved by 74 to 61 votes to do so too, but not independently. In July 1974, in defiance of existing Church law, three retired American bishops and one from Costa Rica ordained eleven women in Philadelphia, one of the ordinands being the daughter of one of the bishops. In 1976 women were ordained canonically in Canada, in 1977 in both the United States and New Zealand. So, by the time the Lambeth Conference of 1978 met, four areas of the Church had already crossed the Rubicon without any more consultation or weighty interprovincial approval than Lambeth 1968's failure to agree a line and an inadequate discussion in a small meeting at Limuru. It seems hardly the best way to do things.

Michael Ramsey was Archbishop of Canterbury until 1974. Like many an Anglo-Catholic, he had started off by being pretty definitely opposed, on principle as well as in practice, to women's ordination. He had thought that the unanimity of tradition was too powerful an argument against. But he changed. He began to see how weak the scriptural arguments against it really were. By his later years, he believed it quite possible for women to be ordained and he thought it would come, but he was not enthusiastic and feared that if Anglicans agreed to do this, it could be profoundly damaging for their relations with both Rome and Eastern Orthodoxy. When ecumenical progress was really being achieved for the first time for centuries, with the Catholic Church in particular, could it possibly be right to create a new barrier and a renewed suspicion that Anglicans were indeed, beneath a more hierarchical veneer, fully-fledged Protestants? He recognized however that Roman Catholic theological opinion on the ordination of women was also changing fast, so he thought that given a little time, this difficulty might well be removed.

Donald Coggan believed far more positively in the ordination of women and it was in his time that the General Synod of the Church

110

of England voted in 1975 that there were 'no fundamental objections' — a pretty unsatisfactory form of words, especially when the following motion, to remove legal barriers, fell. Meanwhile, women priests were multiplying elsewhere in the Anglican Communion: some 150 by 1978. At the presbyteral level at least, developments were already beyond the possibility of central control by the time the Lambeth Conference again met. Nevertheless, so radical a departure from traditional practice, entered into unilaterally by some Churches within a Communion claiming a fair measure of common character, could not but raise basic issues about Anglican identity and some form of supra-provincial authority. Professor John Macquarrie, perhaps the weightiest theological consultant at the 1978 Conference, had this to say in his introductory speech to the debate on the subject:

> The question does arise whether on such an important and potentially divisive issue as the ordination of women to the priesthood, one should not look for a consensus beyond that of the national or regional church. It is true of course that within the Anglican Communion, each constituent church is autonomous. But I must confess that I am not much impressed with the idea of an autonomous church. This is especially the case at a time when we hear a great deal of talk about collegiality, partnership, conciliarity and so on. . . . on the particular matter with which we are concerned today, it would surely have been wise if individual churches had deferred action until this Lambeth Conference of 1978.

But they had not done so. Neither the Conference nor Archbishop Coggan saw any possibility or point in any action beyond one of 'damage limitation': while recognizing that there would be a painful division between those Churches which ordained women and Churches which refused both to do so and to admit women canonically ordained elsewhere to their altars, it was urged that such ordination must not be allowed to lead to a breach of communion. 'Communion' would, in consequence, be nevertheless no longer a quite full communion, but only an 'almost full' one. The Conference however did strongly urge provinces not to consecrate a woman to the episcopate without the widest consultation and local support.

It was at this point that Runcie came into the story, as we saw in Chapter 1. As an Anglo-Catholic of the post-Ramsey era, he was at first deeply perplexed and far from naturally enthusiastic but he soon realized that he was not at heart opposed. By Lambeth 1978, he had been a bishop for eight years and had done much to advance women's ministry in an unrevolutionary way. He had also been Chairman of the

Joint Commission with the Orthodox. He knew how deeply these developments upset the Orthodox and how disastrous they might prove for immediate inter-Church relations with them. And he regarded himself, correctly, as having within the Church of England a special responsibility for averting that disaster. It is not surprising that both in General Synod and at Lambeth 1978 he spoke out fairly emphatically against, at the present time, going further in this direction.

Some people who would have liked him to be promoted to Canterbury thought that in taking this line he was blocking his chances of doing so. Others have claimed that it was the very reason why he got there — he had thereby obtained Anglo-Catholic backing, being seen as a reliable opponent of the ordination of women. It is clear that for Runcie himself such considerations would never have entered his head and it seems unlikely that they could have been decisive for others. If he had appeared a die-hard opponent of change, he would surely not have been chosen to succeed Coggan and preside over a Communion in which there were already a quite considerable number of women priests. He may well have appeared rather as a strategist capable of steering the ship at a time of potential disaster, someone who could see the immediate case against innovation clearly enough, but who was yet not fundamentally opposed; someone, in fact, who followed genuinely enough the Ramsey line, but ten years on.

Of such a kind, at least, the new Archbishop would be. As he remarked in General Synod in 1984, 'In regard to . . . the ordination of women, I have consistently driven down the middle of the road, and I am surprised to find that I have survived this dangerous ordeal!' That is true, but it is also the case that he began his archiepiscopate slightly right of centre and ends it, ten years later, just a tiny bit further to the left. Not perhaps a great change over a decade, but a fairly clearly defensible one. As both Archbishop of Canterbury and President of the Anglican Communion, his point of view was immediately different from that he had held as Bishop of St Albans. A change in his publicly expressed opinion was not a matter of pragmatism, nor even, necessarily, of altered theological and pastoral judgement, but chiefly one of altered personal responsibility. Much as he cared for relations with the Orthodox Church, the internal unity of the Anglican Communion had now to be his primary concern.

Theologically, it may be that his mind did move a little with the years. The fact that, in his words, 'both scripture and Catholic tradition are highly discouraging to the idea' of women's ordination probably weighed more heavily with him in 1980 than in 1990. He had listened to the arguments against female ordination, as expressed, for

Preceding page: A relaxed moment (The Press Association).
Rosalind Runcie *(The Times).*
With Terry Waite in Australia *(Church Times).*
With the Archbishop of York at the York Synod (Jane Bown).

With Pope John Paul II after signing the Common Declaration in Rome, 1989
(John Manning, *The Times*).

With Archbishop Desmond Tutu.

With the Oba of Badagry during his visit to Nigeria for the ACC-6 meeting, 1984.
In the background (wearing glasses), Metropolitan Alexander Mar Thoma of the
Mar Thoma Syrian Church, India.

With George Bush and (centre right) the late Bishop John Walker of Washington
(Church Times).

At General Synod (The Press Association).

Pouring tea at Lambeth Palace for Lord Ramsey of Canterbury (Wm. B. Eerdmans
Publishing Co.).

At the Lambeth Conference (Jane Bown).

With the Queen Mother.

instance by Cardinal Willebrands in their correspondence of 1985, and found them wanting — even dangerous. A fully incarnational theology could actually be impaired by any suggestion that it was the maleness of Christ rather than his full humanity which an ordained priest might in some way be representing. 'I have come to the judgement', he could tell General Synod in 1988, 'that the ordination of women to the priesthood would actually be an enlargement of the Catholic priesthood, an opening up of priesthood, rather than its overturning.' Theologically, Runcie has not sat on the fence in this matter. He has committed himself without reserve to a defence of both the acceptability and the desirability of the ordination of women but not necessarily of its opportuneness. He did this most clearly in his letter to Cardinal Willebrands of November 1985 which centres upon 'the most substantial doctrinal reason', not only justifying but requiring the ordination of women.

Inevitably, as he has himself recognized, in doing this he has distanced himself not only from the official view of Rome but also from the convictions both of Anglican conservatives and of Anglican progressives. His dominant concern throughout has been how to come through a longish period of strain and disagreement with the minimum damage to the unity of communion. Some damage there must be — both within the Church of England, between different Anglican provinces, and between Anglicans and others. Runcie has frequently recognized the inevitability and the reality of a certain, at least temporary, impairment of communion. His aim has been to keep this to a minimum by ensuring that, while there was some recognizable advance towards the ordination of women in England or elsewhere, that advance was sufficiently slow and controlled as to obviate the danger of a schism. In general, he has succeeded in this, but at the cost of a fair amount of abuse and rather little whole-hearted support or understanding. On the one side, those who see the issue of women's rights as the absolutely primary issue for today's Church — a case of the long overdue righting of a major injustice — must judge Runcie's continued temporizing as the subordination of a great moral issue to the successful management of ecclesiastical diplomacy. On the other side, those who regard the whole campaign for the ordination of women as a simple surrender of the Church to the spirit of the age and its secular culture, and had once thought Runcie an ally, now revile him as a traitor to traditional Catholicism.

It is certainly striking that when the ordination of women had already begun in several provinces before he became Archbishop, there should still, after ten years at Canterbury of an Archbishop committed theologically to the rightness of women's ordination, not be a single woman ordained priest in the Church of England nor any immediate certainty that there will be one, though there are, in fact, several hundred women deacons. Of course, this has by no means depended wholly upon Runcie. Indeed, the basic cause is the intransigent opposition of an adequately large minority in General Synod and in the Church at large. But it cannot be doubted that, faced with that opposition, he has himself gone along with delay as the best way of avoiding schism. As Archbishop he sees his function as, beyond all else, one of maintaining unity and communion. However sound an innovation may be in itself, it should in his view wait, if enough people are so deeply opposed to it that its adoption may wreck the Church's existing unity.

On the surface at least, Runcie's position has at times been even more conservative than that of General Synod. Thus in November 1984, on the proposal that the Church of England should now move towards the ordination of women, he spoke against the motion and listed a number of reasons. The first of these seems particularly interesting and subtle:

> While within the Anglican Communion some churches ordain women and some do not, the situation accurately reflects a tentativeness about so radical a change which makes it easier to defend, explain and commend to Orthodox and Roman Catholics. . . . The ordination of women by the Church of England would make the Anglican position considerably more absolute and undermine this experimental quality.

Runcie argued that he could better both defend the Anglican experience of the ordination of women and keep open the full range of ecumenical relationships while for an interim period 'a diversity of Anglican practice' is maintained.

Added to this was the need for the unity of the Church of England itself, the need to avoid the quite devastating effect of a major internal schism:

> I really do question whether we have got far enough along the road in our internal Anglican dialogue to take this step. To demand unanimity would be fanciful and unrealistic but I hesitate to urge action until we come somewhat closer to a consensus.

A priest should be an instrument of reconciliation, not of division. These were strong arguments well expressed, yet General Synod at that point rejected Runcie's advice 'to adopt a doctrine of gradualism as an argument of principle not expediency' and not to proceed to legislation to bring about a change.

So legislation — or alternative forms of legislation — was prepared. Inevitably this meant making provision not only for the ordination of women, but also for the protection of the handful of bishops and many hundreds of priests who remained wholly opposed to women priests. The shape of such legislation appeared horrific, providing for a sort of legalized internal schism within the Church of England whereby either the Church would be divided into dioceses with women priests and dioceses without, or it would be so divided that the principle of episcopal authority within a diocese was endangered. It was, above all, in terms of the destructive effect of this upon the basic order of Anglicanism that in the following years Runcie continued to argue that the time was not yet ripe. Thus in July 1986, when the Maclean Report was presented, he warned Synod of the danger of 'a fundamental departure from episcopal government as the Church of England has known it since the time of St Augustine of Canterbury'. It could be 'a moot point as to whether the Ordination of Women or the abolition of diocesan episcopacy would be the greater change'. If the Church could only legislate for the former in terms approaching the latter, the cost of change would simply be too high: ecclesial 'self-destruction' or 'the dismemberment of the Church of England'. Better to wait until the Holy Spirit had prepared hearts and minds for change.

By February of the following year, the House of Bishops, responding to Runcie's leadership and to a request from the General Synod, had produced a new unanimous report excluding a way forward in terms of parallel episcopates. 'I, for one', declared Runcie, 'do not intend to preside over the abolition of diocesan episcopacy and the parochial system as the Church of England has known it from the time of my predecessor, Archbishop Theodore of Tarsus.' In July 1988 when a Measure and Canons for the ordination of women were actually put to Synod, Runcie once more expressed his reservations:

I am no happier that this legislation is likely to achieve a development which will signal a greater unity in mission and service to our people. I must also confess to a feeling of despondency on reading this juridical machinery for the separation of proponents and antagonists. . . . The reason I cannot with a good conscience vote for this particular legislation, as things stand today, is primarily because I feel as did my predecessor Archbishop Frederick Temple, on another question when he said: '. . . I dread with all my soul, I dread what may come if the Church of England were to break in two'.

Once more he was in a minority and General Synod voted to go forward with the measure subject to revision. In November 1989, the measure came back in revised form and this time, while still confessing 'a yearning for greater consensus', Runcie voted in favour arguing that, in its revised form, the legislation should now be sent to the dioceses for discussion.

Only in Archbishop Carey's time will a final decision and its implementation actually happen. When women are ordained as priests in the Church of England, and doubtless they will be in the 1990s, the ground and the relevant procedures will have been prepared as well as is possible. It seems unlikely that there will be any considerable schism. Runcie may have averted that. On the other hand, if, as he has himself said, 'It cannot be irrelevant to evangelism that so many unbelievers think the place we give to women in the Church is frankly absurd', then it could be held against him that he has over-valued the maintenance of unity as against a reform of the ministry: a reform which he himself recognized as necessary to rescue the Church from an antiquated structure describable as 'frankly absurd' and making for unbelief.

In a speech to General Synod of November 1989, near the end of this long and often fraught decade of debate, Runcie had the following to say:

> The way in which we handle our differences could be the means by which we attract others to the faith. I remind you of some words of that great Anglican John Donne,
>
> > on a high hill truth stands
> > and he that would reach her
> > about must, and about must go.
>
> From the tiller of the Church of England, I recognize the danger of that yachting technique called 'going about'. If you don't 'go about' nimbly enough, your head is cracked by the boom as it swings sharply into the wind. But without 'going about' it is impossible to maintain direction. So with the church. It tacks swiftly to and fro at sharp angles as it slowly approximates to truth. On the ordination of women to the priesthood, there can be no way of avoiding John Donne's 'going about'.

The image here of nimbly 'going about', a swift tack at sharp angles to maintain the basic direction, seems very different from that of a gradualism dependent on consensus. Was Runcie's mistake to cling for the most part to the latter approach with little more than a literary

116

reference near the end of his archiepiscopate to the need for a nimbler adoption of different tacks?

Yet where on a lesser point he did try to move ahead, he did not succeed: the admission of women ordained abroad to temporary ministry in England. As Bishop of St Albans, he opposed this when it was first discussed in Synod in 1978, but as Archbishop of Canterbury, he consistently supported it — in 1982, 1984 and 1986. The reason, paradoxical as it may seem on the surface, was essentially the same as that which led him not to support the ordination of women at home: the unity of the Church. As Archbishop of Canterbury, he was responsible both for maintaining the unity of the Church of England and for maintaining the unity of the Anglican Communion. If the early ordination of women could threaten the one, refusal to offer hospitality to women already ordained abroad would threaten the unity of the other. So he strongly urged General Synod to take this step. It refused to do so and in consequence some of the bishops attending the Lambeth Conference in 1988 refused to celebrate in this country: the 'almost perfect communion' had diminished just a little more.

At Lambeth 1988, the issue was now focused upon the consecration of women to the episcopate. It was clear that several Churches were likely to do this and that indeed only a certain restraint had prevented them from doing so already before the Conference. Once more all that could be done was to call for respect for the integrity of decision of autonomous provinces while not necessarily accepting their theology. The consecration of a woman as bishop could only still further limit communion, as Runcie made clear in his speech to the conference on this resolution: 'We have heard a good deal of the phrase "impaired communion". It exists. And it will increase should a woman bishop be consecrated and should other bishops be unable to recognize such a woman as a bishop in the Church of God.' When later that year Barbara Harris was elected Suffragan Bishop of Massachusetts, Runcie at once made clear in Synod (7 November 1988) that as things stood, he and the Church of England could not legally recognize her as a bishop, nor those she ordained, men or women, as priests in this country. In consequence the Church of England and the Episcopal Church of the United States 'do not share the richness of communion we once did' but do still share more than with other Catholic, Orthodox or Protestant Churches. 'Communion', inside or outside the Anglican Communion, is — Runcie frequently insists — essentially a matter of degree.

None of this Runcie himself would really have chosen. He had long recognized that, if women priests were to be ordained, then women bishops too would be consecrated, and he had long committed himself to belief in principle in the ordination of women. He had also for years urged the Church of England to alter its legislation to recognize women ordained abroad but it had not done so. He would also have much preferred it if other Churches had for the time being not increased the strains of 'impaired communion' by consecrating bishops. He judged it inopportune. He lacked the power either to push the Church of England a little ahead or to hold other parts of the Anglican Communion a little back, yet he had to preside over both. There is, in all this, not the slightest sign of lack of principle. To comment 'Dr Runcie and his closest associates are men who have nothing to prevent them following what they think is the wish of the majority of the moment' (Crockford's Preface) is as wide of the mark as it is personally unfair to the Archbishop's often agonized struggle to be a constitutional monarch responsibly presiding over two bodies, the policy of neither of which he personally either controlled or fully approved.

* * *

All this did not make the dialogue with Rome or Orthodoxy any easier as John Macquarrie already declared at Lambeth 1978. 'It will be sad indeed if the promising *rapprochement* between Rome and Canterbury is halted or slowed down by the ordination of women priests in Anglican Churches. This may very well happen, and I hope we all realize that we may be paying a very high price for what we are doing.' Coggan had in fact kept Rome closely informed of developments in this area and the Roman response at the time, in the pontificate of Paul VI, had been fairly conciliatory—more so than that of Orthodoxy. In the 1980s the official Roman position had, however, hardened and the week Barbara Harris was elected, Pope John Paul II issued a further apostolic letter, on the dignity and vocation of women, *Mulieris Dignitatem*, which once more emphatically rejected the possibility of women's ordination: Jesus freely chose only men as his apostles and that must remain normative for all time. Runcie would have, from now on, to relate diplomatically both to the Pope and to women bishops within his own communion; not only Barbara Harris in Massachusetts, but, a little later, Penelope Jamieson, Diocesan Bishop of Dunedin, New Zealand.

As we have seen, the Roman dimension was both continually in Runcie's mind while tackling the women's ordination issue and in that of many other Anglicans who firmly opposed women's ordination until Rome and Constantinople should accept it as well. It is clear from the correspondence with Cardinal Willebrands, and much else, that Runcie was under considerable pressure from Rome and other places over this; indeed at times little less seems involved than an implicit threat effectively to end dialogue begun twenty years earlier. However, it is also clear that he weathered the threat and, partly at least, through the gradualist tactics he adopted. The dialogue did go on. ARCIC II continues to meet. It has become accepted that the ordination of women, instead of being as Rome and the East at first implied a ground for the termination of dialogue, would become instead just one more subject to be discussed. Moreover it would be discussed less for its own sake than as an instance of the wider issues of Christian development and Church authority.

It is undoubtedly true that by the later 1980s prospects for union between Roman Catholics and Anglicans seemed bleaker than they had for twenty years, and that on the official Roman side the ordination of women would be pointed to as the principal cause of this. Yet it could only be a very partial cause. It is noticeable that Rome has not yet fully accepted any report of its joint commission with Anglicans — neither the Malta Report of 1968 nor ARCIC I. If reunion with Rome were really a near possibility, then many an Anglican would surely not wish to upset it for a moment by raising, in the Pope's eyes, one new obstacle. But such was not the situation even before the present phase of Roman neo-conservatism. There seems not the slightest likelihood that Rome, as it now is, would want to enter into full communion with a world-wide group of Churches full of married priests over which it would exercise no regular jurisdiction. Equally there is not the slightest likelihood that any substantial group of Anglicans would accept papal claims to universal jurisdiction as at present both formulated and practised. To believe anything else is to inhabit an ecclesiastical cloud-cuckoo-land.

Runcie realized this well enough. He could see as well as anyone that, despite ARCIC, despite an extraordinary change in Anglican–Catholic relations at local level as exemplified in the collaboration of David Sheppard and Derek Worlock in Liverpool, despite all his own endeavour, the latter part of his archiepiscopate could be described, not unreasonably, as an ecumenical winter: 'Certainly cold winds threaten our growing together', he declared in his Heythrop lecture on Anglican–Roman Catholic Relations Today. 'I am not unaware that hard winters take their toll in the garden. I am not unaware that the history of ecumenism is littered with the corpses of failed attempts.' If the dialogue with Rome were to continue, it had to be a matter of the long haul. But it did not matter the less to him for that.

What is striking is the effective, practical way he not only kept this alive and active, despite both the new Roman conservatism and the increasing Anglican ordination of women, but also considerably enhanced a relationship of working collegiality, a shared confidence between Lambeth and Rome served on the Anglican side by such people as Christopher Hill, Runcie's Ecumenical Secretary, and Henry Chadwick. It is not insignificant that he appointed as Chairman of ARCIC II Mark Santer, probably the closest to him of the younger bishops.

The focal point of his Roman strategy must, however, be located in his visit to Rome in September 1989. It needs to be noticed first that this was no less than the fifth meeting he had had with the Pope: Accra, Canterbury, Bombay, Assisi, and now Rome. He was the fourth Archbishop of Canterbury in succession to visit the Pope in Rome, but he was the first to meet a Pope more than once. Meeting a Pope five times is a very different thing from meeting him once. The relationship has begun to move from symbolism to a working understanding. Runcie, when in Rome, quoted a remark of Newman, 'Men must have chronic familiarity to understand each other'. Perhaps the modern usage of the word makes the phrase sound odd, but Runcie's relationship with the Pope is important precisely because it has been 'chronic', a matter of 'regular meetings'. And not only meetings involving the two principals. In his visit to Rome, Runcie was accompanied by the Secretary General of the Anglican Consultative Council, the Primate of Nigeria and by Mark Santer, Bishop of Birmingham, as co-Chairman of ARCIC, just as in Canterbury he was surrounded by a number of Anglican Primates and all the bishops of England. The point was to demonstrate that it was a meeting of communions, not just of individuals, and to put flesh on a symbolic bone, even to create by familiarity a sort of pragmatic collegiality — a collegiality which indeed he has regularly practised in England with Cardinal Hume just as Archbishop Worlock and Bishop Sheppard have practised it in Liverpool.

Again, the visit to Rome was long enough to be thoroughly practical. Pope and Archbishop met no less than five times in four days. Runcie also had lengthy meetings with other members of the Curia — not only Cardinal Willebrands and the Council for Promoting Christian Unity but Cardinal Ratzinger and others. As a diplomatist, he realized that you can't ignore the Curia. Often the Curia is simply described by those who disagree with its policies as reactionary and bureaucratic. Many a liberal Catholic tends to feel like that. But Runcie knows that a big ship needs an engine room and he does, perhaps, even slightly envy the Pope his Curia. It certainly comes as a novelty to hear an Archbishop of Canterbury stressing 'the importance and the need for the Roman Curia as a service to catholic unity under the Bishop of Rome' — a line rather different from the more traditional Anglican position that if a Roman primacy could be accepted at all, it will be a purely honorary one. Runcie saw that a primacy should be of service rather than of honour, and that a worldwide service cannot be done without some sort of curia — Lambeth's own staff being still inadequate in number for a very much smaller operation. Runcie's approach to Rome was a combination of realism, diplomacy, a sense of history and above all the building up of good personal relations: 'No theological disagreement will permanently divide us when we know each other no longer as strangers but as friends'. He told the Roman Curia, 'In the theological realm conviviality and communion are closely related to each other'. He is good on words and the lively phrase in the Common Declaration, 'the ecumenical journey is not only about the removal of obstacles but also about the sharing of gifts', was a personal contribution of Runcie, one gladly accepted by the Pope.

What Runcie's approach lacked — and many Anglicans, and Roman Catholics too, would blame him for it — was any public critique of the internal illiberalism of the Ratzinger era. Theologians have lost their teaching posts and been silenced, bishops have been regimented and new ones selected in a very partisan manner, the episcopal synod in Rome is no longer free enough reliably to represent the world's episcopate. Runcie did tackle Ratzinger privately over these matters, but clearly without effect and unknown to the wider world. Here as elsewhere he preferred the diplomatic to the prophetic role. Geoffrey Fisher went to Rome to see Pope John, Protestant as he was, because he saw that Pope John had really changed things, and that was before the Council had begun. He had changed the spirit dominant in Rome. Unfortunately, John Paul II has changed the spirit back again to very much what it was. Publicly at least Runcie has seen his role as a diplomatic one and has remained very silent about what is going on — a development probably far more inimical to Anglican–Roman Catholic relations than the ordination of women.

The most memorable and, for some, shocking aspect of his Roman visit, however, was undoubtedly the stress he quite deliberately laid upon acceptance of a Roman primacy. This, as we have seen, was not a new element in his thinking. It has surfaced repeatedly, and notably at the Lambeth Conference. But its expression at Rome, and in the very presence of the Pope, had a special significance. The address delivered at San Gregorio during Vespers deserves quoting at length. Naturally, in such a place, he began by recalling the mission sent by Gregory to England of Augustine and his fellow monks out of which the Church of Canterbury and of England developed. Gregory was in this the model Pope — the agent of mission and unity. From this he was able to continue:

> Gregory's example of a primacy for the sake of unity and mission — which we also see embodied in the ministry of his successor, John Paul II — begins to find a place in Anglican thinking. I tried to give voice to this at the last Lambeth Conference where I spoke of the need for a personal focus of unity. Within the Anglican Communion my own office is in part a response to this need. But for the universal Church I renew the plea I made at the Lambeth Conference: could not all Christians come to re-consider the kind of Primacy the bishop of Rome exercised within the Early Church, a 'presiding in love' for the sake of the unity of the Churches in the diversity of their mission? In Assisi, without compromise of faith, we saw that the bishop of Rome could gather the Christian Churches together. We could pray together, speak together and act together for the peace and well-being of humankind, and the stewardship of our precious earth. At that initiative of prayer for world peace I felt I was in the presence of the God who said 'Behold I am doing a new thing'.

He had said much the same earlier to General Synod (November 1984):

> At Assisi at least, I did see the possibility of a new style of papal leadership: an ARCIC Primacy rather than Papal Monarchy.... Great care was taken to emphasise our fraternity rather than our hierarchy. We stood in a semi-circle and there was a careful allocation of readings and prayers to all. The Pope's chair was the same as everybody else's. We all bundled into the same buses and the Pope had to look for a seat.

Ian Paisley went to Rome to heckle the Archbishop. Neither an Anglican nor an Englishman, just someone filled with a huge hostility to Roman Catholicism, he seldom gets a good British press. It is strange that on this occasion newspapers should follow a Paisley line and declare a highly successful visit a 'débâcle'. It demonstrated an extraordinary ignorance of the beliefs and policies of the man who had now been Archbishop of Canterbury for almost ten years.

Runcie's archiepiscopate was certainly the first one in which an Anglican Primate had repeatedly and positively urged a papal 'Ecumenical primacy'. But as Runcie stressed in his Heythrop lecture, he had a long and sound Anglican tradition behind him in this. In diplomatic terms it was masterly — Rome could hardly not be pleased with an Archbishop of Canterbury who advocated a Roman primacy but, of course, the primacy he spoke of remained something profoundly different from the jurisdictionally all-powerful modern papacy. In real terms, it is Rome, far more than anyone else, who would have to change in order to accept such a model. But to suggest so much at a time when otherwise the dialogue seems almost to be running out of steam did much to ensure its continuance, as well as place the Archbishop of Canterbury in the position of saying what many Roman Catholic archbishops from Westminster to Vienna must feel, but have not had quite the courage to say. He could in fact, through his dialogue with Rome, act as spokesman for a great deal of Roman Catholicism: such dialogue becomes less a conversation between Churches than an exercise of collegiality within the Church.

As symbolic of his authority to speak brother to brother with the Pope, Runcie wore on his finger, on his visit to Rome, the episcopal ring which Paul VI had given so movingly to Archbishop Ramsey. That ring is itself a symbol of half-acknowledged collegiality. Runcie, referring to this ring in addressing the Pope, recalled the amusing comment of the great theologian Yves Congar, whom he had visited recently in Paris, comparing the ecumenical movement with an engaged couple that is never daring enough to get married. 'This ring given by a much loved Pope to a beloved Archbishop is a sign not unlike an engagement ring' — a token of commitment to fuller unity. In the Roman Vespers at San Gregorio, Robert, Archbishop of Canterbury, was prayed for as well as John Paul II, Bishop of Rome. At the open air Papal Mass at St Peter's, Archbishop and Pope exchanged the kiss of peace at the altar in the face of everyone immediately before the distribution of communion. These are the traditional symbols of episcopal collegiality. The Pope's last words on departure, unscripted and spontaneous, were 'Our affective collegiality will lead us to effective collegiality. Nothing affective, nothing effective.' Certainly, despite all the problems of the 'winter of ecumenism', relations between the sees of Canterbury and Rome have never been so close since the sixteenth century as in the archiepiscopate of Robert Runcie and the papacy of John Paul II. That was no small achievement.

7

From covenanting to togetherness

I wish that I could give the clear lead given by Archbishop Ramsey over the Anglican/Methodist scheme, or by Archbishop Coggan on the ordination of women. But at the moment I cannot and perhaps it is only human for me to comfort myself by remembering that the Church did not follow their lead on those issues.

(To the Canterbury Diocesan Synod, July 1980, in regard to the Covenant)

The Nottingham Faith and Order Conference, held in the optimistic atmosphere of 1964, resolved by a majority of 85 per cent to invite the member Churches of the British Council of Churches 'to covenant together to work and pray for the inauguration of union by a date . . . (which) . . . we dare to hope should not be later than Easter Day 1980'. So Runcie became Archbishop at precisely the moment, the spring of 1980, at which this great hope of the British ecumenical movement failed to be realized. He inherited a situation in which, over many decades, a certain ecumenical strategy had been attempted, but never quite successfully. The strategy was to achieve the organic unity, in one place, of all the Churches stemming from the Reformation through some form of reconciliation of ministries and the adoption of a single Church order and liturgy. It had been, predominantly, an Anglo-Saxon strategy but its most successful fruits had been the Churches of South and North India. Elsewhere it had been tried and failed or, at least, Anglicans had failed to participate in whatever had come into being, such as the United Church of Zambia or the United Church of Canada.

In England this strategy had come near to achieving Anglican–Methodist unity in 1969 and 1972 but it just failed to gain sufficient votes for a two-thirds majority on the Anglican side. Everything ecumenical in subsequent Anglican history has stood beneath the shadow of that failure. In 1972, however, there was one 'organic' success in England — the unification of the Congregational Union and the Presbyterian Church in England which produced the United Reformed Church. It has to be said that this was a relatively small

124

achievement between two bodies, one of them extremely small, which had for long enjoyed particularly close links. Their union had been urged for many decades. Moreover, even in 1972, it did not take place without schism. A minority of Congregational Churches refused to join and continued on their own. Indeed, even in the classic ecumenical model of the Church of South India, there was a significant schism in Nandyal, something from which most devout ecumenists long turned their eyes in distress. Moreover, just as in England the United Reformed Church went almost no way at all to achieving the visible unity of all Christians 'in one place', so in South India, the Church of South India never united anything like a majority of the Christians of South India, as the Syro-Malabar Churches, the Roman Catholic Church and even the Lutherans were not included.

It is, then, reasonable to conclude that the strategy in question had not been a large success, despite the thought, prayer and effort which had gone into it. Certainly, no alternative strategy appeared to offer chances of greater success. It would be more than foolish to blame a long generation of committed ecumenists who put so much of themselves into realizing this model. Nevertheless by the mid-1970s the message should have been becoming clear.

One more attempt was, nevertheless, made in England to break through the road-block. It was an attempt of a particularly audacious kind to outflank the obstacles and achieve the goal of an almost organic unity within the sort of time span envisaged by Nottingham 1964. It was the English Covenant. Its conception had grown out of the energy generated by the inauguration of the United Reformed Church (URC), out of Anglican guilt for the failure of the Methodist unity scheme, and out of the practical needs for providing a framework within which the increasing number of Local Ecumenical Projects could be sanctioned and strengthened. A very widely representative Churches' Unity Commission had been established in 1974 (including even Roman Catholics) in response to a URC invitation to see what might still be done to carry the endeavour of unity forward after the events of 1972. Two years later this commission published an outline of 'Ten Propositions' for a Covenant of Unity, a tentative way to arrive at a working organic oneness without the hassle of institutional and liturgical reconstruction. These propositions were eventually accepted, with qualifications, by the URC, the Church of England, the Methodists, the Moravians, and the Churches of Christ. Late in 1978, this group established a Churches' Council for Covenanting with instructions to complete plans for a Covenant within no more than two years.

There was, it would seem, a cloudiness surrounding the Covenant which was never really resolved. For those most closely involved in its shaping, the Covenant was performative in nature, it was not to be merely a solemn declaration of intention. It would actually achieve the essentials of visible unity. From the moment the Covenant Service took place those participating, or represented by those participating, would be understood as sharing a common Church life with a full inter-changeability of ministers (rather like different rites within the Roman Catholic Church). The separate institutional life of the Churches would continue on a day-to-day basis, but the separation would no longer be underpinned by distinct theologies. 'Common decision-making' would henceforth be required in all matters of common concern though no thought had been given to establishing how that decision-making would actually work. There was no time in which to do so. The Service of Reconciliation, on which the Council spent most of its time, certainly did not involve any notion of possible re-ordination or conditional ordination for those not episcopally ordained (and, indeed, it was not intended that all ministers should attend it anyway). The service was to signify the corporate mutual recognition of different ministries from that point on, without judgement on the past, but the Council regarded any insistence as to the way in which individuals were incorporated into the new common ministry as unworthy of consideration, a surrender to 'sacramental and juridical individualism'. Inevitably, more traditional Anglo-Catholics (like Roman Catholics or Orthodox for that matter, apart from a radical fringe) could not accept such an arrangement.

Still more audacious was the Council's leap across the issue of the ordination of women. If the Covenant had gone through, former URC and Methodist women ministers would from that moment have functioned legally as priests within the Church of England, despite the fact that General Synod had only a little before repeated its refusal to allow Anglican women priests legally ordained abroad to minister as priests in England. Furthermore, Anglican bishops would themselves have had at once to participate in the ordination of women in the very Service of Reconciliation. It seems quite extraordinary that it was not recognized that the Church of England needed to resolve its own mind on this issue, and effect the legal change required, before attempting to commit itself to a package deal of which this was a little-stressed but still unavoidable part. It is hard at this distance of time to conclude other than that the Covenant was a too hastily constructed expression of a form of ecumenical idealism almost at the end of its wits to find a way forward.

126

It needs at this point to be recalled that Runcie had had nothing to do with this endeavour hitherto. The whole enterprise was almost complete before he took office. It was in its way a piece of 1970s agenda left over, a little awkwardly, for the 1980s. Nevertheless Runcie was confronted with it as the first major decision of his archiepiscopate. It was also something with which he was most unlikely to be wholly sympathetic. He made that clear shortly after his enthronement and again in a speech to General Synod in February 1981, when he subjected various aspects of the proposals to quite severe criticism — both the Reconciliation Service itself and the whole area of subsequent common decision-making which he described as possibly 'an energy-consuming bureaucratic quagmire'.

In their final form the proposals for the Covenant came before General Synod on 7 July 1982. They came with a 'Memorandum of Dissent' signed by three Anglican members of the Council for Covenanting. A far from unanimous recommendation from those commissioned to prepare it was hardly an auspicious beginning. The Bishop of Guildford, David Brown, had been the Anglican leader within the discussions and he had, therefore, the responsibility of presenting the Covenant to Synod. Naturally enough, he wished to know in advance the mind of the Archbishop and what he now intended to say. He asked Runcie but was able to obtain no clear reply and had to speak in Synod still uncertain what line the Archbishop would take. The two men, it seems, had always found it difficult to relate but it can hardly be denied that at this point Runcie failed to give what was needed, at least an adequate explanation of where he himself stood. The trouble was that, probably until almost the last moment, Runcie was unable to settle in his own mind what he should do. He was unable to back with full conviction proposals about which he remained deeply uneasy, yet for the Archbishop to speak and vote against the Covenant would have branded him in ways he certainly wished to avoid. Only a few weeks before, he had welcomed the Pope in Canterbury Cathedral and the leaders of all the Free Churches had been with him as he did so. If he now voted against the Covenant to join with Methodists, Moravians and the URC, he could have appeared a very one-sided ecumenist indeed, which in intention he was not. Moreover, a large majority of bishops was in favour. To disagree with them over this looked rather uncollegial.

Nevertheless, the Covenant went deeply against Runcie's better judgement, against his intuition rather than his formal theology, in several ways. It meant accepting in principle for priestly ministry within the Church of England thousands of people who had not been

127

episcopally ordained. Such a step was revolutionary and his reluctance to go along with it may be paralleled by his refusal thirty years earlier to contribute to *The Historic Episcopate*. The fact that some of the people in question were women certainly did not make it any easier. In 1982 Runcie was not quite through his hesitations in regard to the ordination of women, but what mattered most here was not his personal opinion but the fact that the Church of England had hitherto rejected any offering of hospitality to Anglican women priests ordained elsewhere. There was an inherent contradiction in the position the Covenant could easily lead the Church into — a contradiction the seriousness of which the Anglican members of the Council seem to have played down in their discussions with the other Churches but which Runcie could have had the final responsibility for sorting out and endeavouring to defend in parliament. Furthermore, he remained perplexed about the actual way in which decisions would be made in a post-Covenant Church. He was probably unable to formulate his views on all this very clearly even to himself, and he may well have felt more isolated within the House of Bishops at this point of his archiepiscopate than at any other. When it came to his speech he announced that he would vote in favour but then devoted almost all the time to a critique of its deficiencies. It was honest. It was a wiser response to the Covenant than that of its full supporters. But it was certainly confusing and disappointing for supporters and opponents alike. Never did the archiepiscopal trumpet sound a more uncertain note.

The Covenant all the same obtained a two-thirds majority among bishops and laity and it only just missed it among the clergy. It is arguable that if Runcie had spoken more enthusiastically it might have passed, but he would not have been honest if he had done so. It is also far from clear that it would have served the Church's interests if it had passed on 7 July or — having passed that day — would actually have come into existence. There were many other hurdles ahead. There were indeed deep reservations on the part of the URC, but beyond that the issue of accepting women priests through the back door would almost certainly have come to the fore with ferocity. It is only too likely that the Covenant would have foundered on this rock either in General Synod or in parliament. The Bishop of Guildford died a week later of a heart attack and the Churches' Council for Covenanting was immediately wound up. It was a sharply painful ending to a gallant endeavour.

Dr Kenneth Greet, a leading Methodist, commented soon afterwards:

The way marked out by a whole generation of ecumenical leaders has proved to be a cul-de-sac. We must pray that a new generation will succeed where we have failed, for in the end a way must be found. The Holy Spirit does not declare a moratorium just because we temporarily lose our way.

Two years later Runcie declared in General Synod that the complete interchangeability of Anglican and Free Church ministries was 'the rock on which the Covenant sank'. The acceptance of that would require a greater 'consensus over ministry, priesthood and the episcopate' than the Church of England then possessed. 'The debate about the necessity or otherwise of episcopal ordination' had not been foreclosed. 'Like it or not, that is where we are.' It was not that Runcie was personally convinced of the necessity of episcopal ordination; yet he was not quite convinced of the contrary, either. He had some duty to remain the guardian of tradition where so large a deviation from the practice of the Church of England was proposed and where a great many people within the Church were opposed to that deviation. It should not have been difficult to see that if the Covenant was voted through, it could either prove simply unworkable in practice or lead to schism.

What Kenneth Greet said remained to a large degree true but it was a truth which might already have been perceived some years earlier. The way marked out by a whole generation of ecumenical leaders was, alas, a cul-de-sac and the task of contemporary ecumenical leaders was no longer to try and force a way through the road-block but to seek another road. Some of the characteristics of that other road have been becoming more evident in this country in the course of the 1980s. A first characteristic could be the priority of the local, even if that priority seems sometimes almost anarchic. A second characteristic is that the priority of Protestant unity, always implicitly there in the past, is no longer valid. The endeavour to establish some form of 'organic unity' upon that side prior to the task of working upon other relationships in the more distant future is no longer psychologically sustainable or practically useful. A third characteristic is to abandon the priority of the national over the international whereby in the past it was anticipated that international communions would, as ecumenism advanced, give way to national unities. A fourth is to build the wider strategy upon a theology of degrees of communion between different continuing bodies, rather than upon a theology which contrasts disunity and multiplicity with unity and an organic/institutional merger. The implicit strength of a 'degrees of communion' theology lies not only in its more realistic historical grounding but also in a rejection of the idea that ecumenism has failed if 'full communion' or even 'organic unity' has not been attained. If a condition of bitter controversy and non-co-operation has been replaced by a large measure of good-humoured sharing across every side of Christian life between Churches still officially only in 'partial' or 'almost complete' communion, surely 95 per cent of the goal has been gained. The honest recognition of some serious differences does not negate fulfilment of the Lord's command that his disciples be one. The sense that Church history has always been a very anomalous matter, that almost all the structures we know are really profoundly provisional, may make one recognize that it is not wicked, but to be expected, that communion should frequently be experienced as limited, the limits being due not to hate or perversity but to some serious perplexity in regard to the relation of historical experience to a divine norm. 'Full communion' is less a condition to be juridically achieved than a goal always ahead of us, a goal to make the Church what of its nature it is but in the awkwardness of history never will quite be. While Archbishop Runcie would probably not write the characteristics of a new ecumenism down quite like this — it is not the sort of thing he does — these would seem to be the lines along which he has nudged the movement forward in the 1980s.

Two ecumenical addresses of 1984 reflect the current shape of Runcie's thinking in the post-Covenant age pretty clearly. In January he spoke to the Kensington United Reformed Church and, after surveying both the long march from the old days of 'ecclesiastical cold war' and the continued existence of formidable 'road-blocks', he went on to summarize a varied but fairly low-key agenda:

> A concrete and realizable programme will then, I hope, enable us to get over our ecumenical split personality and make actual progress: consolidating the theological gains of the past years of dialogue, particularly the concept of a stage by stage growth towards unity; insisting on the unity of the ecumenical endeavour and so doing everything we can to bring the Roman Catholic Church into the main stream of the ecumenical life of this country; and making progress locally by the Church of England being more flexible in designated ecumenical projects.

Six months later, addressing the Methodist Conference, he declared

> In the end the cause of unity is best served not by the dilution and diminution of the particularities of tradition, but by their rediscov-

ery and re-emphasis as gifts to the wider *oikumene*. Such a diversity of gifts in united christian fellowship will in any case be more appealing to the unbeliever who is unlikely to be attracted to a monochrome ecumenism in his reaction against an increasingly homogenized society.

Where the traditional ecumenist harped on the theme of 'unity for mission' Runcie was now insinuating that 'diversity for mission' might really make better sense.

It is true that none of these suggested characteristics quite copes with the problem of the full recognition by episcopal Churches of ministers not episcopally ordained. The problem was solved at a blow in the Church of North India. It is an example which might still be worth considering. It may be immediately more cathartic but also more creative of a confident future. Its rejection elsewhere may well still say something about backward- rather than forward-looking pre-occupations. Yet it is also true that adequate consensus might very well be found in fully catholic terms, of a none too radical kind, for other solutions. For us the point still simply remains that in 1982 within the Church of England that degree of consensus did not exist at clergy level, and that Runcie had now recognized its non-existence as provisionally decisive.

The sense of numbed uncertainty as to what to do next, a sort of ecumenical despair, was not less acute. For Runcie himself the experience of the Covenant and the realization that his own part in it had hardly been glorious seems to have led to some pretty furious thinking, a considerably increased determination to take the lead in finding as many ways forward as possible. The most immediate problem was that of Local Ecumenical Projects and their sanctioning. Here, only ten days later, Runcie made a strongly positive statement in the Canterbury Diocesan Synod. He had already appealed to leaders of the local Free Churches which had been involved in the Covenant to meet him to discuss ways and means forward at the local level. There can be no doubt that this was seen as an important signal, speedily provided, that there was after all a future. 'For something to be real it must be local' is a maxim he is fond of quoting. He was well initiated into the area of Local Ecumenical Projects during his St Albans years across long hours of discussion with Bishop Christopher Butler and others. He had himself experienced the field and its problems, he had nudged Butler forward and even been nudged forward by Butler, so he felt confidence here and knew it to be important. He recognized too that a lot of the difficulties were technical legal ones, mostly on the

Anglican side. Anglican priests, and bishops too, were prohibited by law from doing things which, within an on-going ecumenical project, were quite inevitable (such as taking a service according to a non-Anglican rite): 'We must not force priests', he declared, 'to choose between their spiritual integrity and the canon law'. It was precisely the multiplication of such tensions which had fuelled the Covenant. Runcie's increased concentration upon them in the post-Covenant period certainly helped a sense of ecumenical hope.

1982 remains in a whole series of ways a crucial ecumenical date: not only the year of the Pope's visit to Canterbury and the failure of the Covenant, but of the publication of the final report of ARCIC I and — of still wider concern — the World Council of Churches' Lima statement on *Baptism, Eucharist and Ministry* (BEM, as it came to be known). It had been prepared over a number of years and showed a close convergence of view with that of ARCIC. From now on BEM and ARCIC would provide the ground for a new kind of ecumenical doctrinal orthodoxy of considerable significance on account of the range of support it included as well as its theological maturity. If the Covenant had been pursued less hastily and had had time to be grounded on and within a BEM–ARCIC consensus, it might conceivably have found acceptance. Henceforward for Runcie and many other people, the joint appeal to ARCIC and BEM could suggest no undue inclination to either Catholicism or Protestantism. It was both authoritative and contemporary.

Runcie's anxiety to be equally open to Protestant and to Catholic relationships, so long as they seemed compatible with Anglican tradition and were not inherently contradictory of each other nor too divisive for Anglicans themselves, was shown best in his enthusiasm to improve relations with Continental Lutherans and in consequence with the Evangelical Churches of Germany as a whole. He visited Germany in 1983 for the anniversary of Martin Luther's birth in November 1483, and his lecture in Leipzig on 11 November on the significance of Luther for the Anglican tradition helped to set him thinking about the need for new initiatives in this area. The Church of England had been for years in communion with the episcopal Lutheran Churches of Sweden and Finland. In 1982 wider Anglican–Lutheran discussions at Helsinki, chaired on the Anglican side by the Bishop of Coventry, had concluded that 'there are no longer any serious obstacles on the way towards the establishment of full communion between our two Churches'. Runcie was impressed by how much Lutherans and Anglicans had in common — in liturgical history and practice, music, spirituality, Church ethos, even the sense of being a national Church. He also felt he could rely on Lutheran theology. The only awkward thing remaining seemed to be the lack of bishops in German churches but he was strongly inclined — like some seventeenth-century Anglican divines — to make excuses for them over this. It had been due to untoward historical circumstances, 'the evil of the times', excuses not so readily made for British Free Churches (though Runcie recognized a comparable excuse over Wesley's ordination of priests for America). Anglicans have never unchurched Lutherans, Runcie often insisted.

Runcie's 1983 German visit and subsequent correspondence led to the discussions which produced the Meissen Agreement five years later betweem the Church of England and the two German Evangelical Churches, an agreement which, while making '*visible* that real but imperfect communion we already share with the two German Churches' (Runcie, November 1988), did not overstep the bounds currently defined, in his view, by the rejection of the Covenant: there is no full interchangeability of ministers. The strong Anglican team negotiating the Meissen Agreement was chaired by the Bishop of Grimsby. No more here than over the Covenant or, indeed, over the reshaping of the British Council of Churches, was Runcie closely involved in the details of ecumenical planning and negotiation. Nevertheless the Meissen Agreement was in a very real way his achievement (and that is how it is seen in Germany, where his lectures on Luther made a deep impression), one of his final and most significant acts as Archbishop being the celebration of the Agreement in Westminster Abbey in January 1991, a last rejoinder to those of his critics who have accused him of only being seriously concerned about Rome. His full sympathy, however, was secure for a line of moderate advance which avoided 'both the seductions of the enthusiasts and the imprecations of the scrupulous', which looked particularly warmly on local projects but avoided larger plans for Church mergers, which was even-handed towards Protestants and Catholics, and which — a final consideration — strengthened Anglican relations with Europe.

1982 was ecumenically interesting for yet another reason. It was the fortieth anniversary of the British Council of Churches (BCC). The Archbishop of Canterbury had always been its sole President, a little oddly for a British, not English, Council, so William Temple was its first President and Robert Runcie its fifth. In celebrating the event he was, as so often, constitutionally incapable of not mixing the comic with the serious, even at the price of the risqué, and succumbed to the 'almost irresistible temptation' of quoting the old song:

Forty years on growing older and older
Shorter in wind and in memory long
Feeble of foot and rheumatic of shoulder
What would it help you that once you were strong?

Runcie well knew that such an image was just a little too close to the bone in regard to the BCC to be entirely happily received by everyone, especially just four months after the rejection of the Covenant, the sign for Kenneth Greet that 'the way marked out by a whole generation of ecumenical leaders has proved to be a cul-de-sac'. Of course, Runcie went on at once and emphatically to repudiate 'very gloomy and dispiriting' talk about the British Council — 'I believe we have never needed the BCC more'. He was undoubtedly correct in saying that in its forty years of existence, the BCC had helped to accomplish a kind of Copernican revolution among the Churches of Britain, so that denomination-centredness had hugely declined, and he reaffirmed his faith and commitment to the future of the BCC. The trouble was, nevertheless, that it had become, mostly for no fault of its own, somewhat unadapted to Britain's current ecumenical needs.

It had never got the England–Britain relationship quite right and it had never included Roman Catholics. By the end of the 1970s Catholics were members of a majority of local Councils of Churches and the National Pastoral Congress held in Liverpool in 1980 requested the bishops to reconsider membership of the BCC. No clear reason for non-membership was ever stated, nevertheless there is reason to believe that a significant minority of the bishops, including Cardinal Hume, remained reluctant to join. Perhaps the BCC seemed too set in its ways, even if it did not wish to be. Perhaps the Catholic hierarchy felt uneasy that it might find itself committed to public statements it did not support or might then feel forced to come forward with awkward public statements of dissent. Catholic bishops were also somewhat unaccustomed to the procedures and openness of discussion customary in the BCC. The precise reasons do not much matter. Most members of the BCC were anxious that Catholics should join and many Catholics were anxious that it should be done, but the bishops were not convinced and were not likely to be so without a wider package deal.

For a long time, Catholic membership of the BCC appeared merely as a valuable strengthening to its work but by the Runcie years it had come to appear instead as a matter of life or death. Catholics were so numerous, influential and capable a part of the British Christian community that a British Council of Churches which did not include them had started to seem too awkward an anomaly, especially in the eyes of the quite exceptionally ecumenical people who guided its policies. Basically, it was another example of the way in which the ecumenical agenda had simply changed. The BCC had been set up in the 1940s, just as the Church of South India was, within a world of Protestant priorities from which Roman Catholics had consistently excluded themselves and which had seemed to make good sense without them. Since the Second Vatican Council Catholics had come half through the door — their liberal representatives rather more than half, their conservative representatives rather less than half. One could no more plan without them but, equally, one could not plan in the old way with them. They might still seem unreasonably awkward, their bishops might be over-cautious, but it simply was not worth going on with a game which left them out. It had become just another cul-de-sac. If the mountain would not come to Muhammad, then Muhammad might have to go to the mountain.

Muhammad was helped in this by a public proposal of the Catholic bishops, again in 1982, following upon the papal visit, to reconsider their relationship to the BCC. The implication was that if Muhammad would be willing to move a certain distance, then the mountain might very well move a little too. Early in January 1984 a widely reported meeting between the Catholic bishops and the leaders of the other British Churches took the matter a bit further and helped lead on to what came to be known as the 'Inter Church process', code-named 'Not Strangers but Pilgrims'. Only a General Secretary of the BCC as undogmatic and flexible as Philip Morgan would have been prepared to consider sinking the BCC in its existing form in order to let something different develop in which Catholics would feel more at home. Perhaps only a President of the BCC as wedded as Runcie to the principle of provisionality would have agreed to try going down that road: to implement the deepest of Christian truths and allow a still thriving forty-year-old institution to die that new life might arise.

Such was the master idea underlying the Swanwick Conference, 'Not Strangers but Pilgrims', of September 1987. To it Cardinal Hume had come with some considerable surviving reluctance, a half-will to withdraw even in the course of it. But he did not. Deeply moved by the warmth of shared experience, particularly of so many 'separated brethren' coming up at the Catholic Eucharist to seek a blessing at his hands, he became convinced that Catholics must indeed fully participate in what Runcie, in a major speech, declared emphatically 'a new beginning'.

The ecumenical story in these islands began long ago. But we now come to an important cross-roads. In a real sense we begin a new part of the journey.

Runcie went on to sketch out a possible new model which would include, upon the one hand, 'meetings of office bearers which will be widely recognized as effectively speaking in the name of the Christian Church in this country', and on the other, 'a large, occasional representative assembly in which the proper dialogue between office bearers and the wider church can take place. The present BCC is, I am afraid, neither the one nor the other.' Runcie's preference for an effective meeting of major office holders over the existing BCC was comparable to his preference within the Anglican Communion for meetings of the Primates over those of the Anglican Consultative Council. In each case it represented a pragmatic authoritarianism because nothing else would cut much ice with the wider world or get results. Cardinal Hume announced Catholic willingness to participate in such a new ecumenical instrument in the warmest terms and Swanwick became, in consequence, indeed a cross-roads and a new beginning.

Archbishop Habgood chaired the resulting negotiations which led up to the establishment in September 1990 of a new, renamed and differently structured body, Christians Together, to replace the BCC. Here again Runcie was not involved in the detailed ecumenical discussions (the only area where he did accept that role was with Rome itself). Habgood was a better chairman with a clearer analytical mind for all the issues involved. Runcie's role was to preside over and symbolize the outcome, which was indeed an expression of the way he wished to go, the determination in particular that no one should be left out — and from this point of view the entry of the Black Churches mattered as much as did that of the Roman Catholics. The new instrument certainly reflected his basic intuition that it was pointless to continue with any model which excluded the largest Church in the world (and the largest practising Church, in terms of Sunday attendance, in Britain) or to hold out for Catholic participation in forms disagreeable to Catholic leadership. If the principle of even-handedness meant, in consequence, going slower with old friends, it was still the only sensible way to proceed.

So in a sense, the events running from Swanwick in September 1987 to the inauguration of the new order in September 1990 did fulfil Runcie's comic quote of 1982: 'Feeble of foot and rheumatic of shoulder, what would it help you that once you were strong?' He was not only the British Council of Churches' fifth President, but also its last. The termination of the BCC and the beginning of Christians Together has come so late in his archiepiscopate that it will be impossible to evaluate its consequences for quite some time. Has it genuinely opened the way to a new era? Or has it, on the contrary, simply dismantled a workable body which did much good to replace it by a nonentity in the forlorn hope of drawing the Roman Catholic leadership out of a self-imposed ghetto? The weight of responsibility now lying with the Catholic bishops to ensure that the sacrifice other Churches have made, and particularly the Free Churches for whom the BCC mattered most, has not been in vain is certainly a grave one.

An evaluation of the contribution of Runcie, or the Runcie years, to the ecumenical history of Britain will certainly have to wait. What is clear is that the failure of the Covenant and the reluctance of the Roman Catholic Church to enter an unreformed BCC both indicated that the ecumenical movement in this country in its classical lines had entered a cul-de-sac. It would be exaggerated to see the new model as principally an invention of Runcie. It was shaped by many hands and the on-going logic of circumstances. None the less he could certainly have impeded its development. Instead, as it closely accorded with his own ecclesiological principles, and particularly that of the provisionality of next to everything, he nursed and encouraged it. It may be that, while he initially appeared as an Archbishop unable to dance in tune with current ecumenical orthodoxies in Britain, to the extent that his two predecessors had been able to do so, he acted rather as a catalyst in leading the movement out of a cul-de-sac and on to a road which might at least conceivably have a solid future.

Runcie ended his speech at Swanwick — perhaps the most important specifically ecumenical speech of his career — with words from Eckhart which we have heard before and which, as he admitted, some of his listeners had probably also heard from him before, but he rightly thought them apt for that occasion. They remain apt as Runcie's comment upon the ending of one ecumenical age and the beginning of another:

> There is no stopping place in this life, no, nor was there ever one for any man no matter how far along the way he's come. This, then, above all things: Be ready for the gifts of God, and always for new ones.

8

The Lambeth Conference and the Anglican Communion

In one of the most remote and rural parts of Uganda lies a diocese called West Ankole. It was established in January 1977 in the time of the worst tyranny of Idi Amin. The districts of Igara, Buhweju, Bunyaruguru, Sheema and Kajara were separated from the diocese of Ankole, which had itself come into existence only ten years earlier. Before that there had been a single diocese for Ankole and Kigezi and that too only began in 1961, the year Uganda became an ecclesiastical province together with the countries to the west of it into which its Church had overflowed. 1961 was also the year Michael Ramsey became Archbishop of Canterbury. Before that year, the two dioceses into which Uganda had long been divided were directly dependent upon the See of Canterbury. At the Lambeth Conference of 1958 they were represented by their two diocesan bishops, both white, and four assistant bishops, three of them black, who were officially described as 'Overseas Bishops of the Canterbury Jurisdiction'.

Lambeth 1968 saw, instead of two white diocesan bishops, a black Archbishop, Erica Sabiti, and nine diocesan bishops, eight of them black. By 1978 the 'Church of the Province of Uganda, Rwanda, Burundi and Boga Zaire' was represented by its Archbishop and 21 diocesan bishops. Then in 1980, Rwanda, Burundi and Zaire were established as a separate province and Archbishop Runcie was present at its inauguration, his first visit to Africa. By Lambeth 1988, the Province of Uganda consisted of 20 dioceses, the Province of Burundi, Rwanda and Zaire of ten. So the two of 1958 had become ten in 1968, 22 in 1978 and 30 in 1988. These figures, for just one part of Africa, illustrate what, all in all, has been the most striking development within the Anglican Communion in the archiepiscopates of Ramsey, Coggan and Runcie: an immense shift from North to South and the rise of Africa as the largest continental section of the Communion. 175 African bishops attended the Lambeth Conference in 1988. It was a shift which their predecessor Geoffrey Fisher had been very consciously preparing for during his years at Canterbury.

Let us return to West Ankole. Its first and only Bishop has been

Jerome Bamunoba. He had guarded his father's cattle and goats on the hillside when he was a boy. He had gone on to schooling, Christian conversion, ordination and a degree from the University of Makerere and later to be chaplain of the university. He was consecrated by Archbishop Janani Luwum. It was the great demonstration of Christian fervour that day, and some things which were said in the sermon by Bishop Festo Kivengere and misinterpreted by the soldiers present which led, a few weeks later, to the Archbishop's murder and to the loosing of a wave of persecution upon the Church. For several months Bishop Bamunoba hid in the woods and hills of his diocese, secretly cared for by his people. He spent the time in planning the future of the diocese. When things quietened down a little, he came out of hiding and presented himself to the district governor.

In 1979 Amin was at last overthrown by a civil war and a Tanzanian invasion but that was not the end of Uganda's troubles by any means. A couple of years of highly indecisive government was followed by the return of Milton Obote, the former President overthrown by Amin and himself a tyrant of lesser proportions. His support had always come principally from Anglicans and it did so again, especially in West Ankole, where his plane actually landed on its return from exile. Perhaps fortunately the Bishop was out of the country at the time and so did not join in the welcome. Obote's return to power was achieved by a rigged election and led to further unrest, his overthrow and yet another civil war. At last, in 1986, a very much more stable and acceptable government was established under Yoweri Museveni. The economy and the political and administrative structures, even the road system of Uganda, had crumbled fearfully in these long years of tyranny, civil war and social confusion — a confusion for which Christians had to bear a fair part of the blame. In this, too, Uganda was not so different from many other parts of Africa in the 1970s and 1980s. Yet the diocese of West Ankole grew and grew. Where it had 32 parishes in 1977, it had 99 in 1990.

After Lambeth 1988, Bishop Bamunoba felt that he needed a sabbatical to think about things: the problems, strengths, needs of his diocese. So he came to the University of Leeds and wrote a fresh and informative MPhil thesis on the subject, which is why western Ankole is so vividly in my mind. The thesis is completed and the Bishop is back in Bushenyi. The Church in Ankole is far from perfect, but it is alive, poor, relevant, full of faith and fellowship, and growing fast. Yet it is only one of more than 120 Anglican dioceses in Africa. Perhaps they have not all grown quite like that, but many have. In many parts they continue to multiply. 'A young Church in a young country full of young people', declared Runcie, preaching at Francis-town in Botswana. 'You fill me with hope.'

If Runcie was present at Archbishop Ndahura's enthronement in Bukavu in 1980, so was he present at Archbishop Okoth's in Kampala in 1984, and Archbishop Desmond Tutu's in Cape Town in 1986. Visiting Africa almost every year, he has witnessed the growth and the struggle, the hopes and the fears, the superb relevance of a gospel of cross and resurrection to a society as torn apart as that of much of Africa. If Archbishop Tutu is the best known Anglican bishop in the world today, it is not just because he is a wise, courageous, merry person who has managed to take over the leadership of the Church in South Africa and preach the gospel of both liberation and reconcilia-tion at a time of political crisis when the world's eyes are focused upon his country. It is also because he has a huge constituency behind him, of black Anglicans and black Christians of many other Churches, and the confidence that comes from being so placed. He, like Bishop Sigisbert Nwandwe, the Suffragan Bishop of Johannesburg who has twice been in detention, or Jerome Bamunoba in Uganda or Bishop Sengulane of Mozambique, has come through fire, his people with him. That gives authority.

Most of the Anglican provinces in Africa are within what used to be the British Empire, countries in which the official language, or at least the language of higher education, most often remains English. It is important, however, to remind ourselves that English is not the language of the people or of worship in these countries. The Anglican Communion has long ceased to be a network of English-speaking Churches. The Eucharist is celebrated in very many languages in Tanzania and Malawi, Uganda and Zimbabwe, Nigeria and Botswana. Relatively rarely is it English. But there are also an increasing number of dioceses and provinces where it will never be English. Within Africa, it will never be so in the Province of Rwanda, Burundi and Zaire. Elsewhere, it will never be so in Japan, Korea, Brazil or Burma. Lambeth 1978 was the first in which a simultaneous translation system was in use. At Lambeth 1988, the Primate of Canada, on the day he presided over the Conference, used French to press the point of the multi-linguistic character the Communion now possesses.

Over the last twenty years, provinces have multiplied. Thus in 1970 the Province of East Africa (created in 1960) was divided into two — Kenya and Tanzania. In 1973 the Province of the Indian Ocean was formed (centred in Mauritius). In 1975 it was the turn of Melanesia and in 1976 of Jerusalem and the Middle East — also of Sudan. In 1977 came Papua New Guinea. In 1979 Nigeria became a province separate from the rest of West Africa (Ghana, Gambia, Sierra Leone and Liberia). In 1980 Burundi, Rwanda and Zaire separated from Uganda. In 1990 the Province of the Philippines was formed. At present Malaysia, Korea and Hong Kong are linked in the Council for the Churches of East Asia, but the Archbishop of Canterbury remains their Metropolitan. It will probably not be long before Korea and Malaysia become separate provinces, indeed one of Runcie's tasks these last few years has been that of preparing them for autonomy, his status of Metropolitan in Churches where he is inevitably 'remote and alien' being in his view 'a serious anomaly'.

The four Churches of South India, North India, Pakistan and Bangladesh have taken a different route. Technically they are not provinces of the Anglican Communion. They are united Churches created in the early post-war period and including former Anglican dioceses which left the Anglican Communion in order to unite with other Protestant Churches locally. This was a characteristic ecumenical model of forty years ago, which put local unity first — and not unreasonably, especially in missionary circumstances. It had, however, a somewhat Protestant ethos and it was sad that its consequence was to weaken international ties, especially in the Anglican Communion. It inevitably eliminated any specific Anglican (or Methodist or whatever) presence in an area. In consequence, while the subcontinent of India had earlier been a principal Anglican missionary field, the modern development of the Anglican Communion has entirely excluded it in theory. If this model had been successfully applied elsewhere, there would — for better or worse — be no world-wide Anglican Communion today. However, many attempts to follow along the same ecumenical lines elsewhere, and especially in Africa, have almost invariably failed. While the Church of South India was at the time rightly hailed as an outstanding ecumenical achievement and a sign of things to come, it proved to be a model which, even in England, it was found too costly to adopt. It derived perhaps from an over-simplified form of ecumenical thinking. As Runcie insisted in a lecture in Bangalore on 'A Global Perspective' for unity, 'there are some perfectly proper reasons why national unity schemes are thought of as less than the fulness of unity Christ wills for his people'. They lack a necessary element of catholicity represented by an international communion of Churches. Full ecumenism needs both dimensions.

What has now happened, with Runcie's encouragement, has been the quiet reincorporation of these united Churches within the Anglican Communion (but still in communion too with other parent

Churches). During the 1980s they have been represented, and increasingly actively, at all meetings of the Anglican Consultative Council as well as at Lambeth. As Runcie remarked at the ACC meeting at Singapore, 'There has been an Indian shaped gap in our family life we are now trying to fill'. Actually the co-ordinator of the preparatory theological studies for Lambeth 1988 was Bishop Michael Nazir-Ali, himself a member of the Church of Pakistan. In 1968 and 1978, the Churches of South India, North India, Pakistan and Bangladesh were each represented at Lambeth by a sole 'Observer'. In 1988 South India, by contrast, was represented by six fully voting members, North India by five, Pakistan by three and Bangladesh by one. This is one of the most striking, but least heralded, effective changes of the 1980s and one particularly close to Runcie's heart with his strong Indian affections. His considerable visits to the Churches of North and South India in 1986 and to those of Pakistan and Bangladesh in 1990 represent this concern. The reincorporation of a full Indian dimension is certainly of great importance for the universality and cultural balance of the Communion, and it was further formalized when Lambeth invited the four Primates of these Churches to join the regular meeting of Primates, which they did for the first time in Cyprus in April 1989. This is not, Runcie has insisted, 'to undo' the ecumenical unions of forty years ago. Rather the presence of 'United Churches' within Anglican Councils should emphasize that 'the hope of union' must be at the centre of everyone's self-understanding.

At Lambeth 1958 the Anglican Communion still appeared overwhelmingly as white, Anglo-Saxon and even (apart from the large American contingent) English. Many of the bishops coming from other parts were in fact English. That was true not only for 'missionary' dioceses but for many old-established ones in English-speaking areas. Thus the first non-English Archbishop of Cape Town was Bill Burnett, appointed in 1974. Even non-English bishops tended to have gained their theological education at Oxford or Cambridge. Thirty years later attendance at Lambeth 1988 was very different. The new life in the Third World Church which had long been sprouting had now fully blossomed forth and the whole balance of the Communion had changed from North to South, from white to non-white, from the first-language English-speaker to those for whom it was either a second language or none at all. While undoubtedly, the 'North', and England in particular, retained much of the theological leadership, it no longer led so clearly in moral leadership or missionary dynamism.

The Communion thus reshaped has obviously required new and rather more formal structures to link it effectively together. It can no longer be held together by its Englishness, by the use of an almost uniform Book of Common Prayer or even by an unquestioning acceptance of the final authority of Canterbury such as largely characterized its members in the past. More has been needed. The deepest underlying problem of the Anglican Communion as a real unity most probably remains the great gap in tradition between England on the one hand and the United States upon the other.

The relationship of an Archbishop of Canterbury to the Episcopal Church of the United States has always been a subtle one. His was part of the authority of the English State rejected by Americans in the War of Independence. The American Church could hardly not remain opposed to any formal exercise of patriarchal authority by Canterbury over the Anglican Communion. Yet the Archbishop shares in the mystique of the British monarchy which is so characteristic of modern America. He is the person who crowns the sovereign, who marries the prince. There remains a very deep Englishness to American culture and loyalties, especially of a symbolic sort. The very fact that in the American Episcopal Church order there is no archbishop, actually enhances the quasi-patriarchal character of the one archbishop they still know about and defer to in honour. This is all the more the case if he frequently visits the United States and is seen as someone of special spiritual authority. Ramsey and Runcie, in particular, have both been felt in the States as people possessing outstanding charisma, to be listened to with exceptional deference. In a way the personal authority of the Archbishop of Canterbury may be actually greater in America than it is in England because it is not belittled, as it so often is in England, by a hostile press or the votes of General Synod disregarding his advice. Different as Anglicanism is on the two sides of the Atlantic, the office of the Archbishop of Canterbury, at least when filled with someone sensitive to this aspect of his role, remains one of the more important unifying organs between the two traditions.

On account of its history the American Episcopal Church acquired a far more Congregationalist and Protestant ethos than the Churches of Britain. In modern times it has also become rather more bureaucratic. Its numbers are relatively small but the number of its bishops and its financial power may seem disproportionately great. Since Randall Davidson, Archbishops of Canterbury have regularly visited the United States but probably none has put more into strengthening the English–American entente than Runcie. While the ordination of women has been seen as the principal threat to unity and discussed as such, this far deeper issue, involving as it does almost amorphous strands of religious culture as well as of ecclesiology, has seldom been examined very openly. It will perhaps, in due course, be surmounted by the growing ascendancy of a 'third force', the Churches of the southern hemisphere. How far, hitherto, has this particular diversity of tradition genuinely enriched the Communion? How far has it, on the contrary, paralysed it?

The last thirty years have seen a mounting effort to establish organs of unity to hold the Communion together. Without this effort it is rather probable that by now even the Lambeth Conference would have been abandoned. Already in 1958 the Conference established the post of full-time 'Executive Officer' of the Communion. The first to be appointed (in 1960) was Stephen Bayne, an American bishop. He was intended to be a 'servant of all the Churches equally' within the Communion, and was succeeded in 1964 by Bishop Ralph Dean, a Canadian, who became secretary of Lambeth 1968. However, one man (plus a rather shadowy 'Lambeth Consultative Body' which had existed in theory since the beginning of the century but hardly, if ever, met) was not enough, and the 1968 Conference proposed the establishment instead of a new 'Anglican Consultative Council' which was due to meet every two to three years, to include laity and priests as well as bishops, and to represent all parts of the Communion. Bishop John Howe took over from Dean, the title of his office being changed to 'Secretary General' of the Consultative Council, which met for the first time at Limuru in Kenya in February 1971. 'Consultative' was a good word. It could not dictate but if a motley collection of autonomous Churches were not to fall very far apart, they would need to do a lot of consulting.

By the time of the Lambeth Conference of 1978, the ACC had met three times (Limuru, Dublin and Trinidad). Its basic role was recognized as indispensable but it was also seen to be somewhat inadequate. The structural shape of the Communion had still not developed adequately in the 1970s to cope with its enlarged scale. Lambeth 1978 was only decided upon rather late, was poorly prepared and not exceptionally satisfactory as a meeting. This was by no means Archbishop Coggan's fault. He was only enthroned as Archbishop of Canterbury in January 1975, by which time the preparations for a conference should already have been well under way. In fact it was only definitely decided to have a conference at all in March 1976 at the Trinidad ACC meeting. Coggan wisely decided to move it from London to Canterbury — to make it in fact no longer a Lambeth Conference but a Canterbury Conference — but he was to retire not long after the Conference and was therefore unable to lead the Communion forward in the way that was now needed. His principal address to the Conference on the subject of authority gave a somewhat negative impression as he played down in turn the idea of a more patriarchal role for Canterbury, the authority of the Lambeth Conference and that of the Anglican Consultative Council. He did, however, helpfully propose yet another body — a regular meeting of the Primates of the Communion, to be linked if possible with the ACC. It was agreed to, and the first Primates' Meeting took place just before his retirement, John Howe becoming secretary of this too, as he had been of the Lambeth Conference.

Thus Runcie, in 1980, took over the presidency of a much more extensive international structure for the Communion than had existed previously. He did not create this structure or greatly alter it, but he did make it work, using it most effectively to strengthen the Communion's sense of inter-dependence while preparing very well in advance for the Lambeth Conference of 1988.

In one way at least the structure seems to have remained less than satisfactory. The ACC consists of three representatives from the larger provinces (one bishop, one priest, one lay person) and two or one from the smaller ones chosen as they like. While, theoretically, this 'synodical' (bishop/priest/lay) pattern is attractive, in practical terms it has its disadvantages. One priest or one lay person from a country has limited representative function and probably little if any authority to carry the ACC's message effectively forward. A 'synodical' structure with such small numbers and an advisory role means rather little. Moreover many Churches send one or two people only and almost invariably choose a bishop, quite often the Primate. The pattern of the 1980s has consisted, roughly speaking, of meetings of the ACC one year, the Primates the next. In practice, the overlap is considerable as so many Primates represent their countries on the ACC while the number of priests and laity remains so small. While a regular Primates' Meeting is something newer than the ACC, it is proving more effective in bringing together the people with the greatest authority throughout the Communion. More and more, Runcie has tended to channel his wider strategy through it. For the future, the two will, doubtless, be increasingly closely co-ordinated. As both are serviced by the same secretariat based in London at Partnership House and headed by Canon Sam Van Culin, an American from Hawaii, this should not be difficult. It is worthy of note that Runcie invited the ACC to meet at Canterbury at the same time as the Lambeth Conference, both to ensure that it was in no way left out and to help strengthen for the future the bonding between it and specifically episcopal meetings. While the Lambeth Conference as such has only bishops, its strength is that every diocese in the Communion is thereby represented and by its principal pastor. While it is important to go on supplementing this internationally with lay and priestly participation at the ACC level, the problem of numbers and expense ensures that the principal linking of the Communion can only be done efficiently at episcopal and primatial levels. Runcie clearly recognized this and has consistently striven to enhance the significance of the role of Primate and the relationship of Primates between themselves.

Runcie proposed that he call a Lambeth Conference in 1988 to the Primates' Meeting in Limuru in 1983. Bit by bit a pattern of four themes was hammered out by the Primates: Mission and Ministry, Dogmatic and Pastoral concerns, Ecumenical Relations, Christianity and the Social Order. These were taken up by the ACC in both their sixth and seventh meetings (Badagry, Nigeria, in 1984 and Singapore in 1987) and in regional meetings in Africa, North and South America, Asia and Europe. But above all, bishops were expected to have discussed them at length with their dioceses making use of the preparatory studies put together under the direction of Bishop Nazir-Ali. Runcie had invited the bishops to bring their dioceses with them to the Conference and it was this that was made possible by the length and scale of preparatory work undertaken. It is generally agreed that the 1988 assembly was the best prepared of all Lambeth Conferences. The preparation was justified by the manifest sense of success it generated, a sense too that doubts about the purpose and cost of the Conference, freely expressed after the 1968 and 1978 meetings, had been laid to rest. This was in a very real way the central and overriding concern of Runcie throughout the decade: a reinforcement of the conviction that the Communion was, and would remain, united despite strains over the ordination of women or whatever, that the Lambeth Conference was worthwhile, and that an adequate model of authority was being developed to lead and hold united the Communion in the future.

The issue of authority was indeed, in Runcie's mind at least, the most important that the Lambeth Conference and Anglicanism generally had to face. It had been the subject for his first Primates' Meeting, held in Washington in 1981. This was chosen in response to a resolution of Lambeth 1978 requesting the Primates 'to initiate a study of the nature of authority within the Anglican Communion'. Besides the more official preparatory material, a major volume of essays was published in 1987 entitled *Authority in the Anglican Communion*. They were dedicated to John Howe and edited by Stephen Sykes, the Cambridge theologian for whom Runcie had a very considerable respect and who would become Bishop of Ely two years after the Conference. The aim here as elsewhere was to develop both a theory and a practice of Church authority, 'dispersed' but not non-existent.

It is clear that Anglicanism has not, and will not have, a papal form of authority. Equally, it has recognized that scripture alone cannot be sufficient. The Church has to decide about many things which are either not referred to at all in scripture or not in a way which is unambiguous for subsequent times. Doubtless authority in the Church is the authority of the Spirit within the Church, but the Spirit can only guide the Church through bishops or synods or prophets or the consensus of the laity or whatever. Through which? In practice historic Anglicanism was limited in any answer it could give by the fact that it was the established Church of England and had no independence of parliament. It held to bishops against both the Pope upon the one hand and Presbyterians and Congregationalists upon the other, but it did not think that bishops were together infallible — certainly not British bishops on their own, and probably not all bishops gathered ecumenically. In the course of the nineteenth century the tension within Britain over ecclesiastical authority between the State upon the one hand and the Church's own organs on the other inevitably grew, as the State became more secular and elements within the Church, both Catholic and Protestant, more restive. Outside England, where by 1920 no Church of the Communion remained tied to civil authority, a balance of episcopal and synodical government had been established within each province. Traditionally there was little in Anglican tradition or practice to shape a pattern of Church authority above the level of the individual bishop, although some jurisdiction of an archbishop over other bishops was admitted. What was important in the nineteenth and early twentieth centuries was the development of the synodical collective authority of the province, a 'local Church' wider than the diocese.

Hitherto, Anglican ecclesiology has hardly gone further than that. The Lambeth Conference has had a merely consultative character not infringing, everyone has been careful to insist, provincial 'autonomy'. But total 'autonomy' or the 'independence' of any part of the Church is not very good ecclesiology. Better than 'independence' is 'interdependence'. Churches belong to one another. Anglicanism has sensed the need but not known, beyond the claims of consultation and charity, how to respond. The issue of the ordination of women has brought the problem more sharply into focus but so has the Roman Catholic rediscovery in the 1960s at the Vatican Council of the idea

147

of 'collegiality' — a collective responsibility of the episcopate, not merely within one province, but for the Church as a whole, a continuation of the collective responsibility of the Apostles in the very early Church. Lambeth 1968, in its sector report on 'Renewal in Unity', took over the idea of collegiality without specifying its implications. The 'college of bishops' within the Anglican Communion, it further asserted, must have a president and that presidency is 'at present held by the occupant of the historic see of Canterbury, who enjoys a primacy of honour, not of jurisdiction'.

Runcie's problem has been how to meet the need for an effective collegiality without papacy, patriarchate or even the possibility of conciliar decision-making. The provinces have gone too far down the road of autonomy to be willing to accept any juridical supra-provincial authority at this stage. The functioning of collegiality has essentially to be within the moral rather than the juridical order, yet it would be a mere will-o-the-wisp if it did not have structures, sufficiently complex and well-recognized, to ensure that individual Churches can recognize the process of collegiality at work and feel, therefore, impelled to abide by it. Collegiality, moreover, needs to be seen as the institutional expression of the Communion, or *Koinonia*, which really constitutes the very heart of the Church's meaning: communion or fellowship with God and with one another. 'Communion' and 'collegiality' were key words for the Second Vatican Council, and 'Communion' especially has passed across to become a key word in the theology of ARCIC. Its latest Agreed Statement is devoted to a study of the Church *as* Communion. It is no new word for Anglicans, yet its central theological use is fairly new. It is characteristic of the way that the Second Vatican Council marked out the lines of convergence for the future, even if in practice the Roman Catholic Church has not subsequently followed those lines as closely as many had hoped. Certainly the Anglicanism of Lambeth 1988 is a post-Vatican II Anglicanism which does not make it in any way substantially unfaithful to the Anglicanism of the past.

The Lambeth Conference in July 1988 was the greatest moment in Runcie's archiepiscopate: the moment at which the long journeys, the many meetings of Primates and the ACC, and the multi-dimensional theological preparation were vindicated. He worked throughout the Conference quite incessantly. Despite the predictions that the ordination of women would tear the Communion and even the Conference apart, it quite failed to do so. It did not do so partly because there was no major Church within the Communion absolutely committed to not ordaining women. If England still continued to refuse to do so, a large majority of its bishops were all the same in favour and it remained upon the English agenda. It did not do so because in the context of the great southern growth of the Communion and the sort of life and death concerns the African bishops brought to the Conference the issue was relativized as, at least in its urgency, a 'Northern' matter. The South was certainly not uniformly against but it was not wildly in favour either. Both enthusiasts for women's ordination and die hard opponents had to recognize that the common mind of the Communion at its most lively was somewhere else. This did not make the ordination of women unimportant but it did mean that any attempt to press the matter too hard would be deeply unwelcome to the large middle ground. Finally, the issue failed to rend the Conference too damagingly because the preparation for the Conference had been so focused upon the deeper issues of communion and authority by Runcie's steady steering that the ordination of women fell into a more manageable place within these wider horizons.

The most authoritative single piece of teaching Archbishop Runcie has given is probably his opening address to the Conference, 'The Nature of the Unity we seek'. So important is it that we need to quote it here at some length. It provides the central core of his theology of the Church and of pastoral practice too: the point at which God and humanity, Church and world, ecumenism and social action all come together. It constitutes the high ground of the whole argument, a ground at once for idealism and for a fair measure of pragmatism too.

In the Book of Revelation we are given a vision: a new heaven and a new earth, and the holy city, New Jerusalem, coming down from God out of heaven. Here is God's disclosure of the unity of the whole human family. The Lord God Almighty and the Lamb are the central focus of the holy City. All the nations shall walk in the light of the glory of God and of the Lamb. The Kings of the earth shall bring with them the glory and honour of the nations. *And the gates of the City shall not be shut* (Rev 21.22–27). Exclusiveness is not a characteristic of the City of God.

In this vision there is ultimately no difference between the quest for the Church's unity and the quest for human healing in the widest sense. The Church is the model towards which the whole human family will look for its healing and reconciliation. To the degree that the Church is effectively gathered in unity in the assembly of worship around God and the Lamb, it is the sign of hope and the bearer of good news to the whole world.

Neither the Church nor the world 'sets the agenda': God has *his* agenda of shalom, unity and communion. *We* must seek to be loyal to it. So the question of Christian unity always needs to be considered in the light of what it is *for*. What would be the value of unanimity without purpose? Human unity is the goal of God's mission to his creation — though in relation to the Lamb on the throne. Christian unity is part of our share in that mission, the sending of God's Son and his Gospel and his Church to the ends of the world. . . .

. . . At this plenary assembly of the Lambeth Conference, I see in so many of you the personal embodiment of God's mission to a broken and divided world. As Anglican bishops, bishops in full communion, and as ecumenical observers, you come with wounds humanity cannot by itself heal: the wounds of Southern Africa and Uganda, Sudan and Ethiopia; the wounds of the Philippines, Korea and Sri Lanka; of Nicaragua, of South America; of Jerusalem and the Middle East; the wounds of Ireland; the great global wounds of distrust between East and West, and the increasing disparity between North and South. Look at each other also as fellow citizens of the heavenly city, as those who worship the Lamb and who are thus constituted within Christ's Church as a sign of hope for the whole human race, the bearers of the Gospel of reconciliation.

Unity within the Anglican Communion

I want to begin what I say about unity within the Anglican Communion with a strong affirmation of gratitude. Our mood is eucharistic, in spite of the conflict and debate we must realistically anticipate. We give thanks to God for our communion with him and with each other as Anglican Christians. As I travel around the Anglican Communion I am filled with enthusiasm for what I see and hear, and especially for the people I meet at the local level.

I think of a hispanic 'street' celebration of the eucharist on the West Coast of the USA; of the consecration of four new churches on one boiling hot day in the outback of Australia; of the indomitable enthusiasm and valour of the Church in South Africa at Archbishop Desmond's enthronement; of the beauty and reverence of worship in Japan; and of the fresh idealism of young Anglicans at their meeting in Northern Ireland. Many of you could tell similar stories, especially from Partnership in Mission consultations and the regional preparatory meetings for this Lambeth Conference.

So I have had to say with some vigour to the British press of late that the Anglican Communion is not about to dissolve. And to the Church of England Synod that it is a little early to be taking the covers off the lifeboats and abandoning ship.

So let us maintain the note of joy and thanksgiving with which we began the Conference at the eucharist yesterday and with which we begin each day. The ecumenical presence among us is also a sign of mutual confidence and trust. Our partners in the Gospel may have their problems with us, though they also say to us, 'There are good things in the Anglican Communion'.

But I want to say too that we must never make the survival of the Anglican Communion an end in itself. The Churches of the Anglican Communion have never claimed to be more than a part of the One Holy Catholic and Apostolic Church. Anglicanism has a radically provisional character which we must never allow to be obscured.

One of the characteristic features of Anglicanism is our Reformation inheritance of national or provincial autonomy. The Anglican tradition is thus opposed to centralism and encourages the thriving of variety. This is a great good. There is an important principle to be borne witness to here: that nothing should be done at a higher level than is absolutely necessary.

So Anglicans have become accustomed to speak of a dispersed authority. And we are traditionally suspicious of the Lambeth Conference becoming anything other than a Conference. We may indeed wish to discuss the development of more solid structures of unity and coherence. But I for one would want their provisional character made absolutely clear; like tents in the desert, they should be capable of being easily dismantled when it is time for the Pilgrim People to move on. We have no intention of developing an alternative Papacy. We would rather continue to deal with the structures of the existing Petrine Ministry, and hopefully help in its continuing development and reform as a ministry of unity for all Christians.

But Anglican unity itself is most characteristically expressed in terms of worship. Here we have much in common with the Eastern churches, whose very name implies a unity through right worship — *Orthodoxy*. This is a proper corrective to an over-institutional view of Christian unity and to an over-intellectual understanding of unity through assent to confessional formulae.

In liturgical worship the Scriptures are proclaimed, the Creed is confessed, the Sacraments are celebrated, and all is given order through an authorized episcopal ministry. You will recognize here the elements of the Chicago–Lambeth Quadrilateral, first formulated one hundred years ago. It is a description of the cohesive ingredients of the worshipping community, the glue which binds us together.

Nevertheless, I do not wish to sound complacent. There are real and serious threats to our unity and communion and I do not underestimate them. Some of them are the result of Gospel insights; for example the proper dignity of women in a Christian society. We need to recognize that our unity is threatened over the ordination of women to the priesthood and episcopate in *whatever we ultimately decide to do*. There are dangers to our communion in this Lambeth Conference endorsing or failing to endorse such developments. And there are equal dangers to communion by trying to avoid the issue together.

Such conflict is particularly painful, because the glue which binds us together is not so much juridical, but personal, informal and expressed in worship. An impairment of communion for Anglicans is not essentially about canon law but at the much deeper personal level of sharing in the eucharistic worship of the Holy Trinity. So we tend to shy away from a conflict which has such destructive potential. This is of course a serious mistake.

We need to recognize the persistence and place of conflict in Christian history. There has never been sharper conflict among Christ's people than the great debate over the admission of the Gentiles to the Church without the ceremonial law. Think of Paul withstanding Peter to the face (Gal 2.11). Nor were the early Ecumenical Councils of the Church any easier. Tempers blazed on the doctrines of the person of Christ and the Holy Trinity, charges and counter-charges were levelled, coalitions were formed. At the Council of Ephesus the monk Shenouda hurled a copy of the Gospels at Nestorius. A gesture at once orthodox and effective, for it struck him on the chest and bowled him over! Mind you, I'm not advocating this as a procedural device here.

And yet in and through such unholy conflict the Church eventually, and never without difficulty, came to a common mind. Through the initiatives of prophets and primates, the deliberations of synods, and the active response of the whole Church, the Holy Spirit has been at work. Conflict can be destructive. It can also be creative. We are not here to avoid conflict but to redeem it. At the heart of our faith is a cross and not, as in some religions, an eternal calm.

The creative use of conflict is part of the process of discerning the truth. As the Rabbinic scriptures put it, 'controversies for the sake of heaven'. This is not to propagate polemics but to explore truth. There is a constant dialogue here between revelation and culture in every age. Tradition is not archaeology but the contemporary expression of 'the faith which was once delivered unto the saints' (Jude 3). Consistency with Scripture and continuity with the past there must be. But this does not entail the mere duplication of the past.

So the Church has a living tradition which develops and grows in the tension between that which has been given and the present experience of the community. At the Lambeth Conference the Anglican Communion tries to discern what is of the Spirit, and what is not, and to express this in a living voice. Conflict, then, far from being an unmitigated evil, is, if handled creatively, an essential part of our understanding of the processes whereby the Church speaks with a living voice today.

In any case the problem that confronts us as Anglicans arises not from conflict over the ordination of women as such, but from the relationship of independent provinces with each other. Although we have machinery for dealing with problems within a diocese and within a Province, we have few for those which exist within the Communion as a whole.

Another reason for looking critically at the notion of the absolute independence of Provinces arises from our ecumenical dialogues with worldwide communions. These require decision and action at more than provincial level. And our own experience as a world Communion also teaches us the importance of a global perspective at a time when political concerns for 'national security' often militate against international co-operation and diminish the significance of world organizations such as the United Nations.

The New Testament speaks more in terms of *interdependence* than *independence*. The relationship of Jesus with the Father in the bond of the Holy Spirit as witnessed in St John's Gospel surely gives us the pattern of Christian relationship. Life together in communion implies basic trust and mutuality. Think of Paul speaking of life in the Body in his first letter to the Corinthians: 'The eye cannot say to the hand, I have no need for you, nor again the head to the feet, I have no need of you' (1 Cor 12.21). The good of the Body requires mutual recognition and deference in Christ. Or think of Paul's collection for the saints in Jerusalem, a practical expression of communion on the theological ground of unity in Christ.

The idea of interdependence is not new to Anglicanism. The Toronto Conference of 1963 which gave us the slogan 'mutual responsibility and interdependence in the Body of Christ' also gave birth to the whole Partners in Mission process. But the full consequence of such mutual responsibility and interdependence have hardly yet been realized. It has taken the conflict over the ordination of women to point up the implications for the Communion. Here is powerful illustration of the fact that conflict has creative potential.

It can be put this way: are we being called through events and their theological interpretation to move from independence to interdependence? If we answer yes, then we cannot dodge the question of how this is to be given 'flesh': how is our interdependence articulated and made effective; how is it to be structured? Without losing a proper — but perhaps modified — provincial autonomy this will probably mean a critical examination of the notion of 'dispersed authority'. We need to have confidence that authority is not dispersed to the point of dissolution and ineffectiveness.

Should our answer be 'yes' to a minimum structuring of our mutual interdependence — that which is actually *required* for the maintenance of communion and no more — we would in fact be challenging the alarming isolationism and impatience I detect on both sides of the debate about the ordination of women. We would challenge not only the 'go it alone' attitudes of enterprising independence but also the 'I and only I am left' attitudes of those who believe they are the sole repositories of 'true' Anglicanism.

Let me put it in starkly simple terms: do we really *want* unity within the Anglican Communion? Is our worldwide family of Christians worth bonding together? *Or* is our paramount concern the preservation or promotion of that particular expression of Anglicanism which has developed within the culture of our own province? Wouldn't it be easier and more realistic to work towards exclusively European, or North American, or African, or Pacific forms of Anglicanism? Yes, it might. Cultural adaptation would be easier. Mission would be easier. Local ecumenism would be easier. Do we actually need a worldwide Communion?

I believe we do because Anglicans believe in the One Holy Catholic and Apostolic Church of the Creed. I believe we do because we live in one world created and redeemed by God. I believe we do because it is only by being in communion *together* that diversity and difference have value. Without relationship difference divides.

This is why I have called the present Lambeth Conference. This is why I have visited many of the Provinces of the Anglican Communion in solidarity with both your joys and your sufferings. I have tried to be a personal and visible presence of the whole Anglican family in places like the Province of Southern Africa where solidarity between the worldwide Church and particular Christians is a Gospel imperative if ever there was one.

So I believe we still need the Anglican Communion. But we have reached the stage in the growth of the Communion when we must begin to make radical choices, or growth will imperceptibly turn to decay. I believe the choice between independence and interdependence, already set before us as a Communion in embryo twenty-five years ago, is quite simply the choice between unity or gradual fragmentation. It would be a gentle, even genteel, fragmentation. That much of Englishness still remains. Nor would it be instant. As I have said, the Communion is not about to disappear tomorrow. But decisive choice is before us. Do we want the Anglican Communion? And if we do, what are we going to do about it?

Lambeth's response to this appeal lay principally in two areas. On the one side, it accepted that the ordination of women did divide the Communion but that it must not be allowed to do so to the point of schism and it requested Runcie to appoint a commission to report precisely on the relationship between communion and women in the episcopate. On the other side, it set out with clarity the 'Embodiments and Agents of Unity' whereby communion and a more than provincial authority would, for the future, be guarded. These 'embodiments' had already been well defined in an important discussion paper (Appendix 5 of *The Truth Shall Make You Free*, the Conference Report) which had gone through several drafts. 'Provinces of the Anglican Communion are certainly autonomous in the legal sense, but exactly how far does autonomy extend in the theological and moral sense?' it had asked. Just as divine authority in the Church is 'dispersed' in its sources, so is the exercise of authority 'dispersed' within the Church — at diocesan, provincial and international level. But it does not collectively exist the less for being dispersed.

At the level of the Anglican Communion, the Conference, in line with the developed thinking of the previous years, found four 'embodiments' or 'agents of unity' — the Archbishop of Canterbury, the Lambeth Conference, the Anglican Consultative Council and the Meeting of Primates. It is the role of the last that the Conference particularly wished to see further 'enhanced'. It remains juridically a consultative role but it seems clearly to be through regular meetings of the Primates that 'the universal coherence of the communion' may best be safeguarded and 'episcopal collegiality' exercised. The Primates may constitute, as the ACC really cannot, a quasi-authoritative central cabinet, the appropriate context for Canterbury's own quasi-patriarchal 'primacy'. It is certainly not patriarchal in a formal sense, and the use of the word, while appropriate, would doubtless still not be generally acceptable. It is a focus of unity, a 'primacy of honour', a task which does include the 'care of all the Churches', but a care which is based on service and not on the power to coerce, a role which includes the provision of leadership and of a 'personal' international ministry, in Runcie's own words 'to gather the Churches not to rule them'. All that surely adds up to a 'quasi-patriarchate'.

Runcie recognizes that all this is still provisional, appropriately enough for a 'provisional' communion. He went on in his presidential address to speak of the papacy and

> the question of an episcopal primacy in the Universal Church: an instrument of unity we have been lacking since Henry VIII's juridical break with Rome in the sixteenth century. . . . Our own Anglican experience of belonging to a world communion points to the need of a personal focus of unity and affection. . . . Could not all Christians come to reconsider the kind of primacy exercised within the Early Church, a 'presiding in love' for the sake of the unity of the Churches?

This is an appeal not only to Anglicans and to Roman Catholics but to the Orthodox and to Protestants too, to 'all Christians'. Its realization would probably involve a greater practical change on the part of Roman Catholics than of anyone else. Of course, Runcie realizes, it is impractical *now*. But 'now' changes. He is speaking from his *Cathedra*, the chair of an authority which extends more widely in Christendom than any other except the papal. He is speaking as the man who fittingly presided over the World Council of Churches' Eucharist at its General Assembly in Vancouver. And he is speaking to over 500 bishops of his Communion, his quasi-patriarchate. It is a solemn moment and he uses it to appeal for the acceptance of the universal primacy of the Petrine see from which initially Canterbury itself was founded. It is an appeal to the Orthodox and to Protestants as well to accept a primacy, an appeal to Rome to abandon a primacy of power and jurisdiction for a primacy of love.

What Runcie is saying is that there is not one form of unity appropriate to Anglicans, another to Catholics, a third to Calvinists. The internal unity of a communion and the re-establishment of unity between existing traditions and communions are all part of the same game, a game which must combine the provisionality of a 'now' with a vision of totality and fullness. Runcie still does not think the Anglican 'embodiments of unity' he has worked so hard to get effectively working are wholly adequate; he cannot think it quite right that 'there are canonical and juridical arrangements which control the autonomy of the diocese within each province' but 'no canonical or juridical arrangements which control the autonomy of the provinces'. He would inwardly prefer even now to go a little further in the overcoming of the old stress upon 'autonomy'. But pragmatically he knows that this is impossible at least for the present. He has gone as far as he can go and with that he has to be satisfied.

Coping with the immediate 'impairment' of communion is another matter. Shortly after Lambeth the diocese of Massachusetts elected Barbara Harris as a suffragan bishop. In 1990 the diocese of Dunedin in New Zealand elected Penelope Jamieson as its diocesan bishop. It was clear at Lambeth that such developments were likely to take place. It was also clear that many other people, including bishops and provinces, would not be able to accept them. Male priests ordained by Barbara Harris or Penelope Jamieson will not be accepted as priests in many dioceses of the Communion, any more than would women priests. That is a considerable impairment of communion within the Communion. Moreover in provinces, notably in the States, in which the ordaining of women is fully accepted and a regular practice, there is a great danger of effectively excommunicating Anglicans who insist on adhering to the traditional practice of the Church of an all-male priesthood — at least until greater consensus has been reached than at present upon the rightness of a change. They may be theologically mistaken, old-fashioned, culturally chauvinist, but on what ground can a provincial authority rightly exclude them from communion and pastoral care by only offering them that which they cannot accept? On traditional Anglican principles, the synodical authority of a province or a Church may be autonomous but it is certainly not infallible. Yet, now, acceptance of its decisions may in practice become a condition for continued communion, at least unless suitable alternative pastoral arrangements are made. If women bishops multiply in some parts of the Communion but go on being rejected in others, if there are some twenty by Lambeth 1998 but the Church of England continues not to recognize them, then it will indeed be hard to claim that in sacramental reality this is still a single Communion.

It was to consider these very grave issues that the Lambeth Conference requested Runcie to appoint a special commission. Archbishop Eames of Armagh, the Primate of All Ireland, chaired it. The value of its conclusions lies in its balanced used of the concept of 'communion'. It was in fact the Second Vatican Council which asserted that one is not necessarily simply in communion or out of communion with someone else; there is instead the possibility of degrees of communion. 'Communion' (and do we really have absolutely full communion with anyone?) may be impaired to a greater or lesser extent. Thus there is an 'almost full communion' between Constantinople and Rome, rather less between Canterbury and Rome but still a great deal — enough to enable them to recognize each other as 'sister Churches' — and so on.

The Eames Report recognizes that there is indeed 'an actual diminishment of the degree of communion amongst the Provinces of the Anglican Communion'. It recognizes the great seriousness of a growing 'impairment' and suggests ways of limiting this so far as possible, but it also stresses that historically 'the Church has lived with less than perfect communion' at almost all times. Church history is a history of anomalies, of pursuing but never fully realizing the ideals of a theoretical ecclesiology. The present anomalous situation needs to be judged within a historical perspective of almost endless anomalies, to be deplored but still to be lived with. In regard to new structures of ministry, of which the ordination of women is one, there needs to be recognition of a certain provisionality until at least it is quite clear that they are accepted by an adequate consensus within the Church. An authority not claiming infallibility has the right to go forward in new ways but it has the correlative obligation to recognize a quality of provisionality in what it does. The thinking of the Eames Commission reflects Runcie's own viewpoint very closely. A wider value of this way of thinking lies in its recognition of the fact that the principles and problems of unity within the Anglican Communion are not different in kind from the principles and problems of wider ecumenical endeavour. There is a single ideal of full communion for all Christians within one visible Church. That ideal has never been realized and may, in a way, be unrealizable. It is, nevertheless, of the nature of the Church to be a communion, a eucharistic fellowship of faith, hope and love. It is obligatory upon all members to pursue full communion and fellowship as realistically as possible with all from whom they are separated to a greater or lesser degree. It is certainly dangerous and undesirable that a new 'impairment' may develop and continue to grow, but in some circumstances it may still be, even with the best of good will, unavoidable. Yet it is certainly the task of an archbishop to struggle against the impairment, to remain an embodiment of unity.

That is what Runcie has continually tried to do and to be by word and deed. He has seen it as his central function. We may end this discussion with two small examples of the way he has done it, over and above the theological analysis, the frequent world tours, the institutional leadership. The first is through the appeal to experience, as in his address at the close of the Lambeth Conference:

When we have met to study the Bible; when we have met at the Lord's Table; when we have shared in fasting and vigil; when we have wept together over the pain of Southern Africa or the Pacific (and there have been *real* tears shed, make no mistake); have we been in 'full' or 'impaired' communion? However real the difficulties those words represent, there is sometimes something almost laughably inappropriate about the question. . . . Some have thought this Conference was impossible. Reason and experience suggested we would fall apart. But keeping our eyes on the Lord we have not sunk.

The second example is more symbolic. One of the things Runcie has most enjoyed doing at Lambeth is restoring the chapel within the Palace — a beautifully elegant early thirteenth-century building badly bombed in the war and then rather unimaginatively restored. The chapel, as he put it, 'had lost its mystery and its meaning'. Runcie gave it back both by returning the magnificent wooden screen constructed in the time of William Laud and by commissioning a contemporary artist, Leonard Rosoman, to paint the ceiling in a highly colourful way to illustrate aspects of Anglicanism. But he wanted beyond the decoration to give the chapel an enhanced symbolic use. It is, after all, a very quiet chapel, tucked into a corner of the Palace, not easily noticeable, hardly publicly used and of late very little known in the wider Communion, but it is still the chapel in which the Archbishop of Canterbury daily says his prayers. It is also the chapel in which, in the past, successive Archbishops of Canterbury have consecrated over 350 overseas bishops. So each stall has now been allotted to one of the Primates of the Communion. The 29 existing provinces will each be identified by a symbol marking its own stall and the stalls were allocated to the Primates at Evensong on the eve of the Conference. Thus the chapel in which Archbishops of Canterbury have celebrated the Eucharist since Cardinal Stephen Langton, in which Laud prayed before execution, will now symbolically represent, as Runcie declared to his fellow Primates, 'our inter-dependence and mutual responsibility, our collegiality'. In these words and this innovation, at once symbolic, aesthetic and practical, the heart of Runcie's concern for the Communion over which he has presided is characteristically expressed.

❧ 9 ❧

Nine readings

From the many hundreds of sermons, addresses and lectures given by Archbishop Runcie during his years in office, the following nine have been chosen as illustrative of his teaching. They cover the period 1981 to 1989 and extend across a wide range of subjects from basic issues of belief to some of the great disasters of our time and to our hopes for the future. Belief in God, the resurrection, the Prayer Book, the Queen Mother, the Falklands War, the Zeebrugge disaster, the Holocaust, the environment: it seems a mixed bag, but the role of an Archbishop of Canterbury essentially consists in responding to such a mix, year in, year out. Christian doctrine, the life of the Church, affairs of state, the personal and the political — it has all to enter into the content of his teaching. It is hard in such circumstances to avoid repetitiveness or the banal, whether it be a purely traditional formula or a trendy expression of the contemporary mood. Runcie tried immensely hard to avoid the simplistic and to say something fresh which was faithful both to the great Christian truths and to the special needs of a particular moment.

I hope that these addresses, while in no way fully representative of his teaching, display the manner of it. The selection is my own. It makes compelling and often moving reading.

1. Passionate Coolness

(Sermon preached in Durham Cathedral on the occasion of the
fifth meeting of the Anglican Consultative Council, 8 September
1981)

I am glad that we are celebrating the Festival of the Blessed Virgin Mary in this cathedral where devotion to Mary has been strong throughout the centuries, even when such devotion was out of fashion. In the 1620s, John Cosin — later Bishop of Durham — scandalized some of his contemporaries by renewing the old ceremony of burning candles to the honour of our Lady. 'He busied himself from two of the clock in the afternoon 'til four, climbing long

160

ladders to stick up wax candles.' In this very cathedral the number of candles burned that evening was 220, besides sixteen torches.

All generations have called her blessed and I believe that Mary can be an emblem and an inspiration to us in the future as the Anglican Communion journeys into the second millennium. A meeting like this, the fifth of the Anglican Consultative Council, is inevitably full of housekeeping matters, but I am glad to see from the agenda that the visionary element has not been submerged beneath managerial needs. Every age is one of decision and crisis and this one is no different. The Church is always under judgement. It is always necessary to ask the question, 'Is the face of the Church turned towards her master, Jesus Christ, or is she preoccupied with her status and survival?' This question is one that should concern us as members of the worldwide Anglican Communion in a very special way.

We have never claimed to be the one true Church, to the exclusion of every other Christian Church. We are part of the one, holy, catholic and apostolic Church throughout the world — a Church, now sadly in fragments, which exists only in parts and whose energies are dissipated by unbrotherly conflict. It is our vocation as Anglicans to seek our own extinction by working for the restoration of the one great universal Church — the coming Church, which Christ promised not even the gates of hell could withstand. We must regularly judge the life of our Churches by this standard — are we working for Christ's coming Church? Are we, like Mary, keeping the things of Jesus and pondering them in our hearts, or are we busy planning for a secure future, like the managers of any other long-established enterprise? This meeting will be reviewing the astonishing progress made in twelve years of consultations between the Anglican Communion and the Roman Catholic Church. I hail this work as a sign that we have not entirely forgotten our vocation, whatever might be said about our complacency as a Church in other respects.

It may be that in some parts of the world we should be serving best by ceasing to exist in separation and instead should attempt to strengthen other Christian bodies, better equipped to represent our Lord in a particular locality. That must be a real question for us in the next two decades, but at present I believe that the example of Mary gives us a clue to a way of serving Jesus Christ which has been cherished in the Anglican tradition and which, I believe, the world particularly needs now. I see in Mary and in the best Anglicans a *passionate coolness*. That sounds like a paradox and you deserve an explanation.

Passionate coolness — certainly we need passion: how is it possible to be a Christian, to love God and his works and to see his finest creation, men and women, so starved that their brains shrivel, without passion? Who could view the spectacle of a world devoting its best talents and a large proportion of its resources to the production of weapons of mass destruction, without passion? Who could witness men and women, God's masterpieces, belittled and under-valued because of their skin colour or sex, without passion?

Passion, however, is not enough. It can be merely destructive, adding to the din and obstructing progress. Self-righteous indignation is an opium which makes people unfit for useful work. Some people are shouting so loudly that they have made themselves deaf. They have made the world a more dangerous and less hopeful place. We need to yoke passion, an urgent desire for change, with cool thought and attention. Passion needs to be married to the receptivity shown by Mary as she kept the signs and sayings about Jesus and pondered them in her heart. The young have given the word 'cool' a positive dimension. Someone who is cool is emancipated from the passions which sway the crowd, from the strident slogans and half-truths which drive out thought and reflection. The cool man is sufficiently collected to observe, to discriminate and to receive a fuller vision of the truth and to put his energies into purposeful and well-considered action. At a time when our airwaves are choked with hateful propaganda, we need this kind of coolness. At a time when some, even in the Christian Church, wish to stop their ears to the clamour of a distressed and threatening world by opting for mindlessness and joining one of the many cults of unreason, we need, in our Communion, to speak and stand for this kind of reasonable coolness.

This coolness, which we must learn from Mary, is not, however, a matter of mere disengagement — a self-indulgent idling in neutral — it is passionate coolness. It is practised, first to free us from the narcotic fumes of self-induced frenzy and then to allow us to pay attention to God and to act in his strength. 'Behold the handmaid of the Lord — be it unto me according to thy word.' Mary was there to be found by God: she was free to listen to his angel, to receive and obey his word. The Church will never do breathtaking things; will never be able to spend itself in bringing healing and peace to the world, unless it is so deeply attentive to God that his word and life flow into our very veins and direct our hands. Passionate coolness is one way to be free enough to hear God and to share his life.

Our Anglican Communion is sometimes mocked for its stately liturgy, for solemn services like this one, for our emphasis on learning and suspicion of rhetoric. It is true that this tradition can produce dull and complacent churches but, at its best, Anglicanism has exhibited this passionate coolness that we see in Mary. I believe that we need to cherish and deepen our practice of this way of approaching God as part of our contribution to the great Christian centuries to come.

I recently made a hugely enjoyable visit to the Episcopal Church in the United States and made many friends. One of those who made the deepest impression on me was the Dean of the Seminary in the University of the South — Terry Holmes. His tragically early death last month, on the Feast of the Transfiguration, was a shock to the great army of his friends. He personified passionate coolness. He was a patient and careful scholar, a crusader against mindlessness, but he was also fired with a passionate determination to attend to God and to build a Church more expressive of God's word and life. The best tribute to this great Anglican would be to cherish the way of passionate coolness. To persevere in it, as Mary herself persevered. At the beginning of the story, we find her ready to respond to God — 'Be it unto me according to thy word' — pondering signs and sayings in her heart, as she sought to understand and do God's will. This was her way to the end — to the passion and resurrection of her son. It was a way she followed in the din and turmoil of the first Holy Week. The streets were full of shouting crowds. Religious leaders were rushing hither and thither to meetings. The city was full of soldiers, clashing their spears, but it was Mary, silent and still, who remained closest to the Lord. Let her be an inspiration to us.

'Holy Mary, full of grace, the Lord is with thee. Blessed art thou among women and blessed is the fruit of thy womb, Jesus.'

2. Encountering God: Why I Believe

(A sermon given in Great St Mary's, Cambridge during an eight-day 'ecumenical exploration' of the Christian faith in February 1985)

We are concerned here to explore some fundamental questions about truth, the existence of God, human destiny, the nature of man — indeed the meaning of life itself. These are fundamental questions, and not to be ignored or dodged. They continue to be asked, despite having been frequently declared meaningless or impossible to answer.

Faith is often the only form of response appropriate to these kinds of ultimate questions. By faith I do not mean an irrational reaction of blind optimism or homespun philosophy displayed by the immature when confronted by complex or trying circumstances: 'It will all turn out for the best, it will all make sense, in the end'. Faith is perhaps more the ability to say 'Yes' to such questions as 'Is there intelligibility, order and purpose in the universe?'

As an undergraduate I well remember Isaiah Berlin telling us it was our duty not to spend our lives lying on a bed of unexamined assumptions. I think one assumption people might be tempted to make is that an archbishop has 'made it' spiritually: he knows what it is all about, he has all the answers.

I would like to examine that assumption. Because I am an archbishop it is obvious that I believe, that I live by faith. But I believe that everybody lives by faith of some kind — only some have articulated and explored their commitment more thoroughly than others. I am here to try to tell you why I believe in God, and find my faith through the Christian way.

Perhaps I should digress just a little and say why, today, I think it is so important that I believe. I was once startled by Bishop Desmond Tutu saying to me, 'I always find it very hard to be a Christian in England, the issues are so blurred: in South Africa everything is so clear-cut'. It does seem to me that audible clashes of principle or the oppressions of tyranny can lead to a clearer perception of spiritual values and the meaning of life — look at Poland and how it has responded to the death of the outspoken priest Father Popiełuszko.

In Britain we are more inclined to spiritual stagnation: both great sanctity and spectacular wickedness are in short supply. Perhaps we should thank God for the latter. But what of the former? Somehow the Church must be spiritually awakened to hear God's voice speaking through today's events and discoveries — otherwise it will end by speaking only to itself. Some time ago I found myself wondering whether the language used in reporting Terry Waite's operation in Libya (words like 'mission', 'faith' and 'miracle') was merely the residue of a decaying Christianity, or the reflection of an unspoken need for spiritual values to be reasserted.

I believe there is an underlying yearning for God and for things spiritual. I shall speak more of this later. I am not (altogether) convinced that it is (or need be) a case of enter progress, exit God; nor that the present-day substitutes for religion (Communism, nationalism, materialism, humanism) will ultimately replace true religion and religious belief. However, we may have to work harder than we do at present to ensure that a sense of religious mystery surrounds our secular humanitarian activities, and that a sense of religious obligation tempers and disciplines our selfishness, if we are to avoid national suicide.

For me it is Christianity which makes sense of more things about the world and about myself than any ideology. But Christianity is not a once for all religion, handed to me on a plate at baptism, completely ready-made, final. One of its greatest strengths is that it does not attempt to explain everything. There is always at its core, as in every relationship, a heart of mystery.

The God who enters into a personal relation with us through Christ is a God of ultimate mystery. We know that saints like John of the Cross and, nearer home, Mother Julian of Norwich, wrestled with these mysteries; there are records of their agonies of mind and heart as their thinking about God was purified in prayer and tested in suffering. They found a faith deeper than would have been possible had they remained superficial and conventional.

Most of us are, at times, like the poet Francis Thompson in 'The Hound of Heaven' — we flee from God when things are hard and the light of faith is flickering. And yet at such times we can say, with the man in the gospels, 'Lord, I believe — help thou my unbelief', trying to make our muted, half-hearted 'Yes' into a fully articulated response that can shape and rule our lives.

These are some of the reasons why I think it is important to believe. But I do not think I have yet approached the question of *why* I believe closely enough. Nor indeed am I sure this is exactly what I am going to do. I think there is a risk in telling or explaining why I believe in God. And the risk is that the God in whom I believe may be obscured or distorted when I state my reasons for believing in him, just as trying to explain why I love a person by describing a particular attribute or talent may imply that they are loved for the attribute or talent rather than for themselves. (So you can tell your girl friend as often as you like *that* you love her, but it's sometimes dangerous to tell her *why* you love her!)

If I say, for instance, that I believe in God because my prayers have sometimes been answered, then I may as well be taken to mean that I believe in the existence of an invisible slot-machine which can sometimes provide me with what I want. And if I say that I believe in God because a friend recovered from cancer when all the doctors had given up hope, I may well seem to be saying that I believe in the existence and effectiveness of an occult healing power.

The God in whom I believe may be, or seem to be, nothing more than my reason for believing in him. I think there are some people of whom this is true: their God simply *is* their reason for believing in him. There is — or was very recently — a well-known American evangelist who regularly appeared on the TV dripping with jewellery, even to the extent of having diamonds set in his teeth! His message was, 'I believe in God, and see how richly he has blessed me. If you believe in him you too will be rich.' The God he preaches is nothing more than the source of riches to those who believe in him.

But I am sure that to most people the God in whom they believe is not simply an answering machine or an occult power-source — just as the person whom they love is not simply a nice voice combined with a talent for dancing and one or two other things. The difficulty is that the more precisely we set out our reasons for believing the more risk we take of suggesting that these reasons for our belief are the actual substance of our belief.

And here lies the danger of putting forward as our reasons for belief those classical arguments or proofs for the existence of God with which some of you will be familiar. They are claimed — and perhaps justifiably — to be logical demonstrations that, for instance, a First Cause must exist and a most Perfect Being must exist. But if they are our reasons for believing in God, then the God we believe in is (or at least seems to be) no more than a First Cause or a most Perfect Being. Well, I suppose one could believe in a God who was simply that, but it would be a very dim and dull and abstract kind of belief. It would not make much difference to anything, and it would hardly be worth recommending to anybody else. It would be no great achievement to persuade an atheist or agnostic to admit the existence of a First Cause or Perfect Being.

In making explicit the reaons why we believe in God there is a risk of misleading people about the kind of God we believe in. Just as the safest (and probably most truthful) answer to someone who asks *why* you love him or her is, 'Just because I do, and I can't help it', so the safest, and perhaps the most honest, course for me would be to say, 'Why do I believe in God? . . . Just because I do — and I can't help it', and, having said that, to go on at once to what I believe. But there is rather more to be said.

To go back to this business of loving. I do not apologize for doing so — for believing in God is much more like loving someone than it is like believing there is no oil in a certain rock stratum or life on a certain planet. You cannot really say why you love someone, and that all this business about her seductive voice, her shapely figure, fails to express or contain the heart of the matter. But let us suppose someone said: 'You *can't* love Susan. She's no sense of humour at all'; or, 'You shouldn't love Susan. She tells lies.' Well, you might respond with a fist or a kick on the shins, or you might say, 'I know that, but I still love her'. But more likely, especially if the speaker was someone you respected, you would say: 'Susan does have a sense of humour, but it's very subtle and it's not everyone who notices it'; or 'Susan doesn't tell lies: it's just that she forgets and gets things muddled up'. These words do not give the reason why you love Susan, but they do give the reason why it is not foolish or improper to love her. They do not explain your love — but they do to some degree defend it and justify it.

Similarly I cannot satisfactorily explain why I believe in God, but I can, at least to some extent, defend and justify my belief. I can say, first and with great conviction, that there is *space* for belief in God: huge space, empty space, sensible space, that is almost crying out to be filled.

It is the space of which we are aware when we *wonder at the mystery* of being. By this I do not just mean wonder at the beauty and order of the world, but something more fundamental than that — wonder at the fact that there is anything at all. Wittgenstein wrote in the *Tractatus*, 'The mystical is not *how* the world is but *that* it is', and in a paper on ethics he referred to occasions when he found himself wondering at the existence of the world and saying to himself, 'How remarkable that the world exists, how remarkable that *anything* exists'. We may trace with increasing scientific precision the 'how' of the world, detect evermore exactly the laws and forces which determine its operations and its history, but *that* the world exists, *that* those laws and forces are there, remains a matter for undiminished wonder.

A still greater matter for wonder is my own presence and awareness and consciousness within the world at which I wonder. Here am I, within the mystery, sensing and seeing the mystery, treading on and handling and making use of the mystery — surviving, one might say, by courtesy of the mystery. It cannot be the height of wisdom simply to swim and swan around within the mystery in mindless oblivion. Nor, on the other hand, can it be foolish to have some kind of attitude to the mystery. And to take a certain attitude at this profound level is, I think, certainly the beginning, and possibly even the core and centre, of belief in God. To perceive and respond to the mystery as a *gracious* mystery would be to have an implicit belief in God. So, there is certainly space — intellectual space — for belief in God.

Now comes the second point of my defence. It lies in the special and remarkable character of moral awareness. Kant said there are two things which move mankind to wonder — the starry heavens above and the moral law within. I suppose that by 'wonder at the starry heavens' Kant meant what I have just been thinking of — wonder at the mystery of being. It is when we look up at the night sky and think of its immensity and of our minuteness that the mystery of being is most profoundly experienced.

By 'wonder at the moral law within' I think Kant meant what I would describe, rather less imposingly, as 'wonder at the fact that things matter'. The cause for wonder, for vision, is not that things matter to me — subjectively. It is that some things matter objectively, they have a right to matter, and that this is so absolute and irrefutable.

The famine in Ethiopia may or may not matter to me: but there is no doubt that it has a right to matter and that, though I and billions of others may be indifferent, it would still have a right to matter. This right confronts us, and if we ignore it it judges and condemns us. In our awareness the world is not simply registered, as it might be on a spool of film or a tape-recorder. At times it confronts us as mattering; it demands from us some kind of response and condemns us if that response is not forthcoming. There are times when the moral imperative is clear and practical: feeding the hungry, freeing the prisoner, protesting against nuclear weapons or racial discrimination, starting a movement like Amnesty International or Christian Aid.

Moral philosophers may argue as to why — in terms of what general ethical principles — the famine in Ethiopia matters and makes its demands on us, but they can hardly deny that it does so. And so do many other things — public and private, large or small. Our awareness that certain things have a right to matter is as indisputable as our awareness that they exist.

Try telling yourself that it does not matter that you have betrayed a friend, stolen a poor man's coat or, long ago, tortured for your pleasure a helpless cat. Would you buy a second-hand car from a moral philosopher who maintained that these things did not matter? Of course in different ages and societies the moral awareness is sensitive to different things, and in some people it has become atrophied and even, in pathological cases, nonexistent. But the conviction that certain things have a right to matter is as widespread among mankind as the conviction that certain things exist.

In the authority with which certain things engage our moral awareness and make their demands there is again *space* — moral space — for belief in God: for the belief that moral demand springs from a source as profoundly mysterious and awesome as does the universe itself.

Let me repeat that I am not stating the reasons why I believe in God: I am simply setting out reasons why it is not foolish to believe — or naive or a mark of senility or wishful thinking. It is with this reminder that I come to the third of these reasons — which is Jesus Christ or, perhaps more exactly, the story of Jesus Christ. This, to put it over-simply, is claimed to be the story of God making himself present, making himself known in and to the world: and in it God is disclosed not as one who exercises a distant and detached supremacy over the world of his creation but as one who, in the greatness of his love for that world, pours out and expends himself 'unto death'.

That story really belongs to the next sermon, but I mention it here for this reason. You may disbelieve the claim made for this story: you may disbelieve the story itself. But I doubt if anyone who seriously attends to the story and the claim made for it can dismiss the whole matter as foolish or trivial or irrelevant — as something of which the truth or falsehood would be immaterial, making no difference to our feeling and attitude about the world in general or our own place in it.

So in and through the story of Jesus Christ and the claims made about it there is again *space* for belief in God. This time I would call it emotional space: if we believe in the God disclosed in the story then there is met the most universal of all human needs — the need to be unconditionally accepted and totally loved.

Here is an illustration. Some time ago I took part in a discussion on transplant operations. A doctor described how that morning after a road accident in Vienna a kidney had been taken from a child's body, frozen, put on a plane, and brought to London where he had put it into another person. 'But', he said, 'I couldn't do this work if I thought that I was simply dealing with a bundle of parts. I don't know how to define life and I'm not very religious, but what I have of faith reminds me that I must respect, no, reverence, every person with whom I have to do.'

It is easy to think of a person as a bundle of parts or a mixture of chemicals — but perhaps that is a case of beginning at the wrong end. See him as the object of God's love, and he comes together as a person. It is easy to see mankind as economic units or racial groups, and it falls apart. See it as the family for whom Christ died and there is emotional fulfilment — a space filled.

So I suppose I cannot say simply *why* I believe in God, but I can point to *space* for such belief — intellectual, moral and emotional space. This at least helps to make sense of Christian belief — belief for which (let me say finally) I remain profoundly grateful. I am thankful for whatever it may be — the example of others, experience of life, the direct touch of God upon me — which has led me to believe and sustained my belief against counter-pressures which are put upon it and against difficulties which are inherent in that belief itself. I do not want to end with pious platitudes about the blessedness of belief, but I have no doubt that if that belief were taken from me I should find the world an intellectual question mark, a moral vacuum and an emotional desert. And those things I firmly do not believe.

3. The Resurrection

(Sermon in Canterbury Cathedral, Easter Day 1983)

'Fear not; I am the first and the last: I am he that liveth and was dead; and, behold, I am alive for evermore, Amen; and have the keys of hell and of death.'

Encouragement was necessary. The first disciples experienced shock, astonishment and fear when they discovered the empty tomb and when they were confronted with the reality of the resurrection.

Since then, there have been nearly 2,000 years of Christian history and, particularly in times of calm and relative security, the shock and reality of the resurrection is elaborated and explained and smoothed down. Sometimes, resurrection is understood just as a picture of some of the natural processes with which we are all familiar.

Some preachers on Easter Day talk of springtime — new life in nature — or the patient's experience of recovery from the depths when health returns or how, after a long struggle in a marriage, a new relationship blossoms.

In one moving meditation on the resurrection, there is this passage:

We know it when doing a piece of work. We reach a point of utter frustration where the whole thing seems to be beyond us and we long to abandon it. But, if we don't abandon it, then almost at the very moment when we acknowledge our inability to go on, the whole thing buds and blossoms in our hands and we see a dozen ways in which to proceed.

We know death and resurrection in our closest loves. In marriage perhaps in particular, we know what it is to struggle on when there are no rewarding emotions. And after, there comes a point where the relationship flowers gloriously beyond our imagination or expectation . . . and it is impossible afterwards to escape the knowledge that joy and happiness sprang out of the darkness of the pain.

Certainly there are experiences of resurrection in all our lives and you don't have to be a Christian to experience them. The resurrection of Jesus Christ, however, is not just a way of drawing attention to some of the recurrent patterns of human experience. It is a unique event which brings hope of a kind that cannot be extracted from the world of natural processes.

I remind you of this because one of the great difficulties which people find in our time when they consider the claims of belief is the way in which the vocabulary of Christianity has been gradually diluted into a mere series of ethical truisms and made to mean what it never meant before. The end of this process is that the message becomes so thin and anaemic that there is really no reason, no impetus, to believe in something that has practically no content.

When the resurrection is simply a spiritual event within the hearts of disciples, and when everything is translated into non-historical terms, then the gospel becomes one more fairy-tale. If you treat the gospel in this way, then it is arguable that there are more entertaining fairy-tales presented with even greater literary artifice.

The gospel which brought the Christian Church into being is proclaiming something which is beyond us and which has the effect of widening our vision at times beyond the bearable. The trouble is that when you add too much water to a glass of wine, it gradually becomes water tainted with wine. It gives you none of the kick which a glass of wine can give.

If God becomes just one of our ideas, imprisoned in the world of cause and effect, and resurrection just an allegory of certain recurrent patterns in human experience, then hope for the human enterprise is short indeed.

Men are always being tempted to live out the lie that they are gods. They try to live as if they are at the centre of the universe; like medieval astronomers, they are tempted to believe that the sun revolves around them. God, if he has a place at all, is a Sunday secret for those people who have a taste for religion as a hobby. Again and again, this arrogance is revealed for what it is and seen to have very bitter consequences.

We are near the end of an historical period in the West in which there has been a particularly vigorous attempt to assert that the sun should orbit around us. For the last 300 years, man has been seeking, through the exercise of his God-given intellect, to manage and control his environment. We now dominate our planet in a way that no previous generation has done. In human organization, we have the capacity to guarantee a reasonable standard of living for all the people in the world. There is doubt, however, about whether we have the will and spiritual energy to do so. But our capacities also extend to a power to regulate the lives of individual human beings as never before. Tragically, man's progress towards god-like management of his fellows and of nature itself has, in our own day, culminated in the unleashing of seemingly unmanageable forces. Nuclear weapons and the horrifying prospect of nuclear warfare are, of course, the most eloquent symbol of this tragic development, but the tragedy can also be seen in the capacity of totalitarian states to subject their subjects to previously undreamed-of manipulation and social engineering which no mortal wisdom can possibly control or justify.

If God were trapped in the world of cause and effect, as just another of our ideas of ourselves as god-like, then there would be little hope indeed.

But: 'Fear not', said Jesus, 'I am the first and the last'. God stands before history and he is the meaning of history. Christ is not to be imprisoned. He has the keys even of death and of hell.

This truth is most obvious and invisible in places and in times when man's effort to become god-like has been exposed as a tragic distortion of the real order of things. The reality of the resurrection and the hope it brings was experienced by the author of the Book of Revelation who spoke to us in the First Lesson. He belonged to a community that was facing the persecution of the Roman state which had pretended to god-like power to the extent even of deifying its emperors. John the Divine was in exile in the island of Patmos. He had tasted the 'tribulation' and was in prison 'for the Word of God and for the testimony of Jesus Christ'. It was then in some Roman Gulag that John was encouraged and sustained by the risen Christ and used by him as his spokesman.

It is not necessary, however, to go back many centuries to find places where the reality of the resurrection has blazed up in the darkness created by the lie that man is a god with no dependence upon the will and word of the Creator.

Perhaps the most vivid experience of the resurrection reality known to me is in the Soviet Union. Michael Bourdeaux has just written an important book called *Risen Indeed: Lessons in Faith from the USSR*. I would advise everybody to read it. No plausible stories can disguise the fact that the Church in the Soviet Union in recent times has experienced very great suffering. Solzhenitsyn, in his Nobel Prize lecture, refers in his oblique way to 'one place where not so long ago there were persecutions no less severe than those of ancient Rome, in which hundreds of thousands of Christians gave their lives in silence because of their faith in God'. In these circumstances, I share with Michael Bourdeaux the perception that Russian Christians do not debate the resurrection. They have experienced its reality in their own lives. 'They have not preserved the faith in hostile surroundings, it has preserved them.'

Christians, like the first disciples, like St John the Divine on the island of Patmos, like Bishop Desmond Tutu, like many Christians in the Soviet Union, know of a God who is not just an idea in the human mind but a God who cares, a God who acts and a God who saves. Their joy at the resurrection event is profound and not genteel. They can teach us that joy and many other things.

I end with one of the lessons in faith from the USSR: Michael Bourdeaux was standing in a church in total darkness, on Easter Eve:

> A hammering and creaking from the back indicated a great door opening. 'Whom seek ye?' 'The body of Jesus.' 'Why seek ye the living among the dead? He is not here, he is risen.' For the first time, the great crowd broke its silence. A murmur as though they could not believe the truth they were affirming, 'He is risen indeed' was their antiphon. But now too there was light. Someone at the back had lit the first Paschal candle . . . swiftly the flame passed from hand to hand . . . each candle lit up a face behind it. That face bore the deep lines of sorrow, of personal tragedy. Yet, as it was illuminated, the suffering turned to joy, to the certain knowledge of the reality of the risen Lord.

We have been given a faith which is strong enough for the darkest shadows in life. I pray that familiarity may not blunt the wonder of an astonishing message which we celebrate together in Canterbury today.

4. The Future of the Past
— Reflections on the Prayer Book

(An article written in February 1984)

Cranmer's Parlour at Lambeth Palace has just been restored. I began using it at the beginning of this year as a room for writing and thinking, and I am sitting in it now as I compose this article. From my chair I can see the Chapel where each day the Offices are still recited from the Prayer Book which Cranmer probably compiled in this very room.

The liturgical diet of an Archbishop is necessarily very varied. As I move around the Diocese of Canterbury, I have many opportunities to observe and share in the liturgical vitality of those parishes which have adopted the Alternative Service Book. The new book has undeniably helped many congregations to transform themselves from mere aggregations into people with a deeper sense of community. The shape and drama of its Eucharist are closer to primitive models and those in other Christian traditions. It has already attracted the loyalty and affection of a new generation of worshippers.

173

What is the future then for the older alternative, the Book of Common Prayer? Will it become merely the preserve of small bands of enthusiastic conservationists, treated as quaint though redundant like the traction engine or stage-coach?

I believe that this ought not to happen. I do not think it is happening. I will do everything in my power to see that the Prayer Book continues to be, in the words of the pastoral letter issued by my brother Archbishop and me in 1980, 'a living element in the tradition of the Church'.

Very few people would deny that the Prayer Book has extraordinary literary merit, but some claim that this sixteenth-century achievement has little contemporary religious relevance and that archaic language estranges people from the Church. I take a contrary view.

The vigour, the rhythm and even the strangeness of Prayer Book language makes it memorable, and what a person remembers shapes his personality. Christianity has its roots in 'a perpetual memory of that his precious death until his coming again'. This memory generates Christian hope. In today's world, unless we are steeped in the language and the perspectives of faith, then we shall all too easily become assimilated to the assumptions of a passing age whose talk and thought assigns no central place to God. I believe that there is no substitute for knowing the sacred texts and prayers by heart, and the Prayer Book, and perhaps particularly its Psalter, is a treasury of memorable texts. 'Treasured words', as Iris Murdoch has observed of the Prayer Book, 'encourage, console and save.'

One of my most moving and humbling recent experiences was taking the Sacrament to a group of elderly people. A number of them had begun to lose their memories of recent events and one was not even sure where she was, but all were able to pray the Collect and recite the Prayer Book service off by heart in a way that transformed a very ordinary room into one of our Father's 'many mansions'.

I am grateful for many things in the Alternative Service Book, particularly for its stress on some of the central themes of our faith such as the activity of the Holy Spirit and the joy of the Resurrection which receive too little attention in the Prayer Book. I am grateful too for modern translations of the Bible, which used in conjunction with the Authorized Version, deepen the worshippers' understanding of the faith. Indeed, as the Archbishops' pastoral letter said, the new is not a substitute for the old, but an alternative.

For well over a decade the new services have been complementing the old and enriching the worshipping life of the Church. There is now a new situation and it is time for some of those reared on the new book to be introduced at depth to the Prayer Book tradition. The 80s are very different from the 60s and perhaps it is clearer now that an impatience with history and an ignorance of our own tradition can deliver us bound hand and foot to the very partial view of reality which happens to be current in the present. Hope for a different vision of reality in the future is nourished by memories, and we dare not casually abandon our living link with the past of the church and nation which is given to us in the Prayer Book.

I can only plead with those who find this argument irrelevant and difficult to hear that they should not seek to prevent the new generation entering into its liturgical inheritance. But it is the total inheritance into which the new generation will enter — the Alternative Service Book as well as the Book of Common Prayer, and it is fair to ask those whose vigour in defending the Book of Common Prayer has thus far prevented them from seriously considering and using the Alternative Service Book to be readier to come to terms with it.

Surveys of current practice recently completed in many dioceses of the Church of England reveal that the Prayer Book is still widely in use. They also show that in many parishes both the Alternative Service Book and the Book of Common Prayer are in use. This is welcome and encouraging. I am also particularly concerned that the Book of Common Prayer should be a regular part of the daily worship of our Cathedrals.

There is, however, no cause for complacency. The House of Bishops has given considerable thought to the subject. One of the difficulties often reported to us concerns the enrichment and development in the Prayer Book tradition which has occurred over the past three centuries. Just to authorize the Book as it left the printer in 1662 does not do justice to the vitality of our liturgical inheritance. Within living memory, very few people have used the wordy exhortations in the Communion Service, and the use of prayers like 'O Lamb of God' has become an accepted part of the Prayer Book tradition. Next week in the General Synod the Bishop of Birmingham, as a spokesman for his brother bishops, will propose that developed forms of the Old Prayer Book communion and baptism services (so-called Series I) should be re-authorized.

The bishops are also very concerned with the place of the Prayer Book in ordination training. It is clearly crucial that the younger clergy should be familiar with the liturgical tradition of the Church of England and should be able to commend it and teach it with conviction. We need to raise up a generation of clergy who realize that loyalty to the old and new books are not exclusive. Just because you have a sympathy for the music of Tippett is no reason to discard Tallis. I am sure that no one ought to leave a theological college without demonstrating a knowledge of the Prayer Book and having experienced it in living worship.

If the Prayer Book tradition is not to become a dignified fossil, then those who have been nourished by it and are attuned to it must be vocal in its support in the councils of the Church. Questions should be asked at meetings of Parochial Church Councils about the use of the Prayer Book in the locality, and whether some of the old texts and their musical settings could be used as part of the new services — as already happens in many places encouraged by the notes of the Alternative Service Book.

Parents and godparents have an especially significant role. Young people, particularly those training for Confirmation, should be as familiar with the Prayer Book and the Authorized Version, as they are with the Alternative Service Book and modern translations of the Bible. They should be encouraged to use them all.

We have a rich inheritance of worship. If within it we are not to lose touch with our 'incomparable liturgy', there is a responsibility for all Church people, clergy as well as laity, who love the Prayer Book, to show 'boldness with fervent zeal' in councils and synods to ensure that it continues to be heard and inwardly digested in the homes and parishes of England.

5. The Queen Mother

(Sermon preached to celebrate the eightieth birthday of Queen
Elizabeth, the Queen Mother, St Paul's Cathedral, 15 July 1980)

I happened to be present recently when the Queen Mother was paying a visit to Kent. She said she was looking forward to further visits and to getting to know the area better, particularly now that she had been appointed Warden of the Cinque Ports. At a time of life when many people have already been retired for twenty years, the Queen Mother continues to display an astonishing taste for new experiences and new friendships, so much so that it would probably be more accurate to say that we are met to celebrate and give thanks for the Queen Mother's *first* eighty years.

On the same occasion, I heard a woman in the crowd make a remark which stuck in my mind and has given me my theme: 'It's a lovely dress, of course, but I just can't take my eyes off her *face*. She looks so cheerful.' Queen Elizabeth's face is known and loved throughout the world and has been endlessly reproduced in every medium from oil painting to postage stamp. In a particularly graceful birthday tribute, the National Portrait Gallery has organized an exhibition of portraits of the Queen Mother which is well worth a visit and which illustrates vividly one of the main functions of royalty.

Royalty puts a *human face* on the operations of government and provides images with which the people of a nation can identify and which they can love. The Queen Mother has over the years helped us to feel that being a citizen of this country is not just being an entry on the central computer, or being an income tax code number, but it is being a member of a *family* where common interests and kinships exist beneath and beyond all our divisions and conflicts. It is very difficult to fall in love with committees or policies, but the Queen Mother has shown a human face which has called out the loyalty and the sense of belonging without which a nation loses its heart and disintegrates.

It is a sobering thought that although we begin life with a certain natural endowment — a bone structure, skin colour, a certain kind of flesh tissue — as life goes on *we* play a larger and larger part in making our own faces. Our faces reflect the influence under which we have been living: our sufferings and the attitude to life we have taken up. The Queen Mother has been no stranger to suffering of a kind that comes to most of us, notably bereavement, but she has accepted what has befallen her and been able to turn it into uncondescending and lively sympathy for the misfortunes of others. I shall always remember her famous remark after the bombing of Buckingham Palace during the Second World War: 'I'm glad we have been bombed, it makes me feel we can look the East End in the face'. That woman in the crowd I mentioned when I began saw a face which had its share of the dignity that comes from suffering, but one which was *also* full of life, affection and cheerfulness and a zest for new things and people.

Cynics and pessimists have been in plentiful supply in recent decades, and sometimes the negativity they express has been confused with sophistication. Hardly any of the institutions of our national life have escaped satire or mockery. The monarchy and the royal family have not been exempt from this kind of criticism, but the Queen Mother has continued to speak and stand for abiding virtues and to express her confidence in things that are pure, things that are lovely, things that are of good report.

The faith and hope which are evident in her way of doing her work can *appear* simple and naive, like the text from Julian of Norwich which began this service: 'All shall be well and all shall be well, and all manner of things shall be well'. It may be simple but it is not naive, as you will see if you consider the contrast between the satirist indulging in repeats and revivals, and the Queen Mother appearing as fresh and forward-looking as ever. By reflecting the great simplicities of faith and goodness, and never simply following the trend, she has occupied the centre of the stage since 1923 without suffering the fate which so frequently befalls the fashionable personality who is played out after ten years or so in public life.

Faith, hope and love which are deep and nourishing are God-given, they come in full measure to those who are turned in the direction of God, *and it shows*. Without being insensitive to suffering, we need encouraging examples that human life is *intended* to be full of delight and celebration: Creator and creature rejoicing over one another in a bond of love. How can we be thankful enough for the Queen Mother's love of life and people in all its rich variety: the dogs and the horses, the flowers, the gardens, the fishing, the pictures and the music? Nothing narrow or second-rate, but unselfconscious artistry in her care for details, her unique capacity to relate to all ages and races — student, scholar, housewife or statesman — and an amazing memory for faces. As much at home in the countryside as in palaces, and ever cherishing a lifelong love affair with Scotland. A human face of deep but unparaded faith, equally able to worship in a splendid cathedral like this, with all its memories, or in a simple Presbyterian chapel over the Border.

The Queen Mother reminds us of a basic religious truth. If you want to know the inmost nature of God you must not look so much to rules, commandments and principles, important as they are; instead you must look at the faces of those who love God and whose lives have been nourished by his life, supremely of course, as St Paul writes: 'The light of the knowledge of the glory of God shining in the face of Jesus Christ'. All of us fall short, and the Queen Mother would be the first to want me to say that. Yet the Queen Mother has reflected *something* of that love which comes from those who try to live facing God. What we have seen in one greatly loved and universally admired lady is a love which has been given through her to us, and returned to her by us, and then given again by her, over and over again. Queen Elizabeth I said: 'Though God has raised me high, yet this I count the glory of my crown, that I have reigned with your loves'. I know that is as true today of the Queen Mother, as of us.

I am conscious that I have not said all that some of you would have wished me to say. But I take heart from some words which Queen Elizabeth herself wrote in a foreword to a certain anthology. She wrote there of 'what in our hearts we believe, but find so hard to say'. And it was there she added: 'We can at one and the same time be truly contemporary men and women *and* have our thoughts and lives rooted in truths that do not change'.

6. Kristallnacht, 1938

(Address at the Kristallnacht Memorial Meeting, 9 November
1988, Friends House, Euston Road, London)

The remembrance of Kristallnacht is primarily a Jewish event. That is why I am so deeply moved by the invitation to be with you this evening, and to share in the memory of Jewish suffering. Perhaps you know that in the final days of the last war, I was a soldier. I was among the first troops to enter the Belsen concentration camp. When people ask me whether I regret my part in fighting, I have often replied — 'The war closed down Belsen and Auschwitz'.

But I recognize that we did *not* go to war to close down the concentration camps. Indeed we, and most other nations, had closed our frontiers to all but a small number of those seeking asylum. The desperate search of many for visas led, literally, to a dead end. We went to war to prevent Germany dominating the whole of Europe. In 1938 Adolf Hitler was already the absolute ruler of the German nation, Austria included. He made it clear that he wanted to erase from Germany all that, in his madness, he chose to describe as 'alien blood'. That much was known. The Munich agreement was but one sign of a great conspiracy of silence and complicity which leaves its legacy of shame.

Kristallnacht has its origins deep in the history of Christian Europe. Without centuries of Christian anti-semitism, Hitler's passionate hatred would never have been so fervently echoed. In his home town of Linz there had been very few Jews, but living in Vienna he developed this phobia. In *Mein Kampf* his twisted hatred was expressed in the language of an established and perverse tradition.

Was there any shady undertaking, any form of foulness, especially in cultural life, in which at least one Jew did not participate?

This horrid perception of the Jew festered in Hitler's mind. Once the Nazis gained control of German government, Jews were eliminated from the Civil Service, the legal and medical professions, and cultural and educational institutions. And then, on November 9th, Kristallnacht.

The news was not kept secret from the outside world. Two days later the *New York Times* reported that:

A wave of destruction and looting swept over Germany as National Socialist cohorts took vengeance on Jewish shops, offices and synagogues. Huge, but mostly silent, crowds looked on, and the police confined themselves to regulating traffic and making wholesale arrests of Jews. In some communities every male Jew was sent to a concentration camp.

Earlier this year I paid a visit to Berlin. There I saw the site of the synagogue in Fasanenstrasse, one of the first to be smashed to pieces. We cannot say, 'we did not know'. We did — and stood by. There are painful reminders of our negligence all over Germany. Cain's eternal question rings out: 'Am I my brother's keeper?'

Nazi barbarism resulted in the construction of the death camps in which six million Jews perished. Tonight, as we remember Kristallnacht, the beginning of the acceleration of the process by which Germany determined on genocide, I want to speak about three things. The first is to acknowledge the guilty silence of the Churches then, both within and without Germany. The second is to ask how we can honour God and trust Him after the holocaust. And thirdly, I want to say how I believe the tragic events of the holocaust have altered the relationship of Christians to Jews.

First, the silence of the Churches. Although individual pastors expressed their disapproval of the excesses of Kristallnacht, Church leaders said little. A good many expressed the view that whilst the violence was extreme, it was understandable because of the harm the Jews were doing and had long done to the German economy and way of life. The Confessing Church, the only continuing opposition to Hitler's German Christians, was beginning to lose its way. Karl Barth was right when he said in retrospect:

Bonhoeffer was the first, indeed almost the only theologian, who in the years after 1933 concentrated energetically on the question of the Jews and dealt with it equally energetically. For a long time now I have considered myself guilty of not having raised it with equal emphasis during the Church struggle.

Dietrich Bonhoeffer was attending a retreat at the time of Kristallnacht. But as soon as he heard the news of what had happened, he wrote to his students and urged them to read Psalm 74. In his own Bible that Psalm is marked and underlined. Every time I read that

Psalm in our own Prayer Book it reminds me of the events of Kristallnacht, so accurately does it seem to be prefigured there.

> Thine adversaries roar in the midst of thy congregations: and set up their banners for tokens.
> ... now they break down all the carved work thereof: with axes and hammers. They have set fire upon thy holy places: and have defiled the dwelling place of thy name, even unto the ground.

The travesty of Kristallnacht and all that followed is that so much was perpetrated in Christ's name. To glorify the Third Reich, the Christian faith was betrayed. The slaughter of the Jews was a desecration of the ministry of Jesus, Himself a Jew.

Neither inside nor outside Germany did the churches recognize this. And even today there are many Christians who fail to see it as self-evident.

And why this blindness? Because for centuries Christians have held Jews collectively responsible for the death of Jesus. On Good Friday Jews have, in times past, cowered behind locked doors for fear of a Christian mob seeking 'revenge' for deicide. Without the poisoning of Christian minds through centuries, the holocaust is unthinkable.

In His teaching, Jesus continually stressed that those who loved God were to do good to all without distinction: they were to forgive all, just as they had been forgiven; they were to respond to the call of need, whatever its origins. And that ethic of love was to extend even to one's enemies. This was to be the sign of the unfolding of God's kingdom on earth. When we recall the gas chambers and the mass graves of the holocaust we see the extent to which that vision of universal love was betrayed. We see why Christians can only meditate on the nightmare of Kristallnacht and the Nazi era with a profound sense of grief.

Which brings me to the question — how can we honour God and trust Him after the holocaust?

God *is* dishonoured but He is *not* dethroned. The distinguished Jewish theologian Emil Fackenheim has eloquently and urgently expressed this conviction.

Through the holocaust, he believes, God issued the 614th commandment: Jews are forbidden to grant posthumous victories to Hitler. They are forbidden to despair of God or of the world as the place of His just and gentle rule. For Fackenheim it is a betrayal of the Jewish heritage to question whether the traditional Jewish belief in God can be sustained after the holocaust.

Fackenheim believes it important to recognize the *religious* significance of the Jewish refusal to give up hope. Pregnant mothers refused to abort their pregnancies, hoping their offspring would survive and frustrate Nazi plans to eliminate every Jew. Hassidic Jews prayed though they were forbidden to do so. Only by affirming life and maintaining dignity could the desire for destruction be defeated.

Fackenheim's message is of course directed primarily to the Jewish community. The 614th commandment is added to the 613 other commandments in the Torah. But it is a message for the Christian community too. We also must not allow Hitler — or that-of-Hitler in each of us — to have any posthumous victories. The Jewish people form part of God's plan for His world, and it is our responsibility not merely to ensure their survival — God has done that — but that they are honoured and respected and loved.

Which brings me to my third point. A new understanding of Christian–Jewish relationships emerges from all this. The Jewish people are the people of God, those who bestowed on us the Hebrew scriptures, who gave the Christian world so much of its heritage of faith. Jewish wisdom and Jewish prophecy have been a light to us and will continue to be a light to the nations, even when Jews fall short, as we all do, of their highest ideals.

God's voice also calls us today as Christians to remember and honour the martyrs of the holocaust. So many Jews met persecution, suffering and death in a truly religious spirit. We have our own martyrs — Christians who perished in their solidarity with the Jewish people. Let Maximilian Kolbe and Maria Skobotsova stand for them all alongside Dietrich Bonhoeffer — Catholic friar, Orthodox nun, and Lutheran pastor. They must not be forgotten. But neither must we forget that even though there were a few great churchmen like Heinrich Gruber who set up rescue organizations and survived to become Provost of Berlin, many Jews knew that it was Christians who pushed them into the gas chambers. It is no good saying they were not *real* Christians anymore than we should say that those who did not go regularly to synagogue were not *real* Jews.

In the light of all that, how can we in our generation go to the Jewish people and say, without shame, 'you have rejected your Messiah', or 'we have the truth, listen to us'. We cannot pretend that recent history has not happened.

Christians have much to learn from the ancient people of God in interpreting their own gospel. Our Christian faith is not shaken by discovering how much Jews have to give us in extending our understanding of God. In particular, many Christian ministers who have had the privilege of discussing the Bible with Jewish scholars will testify how much they have gained from it.

Our task as Christians is to hold sincerely to our faith in Christ and to speak of our desire to be conformed to His life, death and resurrection. This discipleship of Jesus of Nazareth Jews can understand and respect. Hectoring from a position of spiritual superiority they cannot. Nor should they. With St Paul we must recognize that it is God alone who can bring us all into one fold.

Tonight, as we remember the streets of Germany, littered with broken glass, we must not simply despair of the past. It is not enough either merely to *understand* the events leading to the gas chambers. What lies before us is the task of creating a world in which such tragedies do not take place again. The planned destruction of the Jewish people did not succeed. Out of suffering God brought a new found liberty. As we Christians would say, out of death he brought resurrection. Out of the pogroms of Russia, God brought new-found liberty for Jews in the United States. He has also brought new-found liberty for Jews in Israel.

The sacrificial victims of the death camps must live in our memories. These memories commit us to all in our world who are outcast, homeless, hungry and oppressed. We honour the victims of yesterday by standing alongside the victims of today. Our love goes out to the ancient and young nation of Israel, to the people of the Holy Land, Jews, Muslims and Christians alike, who are *all* God's children and neighbours to be loved. We must hearken to the divine command which rings out from the ghettoes and the concentration camps. With one voice we must insist: *Never again!* The Lord our God is one, to be loved with all our mind and heart and soul, and our neighbour as ourself.

7. The Falkland Islands

(Sermon at the Falkland Islands Service, St Paul's Cathedral,
26 July 1982)

The first note in this service is thanksgiving. We began with particular thanksgiving for the courage and endurance of those who fought in the South Atlantic and that is where my sermon starts.

What I have heard about the conduct of the British forces in and around the Falkland Islands has moved and heartened me. I have experienced battle myself and know that it is no mean achievement to preserve the restraint and display the courage shown by so many involved in this conflict. I was particularly impressed by the report of one journalist who admitted that he had started the campaign with a fairly standard stereotyped view of the forces — effete officers leading unreflective men. He was converted by the Falklands experience and returned with a deep respect for those who had fought bravely, without turning into 'automata'. He was moved by the mature way in which grief was openly expressed over the loss of comrades and admired the lack of rancour shown in attitudes towards the enemy. Another eye-witness has described to me the determination shown at every level to achieve objectives with the minimum use of force. At the hard-fought battle of Goose Green the reaction was not the conquerors' triumph, but 'thank God it's stopped'. It is right to be proud of such men.

There is much to give thanks for in all this now that the attempt to settle the future of the Falkland Islanders by armed invasion has been thwarted, but the men who served in this campaign would be the first to say that while we are paying tribute to the armed forces we should not forget the perseverence and courage of those who have been defending the lives and laws of the citizens of this country in Northern Ireland over a number of years.

While giving thanks, however, we also mourn for grievous losses. Thank God so many returned, but there are many in this cathedral who mourn the loss of someone they love and our thoughts go out to them. We must not forget: our prayers for remembrance will not end this day. They remind us that we possess the terrifying power for destruction. War has always been detestable, but since 1945 we have lived with the capacity to destroy the whole of humankind. It is impossible to be a Christian and not to long for peace. 'Blessed are the peacemakers for they shall be called the sons of God.' This was one of the themes to which the Pope repeatedly returned during his visit to this country. His speech in Coventry was particularly memorable when he said: 'War should belong to the tragic past, to history. It should find no place on humanity's agenda for the future.'

I do not believe that there would be many people, if any, in this cathedral who would not say amen to that. War is a sign of human failure and everything we say and do in this service must be in that context. The problem is that war belongs to the tragic present as well as to the tragic past. At the beginning of this century, in a noble book, *The Great Illusion* by Norman Angell, the irrational character of war in a modern world was precisely described. The thesis is that in a world of economic interdependence you cannot injure another state without damaging your own interests. We flourish and become prosperous, not by raiding, and pauperizing our neighbours, but by building them up as ever better markets for our manufactures.

Yet war, demonstrably irrational and intolerable, has left a terrible mark on this century. It has claimed tens of millions of victims and even now occupies some of the best talents and resources of the nations. The great nations continue to channel their energies into perfecting weapons of destruction and very little is done to halt the international trade in arms, which contributes so much to the insecurity of the world. In the most heavily armed area, the Middle East, every day seems to bring fresh bad news of man's willingness to resort to the irrational and the intolerable in pursuit of his territorial and ideological ambitions. Angell was writing at the end of a period of relative peace. We cannot be even as sanguine about the human future as he was. Our hope as Christians is not fundamentally in man's naked goodwill and rationality. We believe that he can overcome the deadly selfishness of class or sect or race by discovering himself as a child of the universal God of love. When a man realizes that he is a beloved child of the Creator of all, then he is ready to see his neighbours in the world as brothers and sisters. That is one reason why those who dare to interpret God's will must never claim him as an asset for one nation or group rather than another. War springs from the love and loyalty which should be offered to God being applied to some God-substitute, one of the most dangerous being nationalism.

This is a dangerous world where evil is at work nourishing the mindless brutality which killed and maimed so many in this city last week. Sometimes, with the greatest reluctance, force is necessary to hold back the chaos which injustice and the irrational element in man threaten to make of the world. But having said that, all is not lost and there is hope. Even in the failure of war there are springs of hope. In that great war play by Shakespeare, Henry V says: 'There is some soul of goodness in things evil, would men observingly distill it out'. People are mourning on both sides of this conflict. In our prayers we shall quite rightly remember those who are bereaved in our own country and the relations of the young Argentinian soldiers who were killed. Common sorrow could do something to reunite those who were engaged in this struggle. A shared anguish can be a bridge of reconciliation. Our neighbours are indeed like us.

I have had an avalanche of letters and advice about this service. Some correspondents have asked 'Why drag God in?' as if the intention was to wheel up God to endorse some particular policy or attitude rather than another. The purpose of prayer and of services like this is very different and there is hope for the world in the difference. In our prayers we come into the presence of the living God. We come with our very human emotions, pride in achievement and courage, grief at loss and waste. We come as we are and not just mouthing opinions and thanksgiving which the fashion of the moment judges acceptable. As we pour into our prayer our mourning, our pride, our shame and our convictions, which will inevitably differ from person to person, if we are really present and really reaching out to God and not just demanding his endorsement, then God is able to work upon us. He is able to deepen and enlarge our compassion and to purify our thanksgiving. The parent who comes mourning the loss of a son may find here consolation, but also a spirit which enlarges our compassion to include all those Argentinian parents who have lost sons.

Man without God finds it difficult to achieve this revolution inside himself. But talk of peace and reconciliation is just fanciful and theoretical unless we are prepared to undergo such a revolution. Many of the reports I have heard about the troops engaged in this war refer to moments when soldiers have been brought face to face with what is fundamental in life and have found new sources of strength and compassion even in the midst of conflict. Ironically, it has sometimes been those spectators who remained at home, whether supporters or opponents of the conflict, who continue to be most violent in their attitudes and untouched in their deepest selves.

Man without God is less than man. In meeting God, a man is shown his failures and his lack of integrity, but he is also given strength to turn more and more of his life and actions into love and compassion for other men like himself. It is necessary to the continuance of life on this planet that more and more people make this discovery. We have been given the choice. Man possesses the power to obliterate himself, sacrificing the whole race on the altar of some God-substitute. Or he can choose life in partnership with God the Father of all. I believe that there is evidence that more and more people are waking up to the realization that this crucial decision peers us in the face here and now.

Cathedrals and churches are always places into which we bring human experiences — birth, marriage, death, our flickering communion with God, our fragile relationships with each other, so that they may be deepened and directed by the spirit of Christ. Today we bring our mixture of thanksgiving, sorrows and aspirations for a better ordering of this world. Pray God that he may purify, enlarge and redirect these in the ways of his kingdom of love and peace. Amen.

8. The Zeebrugge Ferry Disaster

(Sermon at the Memorial Service in Canterbury Cathedral on 15
April 1987 for those who died on the Zeebrugge ferry)

Where there is sorrow there is holy ground. The preacher must tread
sensitively. It is tempting to leave it to music, readings and prayers to
match the varied moods of those who mourn. But our service today
would not be complete without an attempt to put into words of a direct
and personal character the sympathies of a nation, and to articulate
the faith for which this cathedral has stood over the centuries of our
island story.

First we want to express our solidarity with the families and friends
of those who died in this disaster. For them the tragedy remains, and
with it the numbness of loss and grief. The tragedy was so sudden —
the loss so unexpected. To those who carry this burden of pain we offer
our deepest sympathy. And no sympathy will, I know, be so heartfelt
as the sympathy of those who shared the horrors of that night but came
through unhurt, and with their families and friends unharmed.

Not even the firmest faith is enough to insulate us from the pain of
loss and grief, or from that sense that, with the death of someone dear
to us, our own life has lost its meaning. *Time* must help. It is said that
you must survive in grief through the course of a full year before life
begins to knit together again, and threads of purpose begin to appear.
Those of us who have friends who are in sorrow must give them time,
and with it the chance to speak of their sadness. We must not only be
ready to offer our words of comfort — we must also be ready to listen
patiently to their words of grief. There are moments, of course, when
we are so overwhelmed that we can say nothing. There is no reason
to be alarmed at that. The better part of mourning, better even than
patience, is *silence*, silence which touches the edges of the grief which
others must endure. Patience and silence and time — and standing
beside us through all is God.

To some who mourn, the question is bound to arise, inevitably,
bitterly perhaps. *Why* should this happen? *Why* should a good God let
it happen? I do not believe that they will be easily satisfied by argument or explanation. In suffering and bereavement we know that no
theoretical answer will do. Hearts cry out not for answers but for
friends who will share suffering with us. The stilted, agonized-over
lines in a letter; the tongue-tied neighbour who is content just to sit
with us — these are the things which count.

In this disaster it has been the practical, down-to-earth support
given by so many doctors and nurses, rescue-workers, company offi-

cials, police and clergy which has struck us all. Even in the darkest moments at Zeebrugge there were rays of light — light in the instinctive co-operation of helpers from our neighbour nations; light in the gallant rescue work of divers, helicopter crews, harbour workers; light in the extraordinary courage of sailors and passengers who risked and sometimes lost their own lives to save others. Some of this light has already become legend. I think of the seaman who found that his diving gear was obstructing his search. So he discarded it, and stayed down in the dark until he found three lorry drivers, trapped alive in an air pocket. I think of the passenger with spinal injuries carrying his baby daughter to safety in his teeth. I think of the four men trapped in lower decks taking turns to hold above water the head of an elderly woman. I think of the man who acted as a bridge to allow others to crawl across, and the grandmother who tried to save someone in a falling wheelchair.

These are but a few examples of human heroism which this disaster encouraged and inspired. There are many, many others, and some will never be known. Our whole nation joins today with those who were rescued at Zeebrugge in admiration and gratitude for all who saved life at sea, or brought kindness and comfort on land. We owe a special debt to our friends in Belgium — the total commitment and excellence of their rescue and hospital services figure in every account I have heard or read. As so often in the past, tragedy at sea has displayed the human qualities of courage and generosity in all their splendour.

In the last century a terrible earthquake struck Italy. An eyewitness described 'the wreckage and ruin, the apparently blind and stupid carnage inflicted by sheer physical forces'. In the midst of it moved a man carrying two small children: 'Wherever he went he seemed to bring order, hope and faith in that confusion and despair'. The eyewitness said that he made them feel 'that somehow love was at the heart of all things'.

Someone who was in the midst of things at Zeebrugge said later: 'Tragedy does not take away love: it increases it. Perhaps we are more loving people, more sensitive, more concerned for each other because of that moment of grief which overthrew our ideas of what things matter, and opened our eyes again to the importance of our common humanity.'

It is in the selfless heroism of so many at Zeebrugge that we can see God's love at work. For the God and Father of our Lord Jesus Christ is not a God who stands outside us, and sends disaster. He is not even a God who offers comfort from a distance. He is Immanuel, God with us, the God who in Christ crucified plunges into the darkness of human sorrow and suffering, to stand alongside us, even in death.

Christian faith does not mean believing in impossible things. It means trusting that Christ's promises never fail. 'Though a man die, yet shall he live.' Faith is not hoping the worst won't happen. It is knowing there is no tragedy which cannot be redeemed.

These things we shall remember again on Good Friday. On Saturday, on the night before Easter Day, we shall light the Easter fire in Canterbury. With the shadows of the vast vaulted roof above us, it seems such a little, vulnerable thing — and yet it is there, making its way through the darkness, and, as other candles are lit from it, a pool of light and hope begins to spread. Such is our faith and hope in the risen Christ. Not a hope which ignores the shadows of suffering and death, but a hope strong and secure in the assurance that love is 'at the heart of all things', that the eternal God is our refuge, and underneath are the everlasting arms in which are held those who have died, as well as those who mourn their loss.

Those who died at Zeebrugge did not die deserted by God, abandoned by him in an alien element, far away from his care and love. Though for a few who died their graves should be the sea bed, nevertheless they are as truly in God's loving hands as if their bodies lay in the most gracious of country churchyards. There also his right hand shall hold them in death as in life. That is the faith of the Bible.

There is no more beautiful expression of this faith than some words of the poet who wrote the book in the Bible called 'The Song of Songs'. I hope those of you who have suffered loss may be able to take these words home with you, and keep them close to your troubled minds and grieving hearts. The words are these. 'Many waters cannot quench love, neither can the depths drown it' (8.7). Many waters have not quenched your love for those who died. How much less shall the waters quench God's love for them, the God who gave them power to live and be yours — and who gave you the power to love them.

In the words of St Paul to companions physically and emotionally distressed,

In all these things we are more than conquerors through him who loved us. For I am sure that neither death, nor life, nor things present, nor things to come, nor height, nor depth, nor anything else in all creation, can separate us from the love of God in Christ Jesus our Lord.

(Romans 8.37–39)

To that love we commend all those who died at Zeebrugge. To that love we pray for all those who mourn them. Amen.

9. Faith and the Environment

(Address at Festival of Faith and the Environment, Canterbury Cathedral, 17 September 1989)

It was the good pleasure of the Father that in the Son should all the fullness dwell, and through the Son to reconcile all things to himself — through him, I say, whether things upon the earth or things in the heavens.

(Colossians 1.19, 20)

A month ago the world caught its breath. The excitement of a space mission again captured our imagination. Twelve years into its journey Voyager II passed close by Neptune and Triton. We stopped in wonder as we realized that its visit to our outer planets over, it would pass out of our solar system 'to wander for all eternity, the milky way'.

This tiny craft, weighing no more than a family car, reached a target nearly three billion miles away 'within seconds of its twelve years and five days time schedule, only twenty miles off course'.

The achievement was stunning, the photographs unexpectedly striking. The Psalmist's words become suddenly contemporary:

For I will consider the heavens: the moon and the stars, which thou hast ordained.

What is man that thou art mindful of him: and the son of man, that thou visitest him. (Psalm 8)

The Voyager mission brought home to us as to no previous generation the sheer immensity of space. Yet I noticed another startling claim related very simply in a *Times* leader, you could have almost overlooked it. It said:

In addition to giving scientists the final chapters for their encyclopaedia of the planets, Voyager II has shown conclusively that earth is the only oasis in the solar system capable of sustaining life.

Even if 'conclusively' may perhaps be under some question against the possibility, some say, of primitive micro-organisms on the moon Triton, yet there remains a thought of overwhelming force and poignancy — was there ever a moment in human history when the sheer *preciousness* of life on this our planet was revealed so clearly?

190

Not, perhaps, since the first dawning of humankind on this earth. Then human beings were what we might now call an endangered species — few in number, less powerful in physique than many animals, less prolific, easy victims of storm, flood, earthquake and fire. Already, no doubt, humans excelled other animals in intelligence; but even that produced a sense of fear — an awareness of the constant danger arising from forces more powerful than ours.

Gradually human intelligence suggested that these threatening powers might be placated or appeased. These powers were seen as 'gods' that roared in the lion, bellowed in the bull or lashed the waters to fury. And so grew cults offering gifts, homage and sacrifices to these 'gods', the potent threats to human existence.

To just one people it was disclosed that there is but one God — the single creator and ruler of all nature. The people of Israel followed the call of that one God. In doing so they found a confidence to use nature for their needs and subdue it to their purposes. They need not tremble as an endangered species but might walk boldly about the earth as, by divine permission, its appointed inheritors. Judaism, and the religions which have their roots in Judaism, both received and taught a wholly confident attitude to nature. In that confidence our once-endangered species has not only survived, it has advanced in knowledge and skill, in material wealth, in artistic flair, even in spiritual insight. Humankind became the dominant species on the earth. But what have we done with our dominion? Was there ever a moment to have more cause to fear for the world because of our dominion over it?

We know — and this is largely what brings us to this Festival today — that humans are acting imprudently, polluting and squandering the riches of the earth at a pace which far exceeds the rate of natural renewal. We are impoverishing our habitat. We have begun to realize, fearfully, that if we go on this way, we are capable of making of this earth a place dark and cold and uninhabitable. The initially endangered species has become the endangering species. Whether our attention is focused on the seals, the tropical rainforest or the ozone layer, the cause of the crisis is the same — men and women have demanded more than the planet can give. Prudence, and concern for our own future demand that we exercise our dominion over nature with less extravagance and self-indulgence.

But there are motives other than prudence for doing so — motives which since they are formed at deeper levels of the human spirit are likely to be more dynamic, more effective and compelling than prudence.

It is, I believe, at these deeper levels that some people risk themselves in trying to save the whale or the white rhino or any other endangered species from extinction. It is at this deeper level that some people accept for themselves considerable restraints of diet or lifestyle for the sake of sparing pain or stress to non-human creatures. The common motives of these endeavours is the conviction that nature does not exist simply and solely for the benefit of humankind: that nature is much more than the necessary infrastructure for our human survival and prosperity, that it has an intrinsic value by no means reduceable to its benefit to human beings.

This conviction — I have heard it described as 'this new sensitivity' — is becoming increasingly widespread and articulate. Because it finds its source at such deep levels of the human spirit, it must, I think, be called a religious conviction. But it is not a conviction unique to any one religion in particular, and it is shared by some who would profess no religion at all.

For Christians this conviction is based upon and validated by the authority of the Bible. 'The earth is the Lord's and all that therein is': our dominion over nature is no more than stewardship and, as St Paul writes, 'it is required of stewards that they be found faithful' — faithful to the attitudes and purposes of our Lord and Master.

It is abundantly clear in the Scriptures that God is not some absentee landlord of the earth concerned only to receive his rent of gratitude and praise from his human tenantry. God is equally *close* to the earth and all that is in it. So we read in the Psalms that he 'waters the hills from above'; he 'opens his hands to fill all things living with plenteousness'; he 'feeds the young ravens that call upon him'; that 'he will save both man and beast' in the excellency of his mercy. When Job questions the Lord's wisdom, he receives the stinging rebuke, 'where were you when I laid the foundation of the earth?' And then we read, most authoritatively of all, in the teaching of our Lord — God clothes with beauty the grass of the field though it is to last only for a day: he feeds the birds of the air: and the death of a sparrow is known to him.

And as the Bible tells of the intimacy of God's care for all that he has made, so it tells that *all his works* may 'declare his glory' and contribute to his praise.

The Bible teaches us that this is no cheap universe, no throwaway world in which everything except humankind is readily expendable. The world cannot be cheap; for it is the very creation of him whom Christ disclosed, whose very nature and name is love, and nothing made or done in love is made without cost or done without purpose. To Christians the intrinsic value of the world of nature lies in the cost of its creation, in the fragment of the love of God which is expended in and for every fragment of its being. The care and restraint and thoughtfulness with which we exercise our stewardship of nature is nothing less than an expression of our duty and obedience to Him who is the loving creator both of nature and of ourselves.

So St Paul writes that it was the 'good pleasure' of God that in Christ all things should be reconciled to him 'whether things upon the earth or things in the heavens'. That is of decisive importance. In Christ all things in heaven and on earth shall be reconciled to God, won back to him, gathered in to him. From that ingathering from time to eternity nothing that is of God's creation shall be excluded. Can the Christian help the world to see that from our precious earth we hear speaking to us, with all his tender strength, the voice of a loving creator? That is the challenge this Festival poses. It demands hard thinking and complex choices. Yet, at the heart of it all, giving us the courage to act, is the very simple thought which links the glory of the Creator to the most ordinary things of earth. Perhaps no one has expressed this truth more succinctly and profoundly than Coleridge in his words in the *Ancient Mariner*:

> He prayeth best who loveth best
> all things both great and small;
> For the dear God who loveth us
> He made and loveth all.

❦ 10 ❦

An Archbishop and his authority

It is part of an archbishop's task to prevent the Church trying to sting itself to death, like a demented scorpion, and instead to gather the church and remind it of the priority of allegiance to its common Lord. A church without order and without strategy is never likely to be effective in handling change or extending its frontiers.

(Sermon at Canterbury Cathedral, for the 1,300th anniversary
of the death of Theodore, Archbishop of Canterbury,
19 September 1990)

When I came to the throne of St Augustine, I was reminded of the men of power who had sat there before me by the pikes from the Archbishop's private army, which now decorate the walls of Lambeth Palace as museum pieces. And I was reminded by them of the temptation to gain the church's ends by the world's means. That temptation is still with us — until we remember the words: 'But it shall not be so among you'.

So if we have anything to offer the world as new maps of authority are being drawn it will be because we have not only remembered this prohibition but also lived by it.

(*Authority in Crisis?*, p. 29)

The central question posed by the archiepiscopate of Robert Runcie would seem to be one concerning 'new maps of authority' — the true nature, appropriate functioning and limits of Church authority in the contemporary world. Seemingly the central question in his own mind, it is one inexorably raised by the dilemmas which have confronted the Church of England and the Anglican Communion in these years, by the ways he has tried to cope with them, and by the attacks to which he has in consequence been subjected. In 1980 it already provided the principal theme for his enthronement sermon, while the only book upon a specific topic he has published as Archbishop is his *Authority in Crisis? An Anglican Response* (1988).

The quite exceptional effort and care he has put into a specifically archiepiscopal mode of teaching and leadership constrain one to ask

194

questions, not just about his own views, but still more about the function itself as he sees it, and has endeavoured to shape it. This was much less the case for Ramsey or Coggan, each of whom had achieved a much greater measure of personal recognition before coming to Canterbury than had Runcie. Their image was not made at Canterbury in the way that Runcie's has been. Every inch of him has responded to the demands of Canterbury with intense sensitivity, contradictory as those demands at times have seemed to be. They have reshaped him, but he has also greatly reshaped them.

It was not only that Runcie had no established reputation as theologian or writer. It was also that he came from a relatively insignificant and uncomplicated see. The leap from St Albans to Canterbury was valuable precisely because it took him to so very different a kind of job from that which he had been doing for the previous ten years, that it forced him at once, self-consciously and continuously, to ask questions about being Archbishop of Canterbury, about authority in general, but particularly about how he should suitably exercise authority. It is really only as Archbishop that he can be evaluated. Excellent as his work was at Cuddesdon and St Albans, it was not the sort of work about which books are written. Even at Canterbury it is not just on Runcie the person but upon the function of Archbishop and of how he has used it that we have frequently needed to focus. It is upon this that, with both the selflessness and the strategic sense of a very efficient and dedicated man, he too would certainly wish us to concentrate. His acute personal feeling for a job and its specific requirements means that, faced with a unique, evolving and largely undefined office of enormous importance, he has continually ruminated upon the functionality of his authority, and the purposes for which it can best be used — though he could still only do it, being the sort of person he is, rather intuitively, as practitioner rather than as systematic theologian.

He has held archiepiscopal authority in a decade in which the pendulum swung back from the libertarianism of the 1960s to at least a rhetorical reassertion in many powerful quarters of authoritarianism. Runcie was not a natural sixties person. He had lots of friends who were, and he was always open to what they had to say, but his own temperament had too large an element of conservatism within it while his underlying liberalism included a note of Oxbridge scepticism which did not easily go with sixties enthusiasms. Yet the liberalism and the scepticism alike equally prevented him from going very far along the road of restorationism, with its simplistic undertones of one or another sort of fundamentalism, which in the eighties turned its back upon the sixties. The more cautious side of sixties liberalism — the spirit, especially, of the Second Vatican Council — was what Runcie continued to identify with most easily. Vested with authority in an age seeking strong authority, Runcie remained the temperamental traditionalist not averse to some strengthening of order but forced by a liberal conscience to say no to the simplicities of Right as much as of Left. The authority he would defend would inevitably be derided by some as soft, because it could not enter an alliance with, or agree to become a vehicle of, religious, moral or political neo-Victorianism.

He would inevitably suffer by comparison, in the eyes of some, with his exact ecclesiastical contemporary, Pope John Paul II. The Pope has used his authority, for better or worse, to provide an exceptionally strong and unambiguous lead over a wide range of issues, theological, ecclesiastical and moral. To many, outsiders and insiders, he certainly appears a great contemporary religious leader. He is not someone who could be accused of sitting on the fence. He has, in consequence, succeeded in alienating more Catholics than any other modern Pope, not only from him personally but from the very institution of the papacy as it actually functions. While those who agreed with his views have welcomed his pronouncements and even the many attempts to silence Catholic dissenters, those — and they are many — who have remained unconvinced have been driven to question the whole nature of papal authority.

No Archbishop of Canterbury ever claimed authority comparable with that of the Pope. Nevertheless, as exceedingly few papal pronouncements can be held infallible even in Catholic theology (and none, at least hitherto, of John Paul II), the difference between the necessary degree of authoritativeness in their teaching can be overstated. In reality ecclesiastical authority, like all other human authority, can take many forms, some of them divergent, of varying weight. Papal encyclicals, statements of Lambeth Conferences, joint pastoral letters of the American Catholic bishops, statements by the Catholic Synod of Bishops, individual utterances by the Archbishop of Canterbury, Cardinal Hume or the Bishop of Durham, the Kairos document, the ARCIC agreed statements, declarations made by a group of theologians — all have authority up to a point. Probably of all major documents produced ecclesiastically in our time, it is those of the Second Vatican Council which have the greatest, as judged upon the basis of 'reception' by the Church as a whole. Yet they too are far from infallible, or above criticism. Certainly when one considers the mass of 'authoritative' teaching which has been produced in the last quarter century, one problem about it and about the further exercise of authority becomes clear: the quantity may not only have its effect upon the quality, it also increasingly affects the ability of anyone to produce anything truly authoritative. It would certainly be idle for an Archbishop of Canterbury, a Lambeth Conference or a General Synod today to attempt to teach authoritatively on any subject at all without regard to all the other teaching which has of late been provided. Authoritative Church teaching has in principle always been a collective, collegial exercise. More than ever it needs to be seen to be so today. From this point of view an Archbishop like Runcie, temperamentally averse to being a bishop-theologian in his own right, is actually well suited to circumstances. If his primatial role might seem to resemble that of Randall Davidson, archbishop in the first thirty years of this century, someone who was again not a theologian, this may be judged strength rather than weakness. It may actually have contributed to the development of a more collegial exercise of Christian authority within the Anglican Communion.

Thus, Runcie's character has combined with the teaching of the Second Vatican Council, to which he paid great attention, and the inherent needs of the late twentieth century, to stress a pattern of authority at once collegial and cautious. The caution, at least, is characteristically Anglican, a 'tradition of moderation and restraint. . . . no stridency, no false heroics; calm, sober, measured speech', as he told General Synod in 1981. Within the Church of England he has stressed the teaching role of the House of Bishops in General Synod as a group, just as within the Anglican Communion he has tried to build up the collegial authority of the Primates as a group. His chief complaint with the Bishop of Durham upon the one side and the Bishop of London upon the other is that each has a tendency to flout collegiality. Undoubtedly the weight of a collegial authority is normally very much more considerable than that of an individual and nothing is more perplexing to the common man than to have different bishops in the same Church loudly proclaiming different things. Authority in Anglicanism has gained from the current stress upon collegiality, though there is an inherent danger of producing in consequence a rather banal or unconvincing conflation of views.

Runcie would stress that the principal role of a bishop, and still more of an archbishop and a Primate, is to mediate the traditional rather than to be a voice of original theology or prophecy. Yet he would not question that the latter is needed too. It has become customary within the Church of England for a Bishop of Durham to be an intellectual and the role of a Bishop of Durham needs to be recognizably different within the mediation of authority from that of an

Archbishop of Canterbury. Ian Ramsey was a wonderful Bishop of Durham. He might have been a very disappointing Archbishop of Canterbury. Michael Ramsey moved from Durham via York to Canterbury. He is the only Bishop of Durham to have done so in this century. He indeed straddled the two roles. If John Habgood had been chosen to succeed Runcie he would have been a second, as he too, like Ramsey, was at Durham before going to York. But it may well be that it was exactly the qualities which marked him out for Durham which detracted from his suitability for Canterbury. York stands between Durham and Canterbury, functionally as well as geographically. Undoubtedly an Archbishop of York exercises something of the primatial function of Canterbury, but it is inevitably less presidential. York remains a more suitable place for an intellectual, a prophet or a party man — so long as he tempers this sort of role with a semi-primatial one. Temple was a great Archbishop of York. He was so briefly at Canterbury that it is hard to judge him as 'Cantuar', but he was not a good judge of character or a born administrator, and from time to time he developed bees in his bonnet. It may well be that his prophetic and intellectual quality, despite his undoubted gift for presiding and reconciling, made him more suitable for York than for Canterbury.

Within a college it is possible to exercise such a variety of roles. It needs pastors, theologians, prophets and a president. David Jenkins might be a wholly disastrous Archbishop of Canterbury but that does not mean he was an inappropriate choice for the see of Durham. Runcie has suited Canterbury. His use of authority, his approach to teaching, has been very much a Canterbury approach, presidential rather than prophetic. He has a lot of sympathy for the traditionalism of Graham Leonard and he has a lot of sympathy for the radicalism of David Jenkins. He is not frightened to admit, without too much regret, as he did in an address to the West London Synagogue, 'that I am the Archbishop of a Church in which the tensions between Orthodoxy and liberalism remain unresolved. I cannot claim to be above these tensions. They run right through me.' He is not a professional theologian. He is not particularly well read in formal theology of a more systematic kind and he remains somehow averse to its methods. He recognizes that a traditionally-minded bishop like Leonard (who is all the same not a theologian either) can find it hard to relate to someone 'so casual about doctrinal coherence'. With his delight in Catholic symbolism and concern for corporate order he can sympathize deeply with some of the views of Graham Leonard but he is simply not intellectually convinced by conservative theological thinking as a whole. Equally he can delight in the cut and thrust of original thought represented by David Jenkins, and almost nothing that Jenkins says would much upset him, but he is not absolutely sure that Jenkins is right, or at least quite right. He believes that 'a vigorous Church needs leadership which is a mixture of conservative and radical'. He has always had this ability to protect, sympathize with and advance the views of others while not being too sure that he actually shared them, or thought that it mattered much if he did not. Thus at St Albans he appointed Eric James, a radical, as Canon Missioner for the diocese and Peter Moore, a strong traditionalist, as Dean of the Cathedral. Both were his friends. Some might think that he must share Eric James's radicalism or he would not trust him so much in the diocese; others might think he must share Peter Moore's principled opposition to the ordination of women. But, really, he did not quite do either. He felt the tensions between orthodoxy and liberalism running too strongly through him. He was also never very sure, even if he was convinced about something, whether he was right to be so convinced. Collegiality, marketed with all the authority of the Second Vatican Council, has been for him the best solution to a great unease.

It has also been a convenient remedy for the Church. He remarked to his Diocesan Synod in November 1980, 'We have passed through a necessary period of critical examination and the qualifying of crude dogmatic statements. The time has come, however, when even to intelligent and sympathetic outside observers the usual voice of our Church seems to be bewilderingly ambiguous and woolly.' It was now necessary instead, he believed, to put the accent on 'positive and affirmative Christian teaching'. *The Myth of God Incarnate* had been published in 1978. It was symptomatic of the disintegration of academic Christian theology consequent upon an over-large injection of sixties liberalism. There can be no doubt that a yawning gap had developed between much academic theology and customary Church teaching. This gap had, to a large extent, been hitherto obscured. Its demonstration in and around the controversy over *The Myth of God Incarnate* could not but be highly disturbing for the Church. Academic theologians did not, of course, all agree among themselves. Nevertheless, it seems clear enough that the Church could hardly function with the sort of theology dominant in *The Myth*: at least the Church's self-understanding would have to be quite enormously reduced. Theologians, if they see themselves primarily as university professors or lecturers, may interpret their role as they will, but bishops have to be concerned with the public teaching and organic life of the Church. Their role is pastoral, not academic. Unquestionably *The Myth* was a threat to the overall balance of Christian and Anglican teaching.

'Compared with Rome', declared Runcie in a Presidential Address to the General Synod in 1981,

> Anglicanism has a higher evaluation of the primitive over the mediaeval tradition of the Church. Compared with Constantinople, it has a higher evaluation of the European Renaissance and Enlightenment, and a greater respect for the autonomy of the scientific method and the realm of ethics. Compared with Lutheranism, it is less sharply defined doctrinally, but more insistent on the centrality of liturgy and worship in the life of the Church. . . .
>
> In the matter of doctrine, the Anglican tradition has been to insist on adherence to the primitive catholic faith while allowing a greater diversity of theological opinion than is permissible in other episcopal Churches, and not proceeding to what has been seen as the over-systematization and definition of doctrine which was given an unhappy impulse by the religious quarrels of the sixteenth century and which has proceeded to our own day, creating new dogmas out of inessentials, which really ought to be left in the realm of theological opinion.

All good sound Anglican thoughts, but not entirely adequate to cope with the problem of *The Myth*. Maybe the latter had strayed well beyond the boundaries of 'the primitive Catholic faith' but what, precisely, was in that faith and is 'the primitive' always a reliable yardstick of Christian truth for today? Anglican tradition might allow 'a greater diversity of opinion' than other Churches, but how great a diversity could even it rightly allow, and on what basis could it make a decision? It is one thing to describe the general qualities of Anglicanism in a soothing way. It is quite another to use them as some sort of yardstick for coping with contemporary doctrinal difficulties of an exceptionally basic sort.

A year later, in December 1982, Runcie preached a sermon for the centenary of Archbishop Tait's death. Tait was a Scot and something of a liberal with whom Runcie found it easy to identify. As Headmaster of Rugby, his favourite phrase had been, 'there is a good deal to be said on both sides' — a very Runcie sort of remark. Runcie also enjoys his dictum that 'the modern ideal of a bishop is of a man in a chronic state of perspiration' and likes to quote it. Tait had struggled to make the Church of England more liberal and open at a time when it was still largely gripped by a pre-critical fundamentalism but was faced with the scientific and historical revolutions of the later nine-teenth century. All this seems congenial enough but the point Runcie wanted to press home in his sermon was rather the contrary: Tait's problem was not his. Tait was faced with a too dogmatic Church, he with a too liberal one in which the theology of the 1970s had led to what looked to many like 'total incoherence'. 'I some-times fear that the Church of England is less and less in a real and reverent dialogue with its traditions. If the process of discarding forms and models goes very much further, there is a great danger that we shall cease to be a Church in which vertebrate and vigorous Christians can be nourished.' Runcie was coming to see that a general appeal to Anglican values was inadequate and he was grop-ing for a more precise strategy of recovery. Certainly, the Anglican tradition 'does not lend itself to the promulgation of new dogmas or the proclamation of anathemas, but the answer to an excessively dogmatic Church is not a Church that is totally at sea'. He was seeking, not to suppress freedom, but to re-establish nevertheless some sort of workable corporate *magisterium*.

A sense of doctrinal crisis was further excited when David Jenkins, previously Professor of Theology in the University of Leeds, became in 1984 Bishop of Durham and made a number of remarks about the historicity of the Virgin Birth and the Resurrection which the mass media took up with exceeding glee. Jenkins is an exciting teacher and theologian who rather likes to shock in order to make people think. He had had little conventional pastoral experience and believed — quite possibly correctly — that quite ordinary people need to be made to think in much the same way as undergraduates. He enjoyed the publicity and the consequent opportunity to run a sort of extended national theological seminar in which he did all the talking. Beyond the fireworks, however, both his belief in Christ and his conception of the pastoral responsibility of a bishop were far more traditional than many of his critics could see. Little that he said had not been held by other Anglican bishops before him. While the effect of The Myth was likely to make its readers abandon Christian faith, the effect of David Jenkins was far more to renew it. He was such an infectiously enthu-siastic and convinced Christian theologian. He even brought the bishops to sit down and think about theology — a considerable achievement! 'While not all of us will recognize our understanding of miracle in the Bishop of Durham's divine laser beam', Archbishop Runcie remarked to General Synod a few months later, 'I know the whole Synod will be deeply grateful to him for his moving and per-sonal exploration of the questions before us.'

The immediate result was an important debate on doctrine in General Synod on 13 February 1985 in which Runcie made a speech of some importance and out of which came the crystallization of what he had been looking for, a decision that the House of Bishops should reflect upon the nature of Christian belief and report back to Synod. He began by strongly affirming Incarnation and Resurrection and assuring Synod that 'the doctrines of the Incarnation and Resurrection are not in doubt among your Bishops'.

'The issues about the limits of interpreting credal statements which have concerned us in recent months are far from new. A nerve has been touched and exposed with painful effect, but not for the first time. Uncertainty about matters of belief and insecurity about authority — these are never far from the surface in a Church which takes pride in its breadth, its tolerance, its liberty, and in T. S. Eliot's phrase, its "continence in affirmation".' He went on to discuss the bishop as teacher. First of all he is a 'guardian of the tradition' and this 'imposes a certain conservative responsibility. He is a guarantee of historic continuity. He is a steward of the apostolic faith which is our common Christian heritage. He will, of course, take advice from theologians and others, but if he is to be true to his vocation, the bishop must regard himself as pre-eminently the trustee of tradition, in his diocese and with his fellow bishops in the Church at large.'

But it is also true that the bishop is a member of the Church sharing its life and thoughts, the faith, doubts, perplexities and aspirations of every Christian. 'The bishop is no more exempt from the need to examine, test and explore the truth of his faith than any Christian, ordained or lay. The bishop is not an automaton, but a man of flesh and blood, a man of doubt as well as faith.' The bishop's 'conservative responsibility' must not be taken to mean that 'tradition and the apostolic faith is something essentially static and unchanging; something handed down, complete and intact, from one generation to the next'. The historic formulation of dogma does not preclude further enquiry. On the contrary, bishops should stimulate new attempts to interpret belief in ways intellectually, personally and pastorally satisfying. He then quoted the 'prudent and prophetic counsel' of Bishop John Robinson, author of *Honest to God* which caused quite as big a stir in 1963 as anything David Jenkins said in 1984:

A Bishop will be the more aware that his lightest word is liable to be taken up — and sometimes distorted — by the public media. The inordinate attention paid to what he says derives almost entirely from his office, and his utterances and actions will therefore appear, particularly outside the Church, but also to embarrassed faithful within, to commit many others than himself.

Nevertheless in the last resort, Robinson insisted and Runcie repeated, 'The Church must give positive witness to the fact that integrity is a more fundamental theological virtue than orthodoxy. . . . a man of unimpeachable orthodoxy but uncertain integrity is a far greater threat to Christian truth than the man of questionable orthodoxy but undeniable integrity.'

At one and the same time he was defending Jenkins and looking for a positive and collective outcome. From this debate came the task of the House of Bishops to prepare a corporate statement on Christian belief which they published a little over a year later, April 1986, a matter of 39 printed pages. That statement was important, first, in representing a return to greater episcopal confidence after a somewhat self-effacing period in which the claims of theologians and General Synod had been more to the fore. It was, explicitly, an exercise in 'collegial responsibility' and it was unanimous: Durham and London both went along with it and everyone in between. Note that this included the particular points which had prompted the exercise.

We affirm our faith in the Resurrection of Our Lord Jesus Christ as an objective reality, both historical and divine, not as a way of speaking about the faith of his followers, but as a fact on which their testimony depends for its truth.

The statement as a whole was theologically well argued, slightly to the conservative side of centre. It was coherent. It was certainly adequate as a basis of teaching and understanding the Christian faith at the level required for a normal educated lay person or pastoral priest. It was not a statement by theologians for theologians. It was a statement by bishops for the twentieth-century faithful. It provided exactly the sort of thing Runcie believed to be needed. It was done in a way he could not have done personally and it possessed greater authority than if some similar statement had come from him. It was composed during a series of full meetings of the House of Bishops and came out as a genuinely 'consensus document'. As Runcie described it to the Synod, 'Some would want to alter this point, some that. But the result comes from us all. It is our best attempt, without ambiguity and without concealing disagreements, to state where we stand on the issues put to us by Synod.' It demonstrated the worthwhileness of a responsible collegiality just as the better documents of the Second Vatican Council had demonstrated it. Its approach was reinforced by a further report from the Doctrine Commission, chaired for most of its work by Bishop John Taylor of Winchester, entitled *We Believe in God*, which appeared a few months later. Much Anglican theology may fairly be called 'woolly', an adjective Runcie is not afraid of using, but these documents could certainly not be so described. What he rightly found in them was, instead, a 'thoughtful temper — an incapacity to impart doctrine to those who want rough and ready answers'.

In his enthronement sermon Runcie had already rejected the temptation of the over-simple. 'The cry is, "The Church must give a firm lead". Yes. It must — a firm lead against rigid thinking, a judging temper of mind, the disposition to oversimplify difficult and complex problems. If the Church gives Jesus Christ's sort of lead, it will not be popular.' In all Christian teaching there is an area of positive affirmation of the work of God and, around it, an area of comparative unclarity — a necessary frontier area between the normal and the revelational. The danger for Christian doctrine is to try to affirm too much about the frontier area and to make those affirmations of equal weight with the central mystery. Christians must share the central affirmation; their beliefs about its surroundings may vary. 'Faith does not centre on negatives', Runcie told the Synod at York in July 1986, 'the absence of a human father or the emptiness of a tomb. The main-stream of the Church believes that these negatives are entailed by its affirmations, but they cannot be said to be the heart of the matter. It is the action of God, not the passivity of Joseph which is central. It is Christ risen in the completenes of his glorified humanity not the vacating of a tomb which is central.'

Runcie is fond of quoting John Henry Newman and he did so here: 'Truth is wrought by many minds working freely together'. The 'many minds' and the 'freely' are both important for his conception of the kind of Church he was determined to preside over. The conception, of course, is a traditionally Anglican one. His sense of its healthy contemporary functioning very much included the work of David Jenkins, his old friend from Cuddesdon days.

We have seen in this book various different ways in which he has endeavoured to exercise a teaching authority. There are many of them, including the awarding of Lambeth degrees in divinity. The Archbishop of Canterbury is the only person in the country, apart from the universities, empowered to award a degree. The authority to do so dates back to 1533. Runcie has been the first to use it to give a Doctorate of Divinity to somebody who is not a member of any Christian Church. In 1987 he awarded one to Sir Immanuel Jakobovits, the Chief Rabbi, for his learning, his moral leadership and the great contribution he has made to bringing Christians and Jews together. That says something about the range of religious commitment Runcie as Primate of All England wanted to provide space for.

The principal ways in which Runcie has exercised authority may be summarized as follows: there has been the commissioning of reports such as *Faith in the City* and *Faith in the Countryside* produced entirely by a body of experts; the collegial doctrinal activity of the House of Bishops; his own primatial teaching at its most pondered. Of this the most notable example was the opening address to the Lambeth Conference. It came closest to being what one might call a pronouncement from the *cathedra* of St Augustine, to employ a rather Roman conception. There is clearly a difference between this and his more personal and exploratory lectures or, again, the many hundreds of addresses to local congregations of the Anglican Communion from Canterbury to every continent. Clearly, the material of many of these is secondary and highly derivative, though he nearly always succeeds in putting his personal mark on it. The humane and deeply spiritual quality of his preaching at its best can be savoured in Chapter 9. With a Temple or a Ramsey one may distinguish between the teaching of an archbishop and the personal reflections of a theologian and intellectual. With Runcie, there is less point in doing so, but one can still distinguish between the more and the less authoritative in terms of the circumstances of an address, the amount of effort that appears to have gone into it, its relationship to the corpus of his work as a whole. What strikes one, despite his admission of a lack of theological coherence, is really how coherent all the more important pieces are, though one senses a certain slight evolution in firmness, purpose and priorities across his decade of primacy.

Yet it is less the content of his teaching than the methodology of his leadership which has been distinctive. The legacy of his archiepiscopate will be seen above all in four structural areas: the development of a more effective mini-curia at Lambeth Palace; the collegial functioning of the House of Bishops within the Church of England; the less formal collegial activity of the Meeting of Primates within the Anglican Communion; the commissioning of genuinely heavyweight reports. To these may be added his contribution to the functioning of General Synod. He was in no way responsible for Synod. Nevertheless, he has been a highly synodical Archbishop, immensely loyal to its method of working, its decisions (even though he has often disagreed with them) and its underlying principles. Beyond all this he has worked very hard to build up links of an almost organic kind with European Churches, Protestant and Catholic, and he has flown the

205

kite of a new ecumenical papacy. Throughout, it is the sense of an over-all strategy of leadership, rather than the loss or gain of individual decisions, the precise content of particular statements, which has mattered to him.

If one should compare Runcie with his twentieth-century predecessors, it can perhaps best be with Davidson and Fisher — the least intellectual but the most statesmanlike and administratively successful of modern archbishops and the ones who have contributed most to the development of the worldwide Communion. Yet Runcie has been less politically involved than Davidson, less administratively preoccupied than Fisher. He has a more subtle mind than either. Moreover, despite disclaimers, he is also more of a theologian — but, to adopt Eliot's phrase, a very continent one in affirmation. Above all, he has led both the Church of England and the Anglican Communion towards practicable and yet imaginative goals while holding them as firmly together as he can, and he bequeaths to his successor a fairly clearly outlined and demanding programme: the Decade of Evangelism, closer links with the European Churches, Protestant and Catholic, and the reform of General Synod, all apart from the resolution of the issue of women's ordination.

Has Runcie failed, all the same, to give a sufficiently dynamic leadership on crucial issues? Has his conservative temperament and traditionally catholic sympathies blunted the rigour of his mind to grapple with novelty? Has he been too willing to remain sitting on the fence waiting for others to reach a consensus, or for awkward bishops to retire? Has he quite excessively extolled the advantages of seeing both sides of every issue? There is clearly some ground for answering yes to such questions. But really so to answer is to misunderstand not only the man but the function.

There is no doubt and he knows it himself, that he cannot lead with conviction when he remains only barely convinced himself. The matter of the Covenant was a case in point. Still more important, he has reached conviction about the ordination of women but hardly great enthusiasm. His continued tendency to joke about it is always perilous. For many, this is the absolutely central issue facing the Church today, an issue which, until it is resolved, blocks the road to all others. For those who so believe, Runcie's leadership must lack prophetic power and may well be condemned as a lengthy exercise in indecision and temporizing. In regard to the papacy, on the other hand, he has undoubtedly been far more prophetic and effective too. It may simply be admitted that his heart is in the one issue far more than in the other. But it has also to be said that he would, in principle, disclaim any real role of prophecy and certainly any ability to realize his prophecies. Perhaps he was able to be prophetic about the papacy just because it is so absolutely certain that in his own time this is not a practicable option. In regard to things that are practicable options, he has seen his role quite correctly as the presidential one of holding the Church in unity while it makes up its collective mind. He noted that Ramsey threw himself into the battle for Anglican–Methodist unity and Coggan into that for the ordination of women, and neither succeeded. He himself consistently struggled for the authorization of marriage in Church after divorce but he failed to get it through. If he had come more off the fence, would it have helped the cause, and might it not rather have damaged his primatial task of preventing the Church from trying to sting itself to death like a demented scorpion? That at least is the way he judged it, a way which admittedly fitted his temperament, but, arguably at least, it also best fitted the authority appropriate to an Archbishop of Canterbury.

In his enthronement sermon, Runcie appealed to the moral authority of Mother Teresa, an authority of 'deep unsentimental love — part toughness, part sensitivity'. That is an important element in any 'new map of authority'. He certainly recognizes that true Christian authority is always far more a matter of spirituality than of verbosity, of being Christ-like rather than theologizing about Christ. He has emphasised again and again the authority of martyrs and confessors, of those who have suffered much, of the poor. However, even Mother Teresa cannot be wholly paradigmatic for an archbishop. If from one point of view, her life has been incredibly hard, from another point of view, it has been almost easy: she has taken just one side of life, the misery of the poorest, and dealt with it superbly well. An archbishop cannot do that. His concerns have to be exceedingly multi-faceted, and each without contradicting others. It is a great deal easier and more pleasant to live in Lambeth Palace than to live in Mother Teresa's cell in Calcutta, but it is a great deal more difficult to cope with the problems arriving at the door of Lambeth Palace, without being either inconsistent or merely banal, than to deal with the problems arriving at the door of Mother Teresa's orphanage. His 'new maps of authority' include collegiality and the appeal to the expert, as well as holiness. He is continuously conscious of the tension between trying to be Christ-like and trying not to over-simplify, to be platitudinous.

That is the reason, perhaps, why of all his predecessors, it is Thomas Cranmer whom Runcie may most admire — a little oddly, some may judge. 'Complex, controversial, enigmatic', a 'godly, honest and much troubled Archbishop', he has called him while noting that Cranmer has been variously labelled by others 'saint' and 'patriot', 'traitor', 'heretic' and a 'subservient coward'. He was a Cambridge scholar, a master of the English language, and a rather exceptionally humane person according to the standards of his age. Undoubtedly, Runcie has at times found himself identifying with the principal Reformation founder of Anglican order. 'Cranmer lacked the art of popular decisive leadership', he remarked when opening the Cranmer exhibition at the British Library. 'The final portrait here which hangs in Lambeth Palace is of a man wearied by indecision and care; but there is no doubt that he had the more enduring qualities of piety and thoughtfulness.' It is a fair but not a generous self-portrait. Pastoral care, piety and thoughtfulness are certainly the qualities for which Runcie himself would most wish to be remembered, but with the view that 'indecision' is really the right word to denote the kind of leadership Archbishop Runcie has given to the Church, this writer, at least, would wish to disagree.

EPILOGUE

The written word

(Sermon by Archbishop Runcie at the Annual Service at St Paul's
Cathedral of the Worshipful Company of Stationers and Newspaper Makers, Ash Wednesday 1989)

Whatsoever things are true, whatsoever things are honest,
Whatsoever things are just, whatsoever things are pure,
Whatsoever things are lovely, whatsoever things are of good report;
if there be any virtue and if there be any praise, think on these things.

(Philippians 4.8)

St Paul was in prison when he wrote these words. Scribes and printers,
paper makers and publishers — each have played their part in ensuring
that his words from prison are communicated afresh to each
generation. Likewise Hitler in prison wrote out of his inner bitterness
Mein Kampf. Its words overflowed the prison walls and played their
part in plunging a world into war.

But only since the invention of the printing press has the written
word, of whatever kind, become easily available and widely distrib-
uted.

Close on 400 years have passed since the first of these annual
services — the history of your Company covers virtually the whole
period in which the materials for writing have been available at
modest cost, and publication of the written word a possibility.

Not that everyone has found it easy to get into print. Nearly three
centuries ago Bishop Edward Law expressed his impatience at the
slowness of his Carlisle printer. 'Why does not my book make its
appearance?' he asked sharply. Came the reply, 'My Lord, I am extremely sorry: but we have been obliged to send to Glasgow for a
pound of parentheses'.

Lent is a sort of parenthesis, a bracket in the Church's year when
men and women try to find time — so easily crowded out in our busy
lives — to reflect on life, its direction and meaning. I am sure that your
Master of nearly four centuries ago, Alderman John Norton, did not
mean that today all should be cakes and ale; but that here a serious
word, too, should be spoken on this serious day, Ash Wednesday.

The Stationers' Company is, perhaps of all the livery companies,
connected with the most serious business — the communication of
the word. No one writes *by accident*. The spoken word is often blurted

209

out, by habit, by instinct, and — if we hit our thumb with a hammer — by compulsion. As St James wrote, 'The tongue is an unruly member': but the pen is not. Writing is the product of deliberate intention. That is why words spoken in an outburst of temper are much less hurtful than the same words written in a letter and sent by post. That is the bad side of the written word — that it can be especially hurtful. The good side is that it can be especially helpful. A letter of sympathy or congratulations may raise the spirits because, as we say, 'he has taken the trouble to write'. The written word is more *authoritative* than the spoken word. When we want to assure someone that we are certain about something we'll say — '*I have it in writing*' or '*I've seen it in black and white*'.

A word spoken may have uncertain value. Men may often say one thing and mean another. 'Do as a concession to my wits, Lord Darlington, kindly explain to me exactly what you mean.' 'Better not, Duchess. Nowadays to be intelligible is to be found out.' So the cynicism of Oscar Wilde.

In the last four centuries, the authority of the written word has shown much more of its good side than of its bad. It has encouraged the idea that more is to be gained from reading books than from listening to the gossip in the street; it has motivated the many to give attention to the wisdom and knowledge of the few; it has opened the door to education. Who would take the trouble to learn to read or teach a child to read, were it not for the authority which is believed to belong to the written word?

This authority has been based in part on the integrity of writers, but also on the integrity of publishers. Most of those who have taken the trouble to write have been, as we say nowadays, 'reader friendly'. They do not want to mislead, corrupt or damage their readers. And if their writing should have this unintended effect, the publisher has always been there to demand amendments or refuse publication. A responsible publisher circulates a book or a pamphlet and in doing so asserts that it is 'worth reading'.

Thus things have been. But is that era now coming to an end? Radio, and then television, seemed to challenge the written word. But somehow the broadcast word lacks the same sort of authority. It is, as its name implies, cast broadly, on a massive scale and in a kaleidoscope of styles. We tend to look to the broadcast word for entertainment, but to the written word for education.

Not that everyone takes kindly to the tomes of academics. When George III's brother was given a presentation copy of the *Decline and Fall of the Roman Empire*, he protested (you may remember) 'Another

damned, thick, square book. Always scribble, scribble, scribble. . . .
Eh, Mr Gibbon?'

I believe that in these days the serious threat to the written word
lies in the erosion of its own integrity. We live in an age in which we
are overwhelmed by paper, and much of what is written on that paper
comes from sources which are unidentifiable or obscure. Whose is the
word that is printed in the newspapers as a leak or attributed to a
source which may not be disclosed? Whose is the word that comes
uninvited through the door claiming that a certain supermarket is the
cheapest in town, or that one detergent washes whiter than all the
rest? Whose is the word that comes through the post urging my vote
or my money for some cause? Whose is the word that comes in a plain
envelope offering access to unlimited pornography? Whose is this
word? No one is answerable, many will be irresponsible — concerned
only for their own gain and indifferent to the effect of what they write
on those who read it.

This is not a plea for censorship. It would be no remedy to reintro-
duce the right of this Company to burn unlicensed publications —
certainly not, as it once was, the publications not approved by the
Archbishop of Canterbury. What better guarantee of attention and
under the counter sales would there be than an index of banned books
at Lambeth Palace?

Who in these days could censor the products of word-processors,
copying machines and limit circulation not only through the post but
by fax and electronic mail? Far more effective than censorship is the
stamp of the reputable publisher. We look to the reputable publisher
to maintain the integrity and authority of the written word. We need
publishing houses which are jealous both for their own good name and
for the survival, in spite of all that threatens, of the distinct and special
authority of the written word.

This attitude to publishing has a religious quality to it. Our respect
for the word is a respect for human creativity and human communication. It is inspired by qualities of service to our fellow men and
women and an invitation to them to trust what is written. These
qualities only rest secure in a world in which there is reverence for
God. They are qualities which create a capacity to receive the message
which comes from that most serious, yet most joyful, word — the
Word of God. They are qualities which only flourish where there is
freedom.

If love, not force, is to rule the world, there must be freedom. Of
course there will be many failures, much backsliding and a good deal
of irresponsibility in a free world. But our task is to promote the finer

211

things of the human spirit of which Paul spoke from his prison cell. In your varied responsibilities you have great opportunities to do so.

So on Ash Wednesday, this solemn day, this day of penitence for all that is or has been amiss, both in our private and our public life, I ask you to take away from your Service those words so well known, but so much in need for this world.

Whatsoever things are true, whatsoever things are honest,
Whatsoever things are just, whatsoever things are pure,
Whatsoever things are lovely, whatsoever things are of good report; if there be any virtue and if there be any praise, think on these things.

A note about books

1. The Archbishop's own principal publications are as follows:

Cathedral and City: St Albans Ancient and Modern, edited by Robert Runcie (Martyn Associates, 1977).

Authority in Crisis? An Anglican Response (SCM Press, 1988).

The main published collections of his addresses as Archbishop are *Windows onto God*, compiled and arranged by Eileen Mable (SPCK, 1983), *One Light for One World*, compiled and arranged by Margaret Pawley (SPCK, 1988), *The Unity We Seek*, ed. Margaret Pawley (Darton, Longman and Todd/Morehouse, 1989) and *Seasons of the Spirit*, ed. James B. Simpson (William B. Eerdmans, 1983).

See also Robert Runcie, Paul A. B. Clarke, Andrew Linzey and John Moses, *Theology, the University and the Modern World* (Lester Crook Academic Publishing, 1988); Robert Runcie, *Reform, Renewal and Rehabilitation* (Prison Reform Trust, 1990).

The main life is by Margaret Duggan, *Runcie: The Making of an Archbishop* (Hodder and Stoughton, 1983).

2. For the lives of the preceding Archbishops see Margaret Pawley, *Donald Coggan: Servant of Christ* (SPCK, 1987) and Owen Chadwick, *Michael Ramsey: a Life* (OUP, 1990). There is no adequate published life of Geoffrey Fisher. Edward Carpenter's major biography still awaits publication. In the meantime, there is William Purcell, *Fisher of Lambeth* (Hodder and Stoughton, 1969).

Standard lives of earlier Archbishops of Canterbury in this century are G. K. A. Bell, *Randall Davidson, Archbishop of Canterbury* (OUP, 1935), J. G. Lockhart, *Cosmo Gordon Lang* (Hodder and Stoughton, 1949) and F. A. Iremonger, *William Temple* (OUP, 1948).

Edward Carpenter edited a selection of Geoffrey Fisher's addresses and speeches entitled *The Archbishop Speaks* (Evans Brothers, 1958). The best of several collections of Michael Ramsey's may be *Canterbury Pilgrim* (SPCK, 1974), and of Donald Coggan, *The Heart of the Christian Faith* (Abingdon Press, 1978).

3. For a history of all the Archbishops see Edward Carpenter, *Cantuar* (Cassell, 1971; 2nd edition, Mowbray, 1988). For a history of English Christianity up to the First World War, see the three volumes of David Edwards, *Christian England* (Collins, 1982–84), and for the twentieth century, Adrian Hastings, *A History of English Christianity, 1920–1985* (Collins, 1986; new edition,

SCM/Trinity Press International, 1991); K. N. Medhurst and G. H. Moyser, *The Church and Politics in a Secular Age* (OUP, 1988) examines the relations between the Church of England and politics in modern Britain.

4. The General Synod's annual *Report of Proceedings* is essential material regarding recent Church history. Volumes 11 to 21 cover the years 1980–90. *The Synod of Westminster: Do We Need It?*, ed. Peter Moore (SPCK, 1986) provides a sharp critique of General Synod. For a restrained response, see the 1990 *Twenty-eighth Report of the Standing Orders Committee* on 'The Synod's Agenda and Debating Style' signed by Oswald Clark, one of Synod's most experienced members.

The Crockford Preface of 1987–88 may usefully be read in conjunction with those for 1982–83 and 1985–86. The latest edition has no preface. The annual *Church of England Year Book* contains a shorter, less personalized commentary on the year's events which it can be useful to consult.

The Bennett standpoint in the Crockford controversy is provided by the posthumous collection of essays by Gareth Bennett, edited by Geoffrey Rowell, *To the Church of England* (Churchman Publishing, 1988) and William Oddie, *The Crockford File: Gareth Bennett and the Death of the Anglican Mind* (Hamish Hamilton, 1989).

The Truth Shall Make You Free (Church House Publishing, 1989) is a full report of the Lambeth Conference of 1988, while Michael Marshall, *Church at the Crossroads: Lambeth 1988* (Collins/Harper Row, 1988) provides a commentary and Alan Stephenson, *Anglicanism and the Lambeth Conferences* (SPCK, 1978) a background history. See also John Howe and Colin Craston, *Anglicanism and the Universal Church* (Anglican Book Centre, Toronto, 1990); Vinay Samuel and Christopher Sugden, *Lambeth 88: a View from the Two Thirds World* (SPCK, 1989); and for a wide-ranging survey of Anglicanism, *The Study of Anglicanism*, ed. Stephen Sykes and John Booty, (SPCK/Fortress Press, 1988).

5. The most authoritative doctrinal statement produced in Runcie's time is *The Nature of Christian Belief: A Statement by the House of Bishops* (Church House Publishing/Forward Movement, 1986).

Wider issues of authority and theological dispute may be followed up in *Authority in the Anglican Communion: Essays Presented to Bishop John Howe*, ed. Stephen Sykes (Anglican Book Centre, Toronto, 1987), *By What Authority?*, ed. Robert Jeffrey (Mowbray, 1987), Keith Clements, *Lovers of Discord: Twentieth-Century Theological Controversies* in England (SPCK, 1988), and Adrian Hastings, *The Theology of a Protestant Catholic* (SCM/Trinity Press International, 1990).

M. E. Thrall, *The Ordination of Women to the Priesthood* (SCM, 1958) is a good early Anglican account of the issue. *Man, Woman, Priesthood*, ed. Peter

Moore (SPCK, 1978) is a collection of essays, all opposed to women's ordination, edited by a man who was a friend and colleague of Runcie at St Albans. Ruth Edwards, *The Case for Women's Ministry* (SPCK, 1989) argues for acceptance, as does Monica Furlong, *Mirror to the Church* (SPCK, 1988).

6. The *Final Report* of the Anglican–Roman Catholic International Commission was published in 1981 (CTS/SPCK). The earlier Malta Report is to be found in *Anglican/Roman Catholic Dialogue: The Work of the Preparatory Commission*, ed. Alan Clark and Colin Davey (OUP, 1974).

Bernard and Margaret Pawley, *Rome and Canterbury Through Four Centuries* (Mowbray, 1974) covers the historical background. Arthur Michael Ramsey and Léon-Joseph Suenens, *The Future of the Christian Church* (SCM/Morehouse, 1971) is a moving joint work byArchbishop Ramsey and the Cardinal Archbishop of Malines expressing the most positive hopes for unity. Hugh Montefiore, *So Near and Yet so Far: Rome, Canterbury and ARCIC* (SCM, 1986) takes a more critical line. *Modern Catholicism*, Adrian Hastings, ed. (SPCK/OUP, New York, 1990) is a survey of Roman Catholicism since the Second Vatican Council.

The Failure of the English Covenant, Preface by Kenneth Woollcombe and Phillip Capper (British Council of Churches, 1982) analyses one thing that went wrong in the early 1980s. *On the Way to Visible Unity: Meissen, 1988* (Board of Mission and Unity, Church House, 1988) shows, instead, something that was going right in the later 1980s.

7. *Faith in the City: A Call for Action by Church Authorities*, a report of the Archbishop of Canterbury's Commission on Urban Priority Areas (Church House Publishing, 1985).

Living Faith in the City (Church House Publishing, 1990) is a progress report by the Archbishop's Advisory Group on Urban Priority Areas. *Theology in the City*, ed. Anthony Harvey (SPCK, 1989) provides a theological response to the report. Two local follow-up reports may also be mentioned: *Faith in the City of Birmingham*, the Report of a Commission also chaired by Sir Richard O'Brien (Paternoster Press, Exeter, 1988), and *Faith in Leeds: Searching for God in our City* (Leeds Churches Community Involvement Project, 1986). The parallel report by the Archbishop's Commission on Rural Areas is *Faith in the Countryside* (Churchman Publishing, 1990).

❧INDEX OF NAMES❧